Men and Masculinities in Southeast Asia

This book brings together extensive recent innovative research on the study of men and masculinities in Southeast Asia. Drawing on rich ethnographic fieldwork from Vietnam, Cambodia, Thailand, the Philippines, Singapore, Indonesia and Timor-Leste, the book examines both dominant and marginal constructions of heterosexual masculinity and the ways in which these are performed in different localized contexts in insular and mainland Southeast Asia. Through the presentation of detailed ethnographic studies on topics ranging from the professional practices of Filipino merchant seafarers to the sex lives of Thai migrant workers to the stand-over tactics of Indonesian gangsters, the authors in this collection challenge the idea of emerging globalizing forms of masculinities. Where existing studies of gender in Asia tend to concentrate on women, East Asia and gay men, this book fills a significant gap and demonstrates how gender, ethnicity, class, sexuality and nationality shape contemporary understandings of what it means to be a 'man' in contemporary Southeast Asia.

Michele Ford is Associate Professor of Indonesian Studies at the University of Sydney, Australia. She is the co-editor of *Women and Work in Indonesia* and *Women and Labour Organizing in Asia: Diversity, Autonomy and Activism* (both published by Routledge).

Lenore Lyons is Honorary Professor in the Department of Indonesian Studies at the University of Sydney, Australia. She is the author of *A State of Ambivalence: The Feminist Movement in Singapore*.

Routledge Contemporary Southeast Asia Series

Men and Masculinities
in Southeast Asia

**Edited by Michele Ford
and Lenore Lyons**

Routledge
Taylor & Francis Group

LONDON AND NEW YORK

This edition published 2012
by Routledge
2 Park Square, Milton Park, Abingdon, Oxon, OX14 4RN

Simultaneously published in the USA and Canada
by Routledge
711 Third Avenue, New York, NY 10017

Routledge is an imprint of the Taylor & Francis Group, an informa business

© 2012 Michele Ford and Lenore Lyons for selection and editorial material.
Individual chapters, the contributors.

British Library Cataloguing in Publication Data
A catalogue record for this book is available from the British Library

Library of Congress Cataloging-in-Publication Data
Men and masculinities in Southeast Asia / edited by Michele Ford and
Lenore Lyons. – 1st ed.
          p. cm. – (Routledge contemporary Southeast Asia series; 41)
          Includes bibliographical references and index.
     1. Men – Southeast Asia. 2. Masculinity – Southeast Asia. I. Ford,
     Michele. II. Lyons, Lenore.
     HQ1088.M4586 2012
     305.310959 – dc23   2011018659

ISBN: 978–0–415–72627–6 (pbk)
ISBN: 978–0–415–48223–3 (hbk)
ISBN: 978–0–203–19739–4 (ebk)

Typeset in Times New Roman
by Keystroke, Station Road, Codsall, Wolverhampton

Contents

Contributors

Michele Ford is Associate Professor in the Department of Indonesian Studies at the University of Sydney. Her research interests focus on social movements in Southeast Asia and identity in the Indonesia–Singapore borderlands. Michele is the author of *Workers and Intellectuals: NGOs, Unions and the Indonesian Labour Movement* (NUS/Hawaii/KITLV 2009) and co-editor of *Women and Work in Indonesia* (Routledge 2008, with Lyn Parker); *Women and Labour Organizing in Asia: Diversity, Autonomy and Activism* (Routledge 2008, with Kaye Broadbent) and *Indonesia beyond the Water's Edge: Managing an Archipelagic State* (ISEAS 2009, with Robert Cribb).

Trude Jacobsen is Assistant Professor of Southeast Asian History at Northern Illinois University. She has published on Buddhism and politics in Cambodia, justice and reconciliation in Southeast Asia, and the history of women and power in Cambodia, most significantly her first book *Lost Goddesses: The Denial of Female Power in Cambodian History* (NIAS Press 2008). She regularly consults on gender, rights and development issues for international and non-governmental organizations. Her current project, 'Intersections of Desire, Duty and Debt: Sexual Contracts in Burma and Cambodia', was funded by an Australian Research Council (ARC) grant and will be published in 2012.

Pattana Kitiarsa is Assistant Professor in the Southeast Asian Studies Programme, National University of Singapore. He holds his doctoral degree in sociocultural anthropology from the University of Washington, Seattle. His work on transnational labour migration focuses on case studies of Thai migrants earning their living in Singapore's construction industry and of Thai–Farang intermarriage in the countryside of northeastern Thailand. He has published on the topics of village-style transnational ties and migrant institutions, masculine gender and sexuality, and the roles of home cultures, such as popular music and Buddhist merit-making, in the transnational contexts. His research has also expanded to cover some related fields of investigation, such as cross-border sex work, transnational Buddhism and human trafficking.

Don Eliseo Lucero-Prisno III has a BSc in Psychology and a doctorate in Medicine from the University of the Philippines. He earned his Master of Public Health

(International Health and Development) from the Royal Tropical Institute in Amsterdam. He works in the field of international health, maritime medicine, and health research and policy. In 2006, he was a Nippon Foundation scholar at the Seafarer International Research Centre at Cardiff University, where he is a doctoral candidate in the School of Social Sciences working on a dissertation on masculinity and the vulnerability of seafarers to HIV infection.

Lenore Lyons is Honorary Professor in the Department of Indonesian Studies at the University of Sydney, Australia. Recognized as the leading scholar on the feminist movement in Singapore, she is the author of *A State of Ambivalence: The Feminist Movement in Singapore* (Brill Academic Publishers 2004). She recently completed a major study of citizenship, identity and sovereignty in the Riau Islands of Indonesia (with Michele Ford) and is currently working on a project that examines migrant worker activism in support of female domestic workers in Malaysia and Singapore.

Steven McKay is Associate Professor of Sociology and Director of the Center for Labor Studies at the University of California, Santa Cruz. He has a PhD in Sociology and an MA in Southeast Asian Studies from the University of Wisconsin, Madison. Professor McKay researches in the areas of labour and labour markets, gender, migration, diaspora and racial formation in a global context. He is the author of *Satanic Mills or Silicon Islands? The Politics of High-Tech Production in the Philippines* (Cornell University/ILR Press 2006). He is currently writing a book on the Filipino seafarers and the emergence of the Filipino niche in merchant shipping.

Henri Myrttinen is currently a researcher with the German NGO Watch Indonesia, which focuses on West Papua and Timor-Leste. He has previously worked for a number of international NGOs and research institutions, focusing especially on post-conflict and post-disaster societies in Southeast Asia. His academic research has mainly been on issues of gender (especially masculinities) and conflict, having recently completed his PhD on masculinities and violence in Timor-Leste at the University of KwaZulu-Natal.

Hung Cam Thai is Associate Professor of Sociology and Asian American Studies at Pomona College and the Claremont University Consortium, where he concurrently serves as Chair of Sociology and Director of the Pacific Basin Institute. His scholarship has been funded by the Freeman Foundation, Haynes Foundation, Social Science Research Council, Hewlett Foundation, Asia Research Institute of Singapore and Pacific Rim Fellowship Program. His first book, *For Better or for Worse: Vietnamese International Marriages in the New Global Economy* (Rutgers University Press 2008), is a study of international marriages in the Vietnamese diaspora. His current book, *Insufficient Funds: Money in Low Wage Transnational Families* (Stanford University Press forthcoming), is about the personal and social meanings of money in Vietnamese transnational families.

Sophie Williams is a PhD candidate in the Centre for Asia Pacific Social Transformation Studies (CAPSTRANS) at the University of Wollongong. Her doctorate, entitled 'Space, Place and Masculinity: Chinese Singaporean Men's Practices of Sex Tourism in the Indonesian Borderlands', is concerned with the ways in which discursive practices of masculinity shape the reading of (sex) tourist spaces. She presented papers at the 2006 Asia Pacific Futures Research Network's Signature Conference, 'Media: Policies, Cultures and Futures in the Asia Pacific Region', and at the Fifth International Convention of Asia Scholars in 2007.

Ian Wilson is Senior Lecturer in the School of Social Sciences and Humanities, Murdoch University, and a Research Fellow at Murdoch's Asia Research Centre. He has published extensively on the political economy of gangs, criminal networks, protection rackets, ethnic and religious militias and private security in Indonesia. Other research interests include Indonesian youth culture and political geography. He has also investigated corruption, cultural politics and the spatial politics of the informal economy in Indonesia. In addition to his experience in policy formulation, he has worked collaboratively with a number of Indonesian NGOs such as Indonesian Corruption Watch.

Preface

The papers in this collection emerged from a series of conference panels organized at the 2007 International Congress of Asian Scholars (ICAS5) held in Kuala Lumpur, Malaysia. The panels were convened by Lenore Lyons, then Director of the Centre for Asia Pacific Social Transformation Studies (CAPSTRANS) at the University of Wollongong, and Michele Ford from the Department of Indonesian Studies at the University of Sydney. At that time, we were undertaking a study of identity and belonging in the Riau Island borderlands between Indonesia and Singapore, and the topic of masculinity emerged as an important theme in the component of our project that focused on marriage and sex work. In the course of carrying out this research, we were surprised to find that, despite the burgeoning interest in studies of 'men and masculinity' globally, the topic had received relatively little sustained attention in Southeast Asia, particularly with regard to straight men.

Following an international call for papers, we received a large number of abstracts on issues ranging through sexuality; fathering and families; religion and masculinity; masculinity and migration; masculinity and militarization; and the construction of masculinities on the Internet. From the abstracts submitted we selected twelve papers for inclusion in four interlinked panels on heteronormative masculinities. Two panels explored the topic of sexuality and the performance of masculinity; one examined the construction of masculinities; and the final one dealt with migrant transnationalism and the family/household. In addition we convened two other panels on non-normative sexuality under the AsiaPacifiQueer banner. Peter Jackson from the Australian National University and Doug Sanders, a scholar and activist based in Bangkok, provided expert oversight to these panels. While not all papers included under the APQ umbrella dealt with men or masculinities, they created a space for the discussion of queer masculinities. This was particularly important given the hostility that the Malaysian authorities have exhibited towards GLBTQ issues. The panels gave local queer scholars and activists a relatively neutral space within which to interact with foreign delegates. The latter benefited enormously from the opportunity to interact with local activists, and the warmth and hospitality with which we were welcomed by Jeremy Kwan of the Pink Triangle Foundation can scarcely be overstated. The conference panels proved enormously successful, and generated considerable discussion and interest amongst both scholars and activists from the Malaysian non-governmental sector.

This collection, *Men and Masculinities in Southeast Asia*, includes the papers presented at ICAS5 by Pattana Kitiarsa, Trude Jacobsen and Hung Cam Thai, as well as two of our own, one of which is a shorter version of an article published as 'It's about Bang for Your Buck, Bro: Singaporean Men's Online Conversations about Sex in Batam, Indonesia' in the *Asia Studies Review* 32 (1): 77–97 (available on www.informaworld.com). We are grateful to the editor of the *Asian Studies Review* and the publisher, Taylor & Francis, for permission to include this piece as a chapter in this volume. In addition, the book contains three papers – by Steve McKay and Don Eliseo Lucero-Prisno, Henri Myrttinen and Ian Wilson – commissioned after the conference.

In selecting papers for inclusion in this collection we were keen to incorporate recent innovative research on the study of men and masculinities in Southeast Asia that drew on a rich ethnographic base. Ultimately, we have been able to showcase work from seven countries: Indonesia, Timor-Leste, Singapore, the Philippines, Thailand, Vietnam and Cambodia. Although there are a number of obvious gaps, the balance between island and mainland Southeast Asia ensures a broad representation of countries and cultures. Following the brief to deal with the lives of non-elite, heterosexual men, the chapters together reveal a world that has hitherto been hidden in most accounts of gender in Southeast Asia.

Bringing together scholars located in different parts of the globe in a collaborative project such as this has necessitated a considerable degree of patience. Unsurprisingly, given the dearth of work on heteronormative masculinities in this region, this focus pushed many of our contributors to work at the very edge of their research interests and expertise. Less predictably, many of our authors experienced some kind of life-changing event during the course of the project, from relocation across continents and across the globe, to childbirth and parenting, to serious bouts of ill-health, to personal loss and family tragedy. As editors, we have lived through these experiences with our contributors and encouraged them at every stage of writing and review. Unfortunately, in some cases, contributors could no longer participate in the project and we have been unable to include their work here. We look forward to seeing it in press sometime in the future.

From the outset, we have encouraged our contributors to address the intersections between hegemonic and non-hegemonic masculinities by unpacking the meanings associated with hegemony/marginality in localized contexts. Although Raewyn Connell's work is used extensively in the study of gender and masculinity, it does not form an established intellectual tradition in gender studies in Southeast Asia. Studies of masculinity (and femininity) in the region have been dominated by a taken-for-granted assertion of an underlying egalitarianism that shapes gender relations. For example, it has been argued that women, particularly in island Southeast Asia, have not been subject to forms of gender oppression typically associated with the patriarchal systems of East Asia. Although these accounts have been subject to critique, they still largely dominate scholarly understandings of gender relations in the region and have led to the failure to interrogate the complex nature of power relations between men and women or among men.

While recognizing that Connell's concept of 'hegemonic masculinity' has limited applicability in understanding the fluid nature of multiple identities, we felt that it provided a useful starting point to begin to interrogate these complexities. For this reason, the chapter authors were asked to test the usefulness of the concept of hegemonic masculinity for their particular cases, and to develop alternative ways of thinking about how power and masculinities are embedded at the local level. Although the end result has been mixed, we believe that the collection provides a useful starting point for other scholars embarking on a critique of hegemonic masculinity in non-Western contexts.

Having finally brought the collection to fruition, we owe a considerable debt to a number of individuals and institutions who have assisted and supported us. In particular, we would like to thank Routledge commissioning editor Peter Sowden for his support for the original proposal and for his patience with delays in the book's production. Mike Donaldson and Keith Foulcher provided invaluable feedback, advice and help as the project developed. Michele would also like to thank her colleagues in the Department of Indonesian Studies at the University of Sydney and elsewhere, as well as her husband, Muliawarman, who first introduced her to the Riau Islands all those years ago. Lenore would like to thank CAPSTRANS at the University of Wollongong for providing funding for the original conference panels, and the University of Western Australia for financial assistance with the final production of the manuscript.

Michele Ford and Lenore Lyons,
University of Sydney
September 2011

Introduction

Michele Ford and Lenore Lyons

Men and masculinities are the subject of burgeoning scholarly interest, much of it driven by a desire to render masculinities visible. Masculinities scholars argue that men *as men* have rarely been treated as the subjects of scholarly research; the man as 'male' occupies the space of 'the universal, normative subject' (Louie 2002: 5) – a figure rarely problematized or deconstructed. These scholars claim that even within gender studies men have been largely absent (Connell *et al.* 2005: 1). The aim of research on men and masculinities is therefore to put men at the centre of scholarly enquiry as *gendered* beings. This has led to an explosion of writing about men and masculinities. In the context of Asia, much of this work is focused on China and Japan (see Brownell and Wasserstrom 2002; Louie 2002; Roberson and Suzuki 2002; Louie and Low 2003; Geng 2004) or on South Asia (Derné 2000; Osella *et al.* 2004; Banerjee 2005). There has been considerably less research on men and masculinities in Southeast Asia where, according to Peletz (1995: 102), masculinity and its constructions 'have been taken for granted'.

The large body of scholarship on gender in Southeast Asia focuses almost exclusively on the lives of women. Where this work deals with the question of masculinity, it is often in the context of women's interactions with men – as fathers, husbands, employers and agents of the state. Men are rarely treated as the subjects of gender-based research, with the result that what we know about men and masculinity is usually inferred from the study of women and femininities. There are, however, some notable exceptions. These include Ong and Peletz's (1995) seminal work on gender relations in nineteenth and twentieth century Southeast Asia; and a few chapters in edited collections on gender in Asia (cf. Atkinson and Errington 1990; Manderson and Jolly 1997). There is also a growing body of work on male homosexuality in Southeast Asia, including Boellstorff's (2005) work on gay men in Indonesia; Jackson's (1996) work on Thailand; and two edited collections by Jackson and Sullivan (1999, 2001). A noticeable gap remains, however, in the study of heteronormative masculinities – studies of 'straight' men are largely lacking (but see Nilan *et al.* 2009; Clark 2010). In particular, there is an absence of any sustained analysis of the interaction between hegemonic and non-hegemonic masculinities or examination of how the performance of heterosexuality is linked to dominant constructions of masculinity. This collection, *Men and Masculinities in Southeast Asia*, seeks to address these gaps by examining male heteronormative models of sexuality in a range of different Southeast Asian countries.

Studying men and masculinities

Scholarly calls to recuperate 'men' and 'masculinities' stand in contradistinction to the claims of second-wave feminists who argued that women's absence from scholarship created a body of knowledge that was primarily about men's behaviour and practice. This 'malestream' knowledge not only served to obscure women's behaviours and practices, but did so by denying the gendered basis of such knowledge. In other words, it made men the subject of research without ever acknowledging their gendered position as men. Feminist scholarship sought to challenge these assumptions by drawing attention to the gendered basis of all knowledge claims. Recent literature on men and masculinity thus 'uncannily mirrors' its feminist forebears: 'it focuses upon men's own experiences, generates evidence of men's gender-specific suffering and has given birth to a new field of enquiry, "Men's Studies"' (Segal 2000: 160). There is a danger, however, that in carving out a space that is analogous to that of 'Women's Studies' such accounts overlook the political role of women's studies as a space within which women were able to embark on the process of critical self-knowledge as a subordinated group. The central focus on the study of gender and power may be obscured, or, even more worryingly, men's studies may make equal claims to gender inequality as victims of patriarchy and/or feminist gains. For this reason, many scholars have rejected the term 'Men's Studies' in favour of 'critical studies on men' (CSM), 'critical men's studies' or 'studies of men and masculinities'.

Connell *et al.* (2005) claim that, as a field of study, CSM is inspired by but not parallel to feminist research on women. This claim leaves unaddressed a number of questions, including: How do CSM scholars position their work in relation to feminist research on men? If 'critical men's studies' is a body of research inspired by feminist research, what distinguishes it from other critical studies of gender? What is the relationship between CSM and other bodies of gender-based research, including queer studies and post-colonial studies?[1] One response to these concerns is to argue that CSM is by and large undertaken by men about men and masculinities, while feminist studies are primarily about women by women. Such a claim is not about an assumed sex-based division of research personnel and interests (although there may be evidence to support this conclusion), but points to a view present in much recent scholarship on men and masculinities that feminist research is not about the study of men. Even a cursory review of the last four decades of feminist scholarship demonstrates the spurious nature of such a claim. Feminist theorizing is about understanding the intersection of gender and power, and is thus always already about men. The significant contribution of feminist theory to the study of men and masculinities, however, is often overlooked in CSM. Neglecting the insights of feminist theory has left much of the recent research on men and masculinities without a strong grounding in gender analysis, with the consequence that it is often theoretically weak.

This weakness is evident in the ongoing debates within critical men's studies about the meaning and significance of such fundamental concepts as 'men' and 'masculinities' (Donaldson 1993). The concept of 'masculinity' has become congruent with studies of men.[2] It has become shorthand for the meanings and experiences associated with 'being a man' in a particular sociocultural context (cultural representations), the everyday lived experiences of men (practices or identities), and a way of understanding the unequal relations between women and men, and between men (social power). The multiple meanings associated with the concept of masculinity/masculinities have led to claims of conceptual vagueness (Hearn 1996). For this reason, Hearn and Pringle prefer to talk about men's individual and collective practices – or men's identities or discourses on or of men, rather than about masculinity. They acknowledge, however, that the term 'masculinities' is 'convenient shorthand to refer to how men act, think, believe and appear, or are made apparent' (Hearn and Pringle 2006: 7).

The linking of men with masculinity appears to be based on an implied (and essential) heterosexual dualism – men/women – which gives primacy to the sexed body in understanding the performance of gender. Queer theorists and many feminist scholars have criticized such static and normative understandings of gender by arguing that the male/female dichotomy has no intrinsic biological or other essential reality; the sexed body is no more primary or 'real' – it is culturally constructed (cf. Gatens 1983; Butler 1990; Haraway 1991). As Cornwall and Lindisfarne (1994: 35) argue:

> While the social construction of gender categories is carefully described in terms of particularities, the very notion of 'gender categories' usually presupposes an incontrovertible gender dichotomy, which in turn rests on notions of essential biological difference . . . Cultural and historical specificity has been laid on to presupposed biological universals – male and female bodies.

Comparative ethnographic research shows that each of the terms in the triad 'men/male/masculinity' (and women/female/femininity) has multiple and ambiguous meanings which alter according to context and over time.

This longstanding feminist and queer critique of the sex/gender distinction does not appear to have influenced scholarly writing within the tradition of CSM, much of which rests on a foundational distinction between men and women (but see Louie 2002). This is evident in the way in which the discipline is described ('men and masculinity studies' rather than 'gender studies') and the ways in which the concept of masculinity is used and debated. The term 'masculinity' is often used in a way that presents it as the singular preserve of men (Mac an Ghaill 1996). Such a view serves to portray an essentialist view of masculinity in which biology is intrinsically tied to the social construction of gender (Hoven and Hörschelmann 2005). This has led some scholars to call for the need to distinguish 'being masculine' from 'being a man' (Clatterbaugh 2004), and to recognize that the terms men/male/masculinity and women/female/femininity can be used to describe a wide variety of different and even contradictory aspects of human bodies and behaviour

(Cornwall and Lindisfarne 1994). For example, although masculinity evokes images of maleness, it is not necessarily shared by men and can be adopted by or attributed to women. As Sedgwick (1995: 13) notes: 'As a woman, I am a consumer of masculinities, but I am not more so than men are; and, like men, I as a woman am also a producer of masculinities and a performer of them.' Masculinity and femininity mean different things depending on whether they are lived out and experienced by male or female bodies. However, the implicit coupling of men with masculinities that is present in much critical men's studies ignores the complex intersections between sex and gender.

Much work in the field of masculinity studies also fails to incorporate the insights of feminist thinking about gender, sexuality and power. Butler's concept of 'performativity' provides a useful way of theorizing the processes out of which identities are constructed. For Butler, the self is produced in the process of making performative gestures. In this sense, the performance of gender is compulsory and unconscious. The gender binary of masculine/feminine is perceived as natural via a process of sedimentation that 'over time has produced a set of corporeal styles which, in reified form, appear as the natural configuration of bodies into sexes which exist in a binary relation to one another' (Butler 1997: 407). Rather than understanding a person to be female or male, she theorizes that a person's gender is performative – that is, one's gender is created through a series of repeated performances: 'Consider gender, for instance, as a corporeal style, an "act", as it were, which is both intentional and performative, where "performative" suggests a dramatic and contingent construction of meaning' (Butler 1990: 190). This analysis suggests that gender is not an identity but a 'set of repeated acts within a highly rigid regulatory frame' (Butler 1990: 33).

Another significant limitation of much of the critical men's studies literature is that it deploys the figure of 'men' as a unitary, essentialist category. Feminists long ago rejected the concept of 'women' as both a political and an analytic category because it has the homogenizing effect of suppressing women's diversity and overlooking the ways in which *all* men and women are simultaneously racialized, classed and gendered subjects (hooks 1981; Mohanty *et al.* 1991). Rather than focusing on gender as the source of women's oppression and men's domination, third world feminists and women of colour call for an approach which examines the myriad ways in which women and men benefit from, or engage in, the exploitation of 'other' women and men. Such an approach is able to acknowledge that men have political interests in common with women, especially in the face of poverty, national insurrection and genocide. It is premised on an exploration of how both men and women are differently located within structural hierarchies. This is meant not to suggest precise ethnic, racial, sexual or cultural identities, but rather to describe a 'position in a structural hierarchical interrelationship' (Ang 1995: 60). Collins (1999: 263) uses the term 'intersectionality' to refer to these cross-cutting hierarchies of power, arguing that 'viewing gender within a logic of intersectionality redefines it as a constellation of ideas and social practices that are historically situated within and that mutually construct multiple systems of oppression'. Although the concept of intersectionality has been taken up by some CSM scholars (see Hearn 2004), the notion of 'difference' is often poorly articulated. In part, this can be explained by the enormously influential role that Connell's concept of 'hegemonic masculinity' has had in the development of critical studies of men and masculinity.

Hegemonic masculinity

The concept of hegemonic masculinity emerges in Connell's attempt to provide an alternative way of thinking about gender relations and the relationship between masculinity and power. Connell (1995: 77) defines hegemonic masculinity as 'the configuration of gender practice which embodies the currently accepted answer to the problem of legitimacy of patriarchy, which guarantees (or is taken to guarantee) the dominant position of men and the subordination of women'. According to this view, two types of relationships shape the gender order – 'hegemony, domination/ subordination and complicity on the one hand, and marginalization/authorization on the other' (Connell 1995: 81). In any given historical moment, 'one form of masculinity rather than others is culturally exalted' (Connell 1995: 77). Although Connell sees some correspondence between the cultural ideal and institutional power, this does not mean that the most powerful bearers of the cultural idea of hegemonic masculinity are the most powerful individuals. In this sense, hegemonic masculinity is assumed to be not normal (only a minority of men might enact it) but normative – it embodies 'the currently most honored way of being a man, it require[s] all other men to position themselves in relation to it, and it ideologically legitimate[s] the global subordination of women to men' (Connell and Messerschmidt 2005: 832). In other words, the hegemonic ideal may not correspond to the lives of actual men but is an ideal to which the majority of men aspire.

Within the gendered order, in addition to hegemonic masculinity, Connell identifies subordinated, complicit and marginalized masculinities which are in constant interaction with each other. For Connell, marginalization is

> always relative to the *authorization* of the hegemonic masculinity of the dominant group. Thus, in the United States, particular black athletes may be exemplars for hegemonic masculinity. But the fame and wealth of individual stars has no trickle-down effect; it does not yield social authority to black men generally.
>
> (Connell 1995: 80–1, emphasis in original)

Subordinate masculinities are those relations labelled as deviant (e.g. gay men), whereas marginalized masculinities are those structured around the concepts of race, class and ethnicity (Howson 2006: 63). Subordinated masculinities have the potential to become protest masculinities when they challenge the defining hegemonic principles. Complicit masculinities are 'lesser versions of the hegemonic ideal' (Howson 2006: 65). Connell (1995: 81) reminds us that these are not fixed character types but 'configurations of practice' generated in particular situations in a changing structure of relationships.

Connell's work has been extremely influential, but it is not without its critics (see Donaldson 1993; Demetriou 2001; Hearn 2004). Much of the critique rests on the lack of precision about the meaning of the term 'hegemonic masculinity'. Beasley (2008: 3) identifies three main ways in which Connell uses the term: (1) a political mechanism (drawing on a Gramscian notion of hegemony that refers to cultural/moral leadership) to ensure popular or mass consent to particular forms of rule; (2) the most dominant (most powerful and/or most widespread) versions of manhood; and (3) actual groups of men. She argues that the links and relationships between these different understandings of the concept of hegemony are not clearly articulated, not least because they are not 'entirely discrete definitional entities' (Beasley 2008: 4).

Some of the problems with the concept of hegemonic masculinity have to do with the way in which it has been used. Some researchers attribute its qualities to individuals or groups of men (i.e. the masculinities of men who occupy elite or ruling-class positions in society) rather than hegemonic power relations (Chen 1999). In other words, these accounts frequently overlook that gender is a set of power relations rather than an internalized characteristic. The most dominant ideals of masculinity are not necessarily the same as those that work to guarantee men's authority over women and those that do legitimate it may not always be socially celebrated or common. For this reason, Beasley (2008: 6) calls for the need to 'distinguish hegemonic from merely dominant men, from actual men or from their specific personality traits'. As Lusher and Robins (2009: 390) point out, however, it is not easy to envisage gender as a set of power relations (as Connell intends it to be understood) rather than a set of personal qualities.

The tendency to equate hegemonic masculinity with dominant men is reinforced by the continual use of the term 'hegemonic masculinity' in the singular. While a relational approach implies multiple, context-specific strategies, Connell and others write as if there were only ever one hegemonic masculinity at any given historical moment (Jefferson 2002). Thus, the fundamental problem with the concept of hegemonic masculinity is that it is grounded in the notion of a fixed (male) structure rather than hegemonic strategies that can 'vary across different parts of a social formation, creating conflicts or tensions for individual men between different hegemonic forms as they move across social practices' (Wetherell and Edley 1999: 337). This formulation is a useful starting point for thinking about the competing positions that men take up in patriarchy but it does little to account for the complexity of masculinities and how they are interconnected. So, although Connell's model insists on a 'distinct and legible hierarchy of masculinities' (Moller 2007: 265) within which some men exercise significant power and other have less, the precise articulation between hegemonic masculinity and dominant men remains unclear. In his critique of Connell, Demetriou (2001: 337) argues that 'hegemonic masculinity is not a purely white or heterosexual configuration of practice but it is a hybrid bloc that unites practices from diverse masculinities to ensure the reproduction of patriarchy'. In other words, hegemonic and marginalized masculinities should be understood as mutually constituting processes.

Other scholars argue that, although recognizing the importance of racial and ethnic hierarchies in the construction of 'marginalized' masculinities, Connell overlooks the complex ways in which femininities and masculinities are constructed in and through other dimensions of oppression (Sinha 1999). Masculinity is not simply about 'male–female relations', but traverses multiple axes of race, class, sexuality, religion and ethnicity. So, although Connell's concept of 'hegemonic masculinity' helps us begin to interrogate these complexities, it has limited applicability in understanding the fluid nature of multiple identities. This has led some scholars to question whether Connell's approach is at all relevant to an understanding of men in non-Western contexts (Lindsay and Miescher 2003). For example, Ouzgane and Morrell (2005) caution against adopting European/American concepts of masculinities in the study of men and women in traditional African societies where age and not gender was significant in determining the distribution of material resources (Schiele 2000).

Writing about Indian men, Osella and Osella (2006) reject the concept of hegemonic masculinity altogether because of its focus on singularity and homogeneity. Their work reveals two hegemonic forms of masculinity – 'one appealing mostly to the hegemonic ideals of control and detachment and the other appealing to equally hegemonic ideals of non-vegetarianism, sociability and providing for the family' (2006: 50). They argue that the concept of hegemonic masculinity is unable simultaneously to incorporate these two idealized forms of masculinity. They therefore reject it in favour of an alternative understanding of dominance based on multiple ideals of masculinity (2006: 51). In her study of a male prison in India, Bandyopadhyay (2006: 187) argues that 'the notion of hegemonic masculinity is not juxtaposed with subordinate masculinities but rather with competing and alternate masculinities which challenge the homogenous idea of hegemonic masculinity'. While she accepts that hegemonic masculinity is always constructed in relation to both subordinate masculinities and women, she demonstrates that, within the prison, hegemonic masculinity is a 'seriously contested idea' (Bandyopadhyay 2006: 188).

The latter issue signals a need to move away from the structural dimension of hegemonic masculinity to the analysis of how masculinities are constructed and how different configurations of masculinity prescribe or regulate men's lives. As numerous scholars have attested, masculinity does not mean the same thing to all men – it varies in how it is understood, experienced and lived in daily practice (Coles 2009; Lusher and Robins 2009). The concept of hegemonic masculinity considers dominant, subordinate and marginalized masculinities at the structural level without taking into account men's lived realities. Attention to the ways men experience gender may reveal that marginalized men feel dominant in relation to other men. This leads Pringle (2005: 267) to conclude that although the concept of hegemonic masculinity is 'useful for helping understand big picture accounts, [it] can be problematic for understanding the constitution of individual subjectivities'. Moller (2007: 275) goes as far as to suggest that it reduces 'our capacity to understand the ways in which the performance of masculinity may be productive of new socio-cultural practices, meanings, alliances and feelings'. Although Connell has always insisted on the dynamic nature of the gender order and thus of hegemonic masculinity, such a theorization provides few positive accounts of how hegemonic masculinity can be subverted (Howson 2006).

Another shortcoming of Connell's thesis is its inability to give sufficient attention to the operation of hegemony on femininities (Howson 2006: 66). Although the relation between masculinities and femininities is a constant theme in the work of Connell and others (see Kimmel and Messner 1992), there is tendency to focus on hegemonic masculinity in relation to patriarchy and male power over women. Part of this problem is that Connell fails to problematize the notion of masculinity itself and elides the terms man/male/masculinity. This has the effect of focusing exclusively on *male masculinity*, with the result that the relationship between men and masculinity seem incontrovertible (Cornwall and Lindisfarne 1994: 20). In response to these critiques, Connell and others acknowledge that not enough attention has been given to the role of women in the construction of hegemonic masculinity, and to the role of what was originally called 'hegemonic femininity' but later 'emphasized femininity'. Connell and Messerschmidt call for greater recognition to be given to the 'practices of women and to the historical interplay of femininities and masculinities' and to the incorporation of 'a more holistic understanding of gender hierarchy, recognizing the agency of subordinated groups as much as the power of dominant groups and the mutual conditioning of gender dynamics and other social dynamics' (Connell and Messerschmidt 2005: 848).

Most critics do not dismiss Connell's theory but seek to elaborate and expand the analysis of hegemonic masculinity.[3] A number of scholars have sought to use Bourdieu's notion of 'habitus' as a way of highlighting the role of corporeality in the construction of gender (Light and Kirk 2000; Light 2003; Coles 2009). Light (2003), for example, argues that theorizing gender as a form of embodied capital can illuminate the ways in which particular bodily regimes act to embody particular forms of culture- and class-specific forms of masculinity. In other words, not only are bodies inscribed with culture, but the body's engagement in social and cultural practice also shapes the dispositions and tastes that structure behaviour, social action and access to resources (Light and Kirk 2000).

To account for the ways in which men's identities shift and change over time, other scholars incorporate Butler's concept of performativity in their analysis of masculinity (Evans 2005; Hoven and Meijering 2005; Moller 2007). According to Evans:

> Masculinity is a performed social identity rather than a state of being . . . There are hierarchies of masculine performance and exceptional performance is equated with exceptional masculinity. How well one performs tasks and the actual performance of those tasks determines one's place in a masculine hierarchy, and that place is never full or permanent. For men, as well as for women, in other words, *not only must gender be done, but it must be seen to be done, again and again* – it must be iterated and, performed within a social space.
>
> (Evans 2005: 201, emphasis in original)

Butler's insights allow us to see masculinity as a fluid, socially constructed concept that changes over space and time. Such an approach destabilizes gender binaries by de-emphasizing the study of 'masculinity' (or 'femininity') and focusing instead on the construction of 'gender' as multiple and variable. Not only does such an approach provide a means to acknowledge female masculinities and male femininities, but it also affords a means to examine how men negotiate masculinities in their daily lives.

While the concept of performativity provides a means to theorize fluid gendered identities, the focus on multiple and/or contested masculinities risks overstating the ways in which men actually experience masculinity. Ethnographic research reveals that, for many men, 'masculinity' is an unfamiliar concept, and when asked to speak about it with scholars they are at a loss as to what to discuss. The notion of 'what it means to be a man' is much more readily understood. And yet, despite the scholarly focus on multiple and fluid identities, most men describe their gender identity as stable and unitary. In their study of migrant men in Australia, Donaldson and Howson (2009: 215) point out that men 'understand their masculinity to be most often quite solid, reliable, dependable, durable and transportable, rather like themselves, in fact'. While the experience of migration may challenge the men's sense of identity, they recognize and respond to familiar patterns of masculinity. These similarities suggest the need to look beyond the local to understand the structuring practices that shape the gender order at a global level.

Globalizing masculinities?

An interest in the global is another enduring legacy of Connell's work on men and masculinity. Connell asserts that a 'world gender order' exists that connects the gender orders of local societies on a world scale. She describes two basic links that constitute this global gender order: (1) interactions between existing gender orders brought about through their contact with each other (through imperialism, neo-colonialism, globalization and labour migration and so on); and (2) the creation of new transnational spaces (for example, those created by multinational corporations, supra-state agencies and the global media). The current global gender order, characterized by the patriarchal organization of society, has been shaped by the emergence and reconstitution of masculinities of conquest and empire, and more recently by neo-liberalism and post-colonialism (Haywood 2007: 93). According to Connell, global history and contemporary globalization must be part of our understanding of masculinities because

> the net result of these two forms of linkage is a partially integrated, highly unequal, and turbulent set of gender relations, with global reach and uneven impact. This is the context in which we must now think about the construction and enactment of masculinities.
>
> (Connell 2005: 74)

The notion of a world gender order implies that hegemonic masculinity is a multi-level concept operating at local, regional and global levels and that masculinities at each level are linked and can influence each other (Connell and Messerschmidt 2005: 849). Connell and Messerschmidt (2005: 850) claim that a regional hege-monic masculinity provides an exemplary masculine model that influences, but does not wholly determine, the construction of gender relations and hegemonic masculinities at the local level. They suggest that processes such as economic restructuring, long-distance migration and development agendas reshape local patterns of masculinities and femininities, describing the relationship between local and regional masculinities in this way:

> [L]ocal plurality is compatible with singularity of hegemonic masculinity at the regional or society-wide level. The 'family resemblance' among local variants is likely to be represented by one symbolic model at the regional level, not by multiple models.
>
> (Connell and Messerschmidt 2005: 850–1)

Global masculinities are formed in a world gender order that privileges men over women. While there are always local exceptions, the 'patriarchal dividend' gives men greater access to power as well as cultural and sexual privilege (Connell 1995: 261). Globalization has thus created the conditions for the production of a hegemonic masculinity on a world scale: 'a dominant form of masculinity that embodies, organizes and legitimates men's domination in the world gender order as a whole' (Connell 1995: 261). Writing in a similar vein, Kimmel argues that globalization is changing masculinities and transforming the lives of individual men. He claims that the patterns of masculinity embedded within gendered institu-tions are

> rapidly becoming the dominant global hegemonic model of masculinity, against which all local, regional, and national masculinities are played out and to which they increasingly refer . . . The processes of globalization and the emergence of a global hegemonic masculinity have the ironic effect of increasingly 'gendering' local, regional, and national resistance to incor-poration into the global arena as subordinated entities.
>
> (Kimmel 2005: 415)

Kimmel's view that gender is becoming the chief means of resistance to globalization is shared by Derné (2002, 2005) whose research amongst Indian men in North India and Fiji reveals that gender is affected by both transnational influences and local arrangements and concerns. Derné found that Indian men who are attracted to transnational media representations of male dominance simul-taneously distance themselves from transnational media depictions of new possibilities for women (Derné 2005). His findings support Connell's assertion that global forces that challenge men's identity and power often lead men to reaffirm local gender orthodoxies and hierarchies. By contrast, Hooper (2000) is less convinced that globalization has reconstructed gender relations in patriarchal ways. She argues that new technologies and new social divisions of labour may in fact fracture the male breadwinner role and 'soften' the hegemonic masculinity of early modernity.

A number of scholars have been critical of claims for a gendered world order. Among their concerns are the meanings attached to the concept of the global: 'what constitutes the global frontier? Where is it? And, if we are unsure where it is, what is the masculinity that it inscribes?' (Kenway *et al.* 2006: 30). Others focus their critique on the micro level and argue that Connell's study of the global rests on a tenuous and limited understanding of the local. For example, Louie (2003) is critical of Connell's call for a global approach to the study of men and masculinities because, in the urgency to capture the global facets of masculinity, she ends up missing the importance of local factors and interactions at the local level.

Louie (2003: 13) states that the consequence of Connell's call for the study of a global gender order is that:

> [O]ne of the most exciting areas for research – the comparisons of masculini-
> ties between cultures within Asia itself – will be subsumed by more global
> concerns. We still need to dislocate researchers' comfort zones. While I
> applaud an internationalist vision, I believe that the groundwork for under-
> standing local masculinities must still be done.

He does not dismiss the significance of globalization in the study of men and masculinities and acknowledges a hybridization process in which 'the mixing of different cultures has already produced global masculinities' (Louie 2003: 13). But, he argues, Connell's work on globalizing masculinities is in fact almost always from a Western perspective (Louie 2003: 1). For Louie, any understanding of the global must rest on a thorough knowledge of the local.

Like Louie, Hibbins is concerned about the potential ethnocentrism implied by the attempt to categorize a global hegemonic masculinity:

> This would lead us to ignore diversity and heterogeneity, eliminate the
> possibility of different types of hegemonic masculinities across different
> cultures, and undermine the potential or actual power of marginalised and
> subordinated masculinities.
>
> (Hibbins 2003: 198)

Louie and Hibbins both point to the need for sustained analysis of localized expressions of masculinity in non-Western contexts.[4] They caution, however, that such analysis should not simply replicate Western notions of masculinity or generate simple and reductive comparisons between the two (Wang 2003: 42). In making this point, Louie's study of Chinese masculinity establishes that 'the cerebral male model tends to dominate that of the macho, brawny male' (Louie 2002: 8). Western paradigms of masculinity are thus largely inappropriate to the Chinese case because 'their application would only prove that Chinese men are "not quite real men" because they fail the (Western) test of masculinity' (Louie 2002: 8–9).

The ubiquitous association of masculinity with Western models and ideals has led some scholars to suggest that the concept is of limited value in non-Western contexts. Haywood (2007: 90) warns that while the concept of masculinity (or masculinities) 'makes sense' within a Western sensibility it may have little analytical or conceptual value in other societies. In cross-cultural contexts, we must therefore be careful not to practise a form of 'conceptual imperialism' in which descriptive and analytical categories are extrapolated to other cultures. The alternative is to develop questions or paradigms that are generated from within specific cultural contexts (Louie 2002: 9). Such research contributes to the process of contesting taken-for-granted ideas about men, masculinity and sexuality. This is not to say that such research aims to reveal an 'uncontaminated' space of difference; after all, 'it is no longer even possible to conceive of a pristine theoretical and cultural world of "non-Westernness", unmarked by a history of asymmetrical interactions' (Srivastava 2004: 27–8). Instead, what is required is research which seeks to foreground the specificities of the local while also taking into account sites of engagement and interaction with the global. This includes an analysis of the ways in which masculinities are shaped by multiple engagements with imperialism, colonialism, nation-building and economic development programmes. Cross-cultural research can further explicate these processes by demonstrating how gender categories are assembled in local contexts.

Overview of chapters

Through the presentation of detailed ethnographic studies of localized masculinities, the authors in this collection add weight to the critique of hegemonic global masculinity. At the same time, they assert the importance of paying attention to the flows of ideas and people that constitute the processes of globalization. The chapters challenge the idea of emerging globalizing forms of masculinities. In doing so, they focus on two inter-related issues: the impact of cultural flows on the construction of what it means to *be* 'a man'; and the way global systems of production impact on the working lives of men. Chapter authors examine how flows of ideas, people and capital shape masculinities, and examine the debates that emerge in particular local settings about the meanings associated with 'traditional' and 'modern' masculinities. In this way, the collection contributes to a better understanding of how cultural and economic globalization is shaping the nature of gender relations in contemporary Southeast Asia.

Global economic restructuring has brought about significant changes in the organization of labour in the Asia-Pacific. While a considerable amount of research has been conducted on the ways in which global production has become dependent on women's labour in Southeast Asia, men are marginal to this analysis. The chapters by McKay and Lucero-Prisno, Kitiarsa and Thai address this gap. In their chapter, Steven McKay and Don Eliseo Lucero-Prisno III focus on the constructions and transnational performances of manhood among Filipino seafarers. They demonstrate that, within the Philippines, Filipino seamen are often constructed as 'exemplars of masculinity'. This image sits in contradistinction to their location in the lower rungs of an occupational and multinational hierarchy with limited opportunities for upward mobility. They argue that consequently Filipino seafarers are caught in a 'masculine dialectic' between models of middle-class professionalism on the one hand and working-class hyper-masculinity of adventure on the other. Their research suggests that because of the greater separation of workplace and home, migrant men are able to enact a range of multiple and sometimes conflicting masculinities.

Pattana Kitiarsa's chapter on the working lives of Thai migrant men living in Singapore also reveals the resourcefulness of migrant men who occupy marginal and relatively powerless social positions in the host society. His research shows that sexual intimacy forms a core part of migrant men's subjectivity as transnational actors. Male foreign workers actively engage in patterns of sexual intimacy despite the strict regulation of their work and social life by their employers and authorities. Kitiarsa suggests that, to understand male migrant manhood, we must look beyond the men's experiences of exploitative labour and acknowledge the fact that workmen are actors with purposeful intent, especially in their pursuit of everyday romance and sexual intimacy away from home.

Hung Cam Thai's chapter on Vietnamese low-wage immigrant men living in the United States reveals another dimension to the intersection between international migratory flows and constructions of masculinity. His research explores the way these men's sense of masculinity and social class is altered through their return visits to their homeland to seek a bride. These return visits enhance the immigrant men's socio-economic worth, as they are able to assert 'high status' when they return to Vietnam to visit because of their foreign passports, even when they live in dire conditions in the USA. Thai argues that the intersecting categories of social class and masculinity need to be expanded globally because much of what we know about both concepts in the West is still nation-specific despite the enormous increase in transnational flows of capital and people in recent years. A fundamental concern here is the question of how transnational migration and transnational mobility can simultaneously challenge as well as reinforce patriarchy.

The themes of social subordination and mobility are taken up in the chapter by Sophie Williams, Lenore Lyons and Michele Ford, which describes Chinese Singaporean men's participation in a members-only online forum about sex tourism to the Indonesian island of Batam. While descriptions of sex acts are ever present in the forum's 'international field reports', they are a vehicle for fraternity rather than eroticism or competitiveness. Williams, Lyons and Ford argue that the men's participation in this online community not only helps them escape from the demands of a heteronormative expression of masculinity predicated on the reproduction of the Singaporean state but also allows them to produce a localized form of brotherhood in which they share information and look out for each other's welfare in their encounters with Batam's sex workers.

While these chapters focus on the movement of people, those that follow address the global flow of ideas. The chapter by Trude Jacobsen explores the influence of traditional texts and discourses on the shaping of post-colonial masculinities, and how notions of 'tradition' intersect with dominant ideas about 'modernity'. In her study of Cambodian constructions of manhood, Jacobsen examines the tropes of 'good' and 'successful' men. International development agencies express concerns about Cambodian men's sexual promiscuity and the seeming contradiction between the two dominant 'manhood scripts' they are encouraged (and expected) to act out. Jacobsen argues that these conflicting scripts reflect the tension between modernity and the perception of tradition at work in Cambodian society. At the same time, the Cambodian past – including its social norms and gender roles – is persistently asserted as inviolable and bound up with national identity. Jacobsen's chapter challenges Western notions of the 'endlessly variable' nature of gender constructs and identities by revealing that in the Cambodian context it is 'culturally essential that the manhood script remain static'. Her critique of hegemonic masculinity focuses on the dominance of masculine ideals rather than the performance of multiple masculinities.

In his chapter on public violence and gender-based violence in Timor-Leste, Henri Myrttinen explores the intersections between the country's violent past and a patriarchal culture in which hegemonic forms of masculinity condone the use of violence. His research amongst young, urban men reveals an ambivalent attitude towards violence – on one hand it is denounced, but on the other hand it is legitimated as a form of discipline or an appropriate avenue to settle differences. Myrttinen concludes that Timor-Leste society is defined by a patchwork of co-existing patriarchies produced by local culture and the cataclysmic impacts of conflict and displacement as well as those of urbanization, modernization and globalization.

The remaining chapters examine the intersections of race, class, sexuality and culture in the shaping of marginal men's relationships with hegemonic ideals. The chapters by Wilson and Lyons and Ford examine how marginal men seek to subvert hegemonic and/or dominant constructions of masculinity. Ian Wilson's chapter examines how latent class and ethnic resentments over the perceived institutionalized inequalities of Indonesia's New Order government, and the failure of the post-New Order state to adequately redress them, have shaped local idioms of masculinity and power. At the centre of his analysis is the *jago* (strongman) who has been revived and has gained increasing currency amongst many disenfranchised young men in Jakarta's slums and poor neighbourhoods. In the context of decentralized and democratized Jakarta, post-New Order *jago* identity has become an assertion of exclusivist rights over resources in a given place. Wilson argues that as affluence, consumerism and global mobility become more inaccessible than ever to working-class men, *jago* masculinity is a means for demanding respect and achieving social status with a minimum of resources.

In their chapter, Lenore Lyons and Michele Ford explore the relationship between military service, masculinity and citizenship as experienced by Malay Muslim men in Singapore. Their study examines the nexus between class and ethnicity in the construction of Malay masculinities and in their juxtaposition against hegemonic middle-class Chinese norms. For the men in their study, Islam is a means to demonstrate a Malay man's superior loyalty to the nation, standing as it does in stark contrast with the materialism and promiscuity they associate with the Chinese.

Lyons and Ford conclude that Malay subaltern masculinity is not subversive of the existing hegemony because the men also gain from National Service, which they see as a positive experience where they grow up, learn respect and gain knowledge of the world – and thus as a means to achieve the status of normative Singaporean manhood. At the same time, however, their achievements are always partial because of their marginal location in class and ethnic hierarchies.

The study of men and masculinities in Southeast Asia is an under-examined field of research. Despite the strong and growing scholarly interest in issues related to gender and sexuality, much contemporary scholarship on the region continues to focus almost exclusively on the lives of women. The chapters in this collection address that gap by providing important new insights into the ways in which masculinities are (per)formed in different Southeast Asian contexts. In this way, *Men and Masculinities in Southeast Asia* contributes to the growing critique of hegemonic masculinity and offers innovative ways of thinking about the intersection between the local and the global, and between the traditional and the modern, in the lives of men and women in the region.

Notes

1 Both queer theory and post-colonial theory take men and masculinities as the objects of their analysis. Queer theory seeks to problematize the categories 'man/male/masculinity' and 'woman/female/femininity'; while post-colonial theory has pointed out that the unspoken, silent man of history is heterosexual, white and Western.
2 In contrast to the almost exclusive focus on masculinities in the study of men, few studies of women address the related concept of 'femininities'. This fact points to a fundamental difference in the ways in which gendered identities and practices have been conceptualized within feminist studies.
3 Hearn (2004) is less positive about its continued centrality in CSM. He calls for a movement away from the study of hegemonic masculinity to the hegemony of men.
4 This call is not limited to studies of Asian societies. Morrell and Swart (2005: 91) argue that despite the emergence of post-colonial theory, and the strong influence of feminism, little has been done to rectify this omission.

References

Ang, I. (1995) 'I'm a feminist but . . . "Other" women and postnational feminism', in B. Caine and R. Pringle (eds), *Transitions: New Australian Feminisms*, St Leonards: Allen and Unwin, pp. 57–73.

Atkinson, J. and Errington, S. (eds) (1990) *Power and Difference: Gender in Island Southeast Asia,* Stanford: Stanford University Press.

Bandyopadhyay, M. (2006) 'Competing masculinities in a prison', *Men and Masculinities* 9(2): 186–203.

Banerjee, S. (2005) *Make Me a Man! Masculinity, Hinduism, and Nationalism in India,* Albany: State University of New York Press.

Beasley, C. (2008) 'Rethinking hegemonic masculinity in a globalizing world', *Men and Masculinities* 11(1): 86–103.

Boellstorff, T. (2005) *The Gay Archipelago: Sexuality and Nation in Indonesia,* Princeton: Princeton University Press.

Brownell, S. and Wasserstrom, J. N. (eds) (2002) *Chinese Femininities/Chinese Masculinities: A Reader,* Berkeley: University of California Press.

Butler, J. (1990) *Gender Trouble: Feminism and the Subversion of Identity,* New York: Routledge.

—— (1997) 'Performative acts and gender constitution: an essay in phenomenology and feminist theory', in K. Conboy, N. Medina and S. Stanbury (eds), *Writing on the Body: Female Embodiment and Feminist Theory,* New York: Columbia University Press, pp. 401–17.

Chen, A. S. (1999) 'Lives at the center of the periphery, lives at the periphery of the center: Chinese American masculinities and bargaining with hegemony', *Gender & Society* 13(5): 584–607.

Clark, M. (2010) *Maskulinitas: Culture, Gender and Politics in Indonesia,* Melbourne: Monash Asia Institute.

Clatterbaugh, K. (2004) 'What is problematic about masculinities?', in P. F. Murphy (ed.), *Feminism and Masculinities,* Oxford: Oxford University Press, pp. 200–13.

Coles, T. (2009) 'Negotiating the field of masculinity: the production and reproduction of multiple dominant masculinities', *Men and Masculinities* 12(1): 30–44.

Collins, P. (1999) 'Moving beyond gender: intersectionality and scientific knowledge', in M. M. Ferree, J. Lorber and B. B. Hess (eds), *Revisioning Gender,* Thousand Oaks, CA: Sage, pp. 261–84.

Connell, R. W. (1995) *Masculinities,* St Leonards: Allen and Unwin.

—— (2005) 'Globalization, imperialism, and masculinities', in M. S. Kimmel, J. Hearn and R. W. Connell (eds), *Handbook of Studies on Men and Masculinities,* Thousand Oaks, CA: Sage, pp. 71–89.

Connell, R. W. and Messerschmidt, J. W. (2005) 'Hegemonic masculinity: rethinking the concept', *Gender and Society* 19(6): 829–59.

Connell, R. W., Hearn, J. and Kimmel, M. S. (2005) 'Introduction', in M. S. Kimmel, J. Hearn and R. W. Connell (eds), *Handbook of Studies on Men and Masculinities,* Thousand Oaks, CA: Sage, pp. 1–12.

Cornwall, A. and Lindisfarne, N. (1994) 'Dislocating masculinity: gender, power and anthropology', in A. Cornwall and N. Lindisfarne (eds), *Dislocating Masculinity: Comparative Ethnographies,* London: Routledge, pp. 11–46.

Demetriou, D. Z. (2001) 'Connell's concept of hegemonic masculinity: a critique', *Theory and Society* 30(3): 337–61.

Derné, S. (2000) *Movies, Masculinity, and Modernity: An Ethnography of Men's Filmgoing in India,* Westport, CT: Greenwood Press.

—— (2002) 'Globalization and the reconstitution of local gender arrangements', *Men and Masculinities* 5(2): 144–64.

—— (2005) 'Globalization and masculine space in India and Fiji', in B. van Hoven and K. Hörschelmann (eds), *Spaces of Masculinities,* London: Routledge, pp. 86–96.

Donaldson, M. (1993) 'What is hegemonic masculinity?', *Theory and Society* 22(5): 643–57.

Donaldson, M. and Howson, R. (2009) 'Men, migration and hegemonic masculinity', in M. Donaldson, R. Hibbins, R. Howson and B. Pease (eds), *Migrant Men: Critical Studies of Masculinities and the Migration Experience,* New York: Routledge, pp. 210–17.

Evans, R. (2005) '"You questioning my manhood, boy?": using work to play with gender roles in a regime of male skilled-labour', in B. van Hoven and K. Hörschelmann (eds), *Spaces of Masculinities,* London: Routledge, pp. 193–204.

Gatens, M. (1983) 'A critique of the sex/gender distinction', in J. Allen and P. Patten (eds), *Beyond Marxism? Interventions after Marx,* Sydney: Intervention Publications, pp. 3–20.

Geng, S. (2004) *The Fragile Scholar: Power and Masculinity in Chinese Culture,* Hong Kong: Hong Kong University Press.

Haraway, D. (1991) *Simians, Cyborgs, and Women: The Reinvention of Nature,* London: Free Association.

Haywood, C. (2007) *Men and Masculinities,* Maidenhead: McGraw-Hill International.

Hearn, J. (1996) 'Is masculinity dead? A critique of the concept of masculinity/masculinities', in M. Mac an Ghaill (ed.), *Understanding Masculinities: Social Relations and Cultural Arenas,* Buckingham: Open University Press.

—— (2004) 'From hegemonic masculinity to the hegemony of men', *Feminist Theory* 5(1): 49–72.

Hearn, J. and Pringle, K. (2006) 'Studying men in Europe', in J. Hearn, K. Pringle and members of CROME (eds), *European Perspectives on Men and Masculinities: National and Transnational Approaches,* Houndmills: Palgrave Macmillan, pp. 1–19.

Hibbins, R. (2003) 'Male gender identities among Chinese male migrants', in K. Louie and M. Low (eds), *Asian Masculinities: The Meaning and Practice of Manhood in China and Japan,* London: Routledge, pp. 197–219.

hooks, b. (1981) *Ain't I a Woman: Black Women and Feminism,* Boston: South End Press.

Hooper, C. (2000) *Manly States: Masculinities, International Relations, and Gender Politics,* New York: Columbia University Press.

Hoven, B. v. and Hörschelmann, K. (2005) 'Introduction: from geographies of men to geographies of women and back again?', in B. v. Hoven and K. Hörschelmann (eds) *Spaces of Masculinities,* London: Routledge, pp. 1–16.

Hoven, B. van and Meijering, L. (2005) 'Transient masculinities: Indian IT-professionals in Germany', in B. van Hoven and K. Hörschelmann (eds), *Spaces of Masculinities,* London: Routledge, pp. 75–85.

Howson, R. (2006) *Challenging Hegemonic Masculinity,* London: Routledge.

Jackson, P. A. (1996) *Dear Uncle Go: Male Homosexuality in Thailand,* Bangkok and San Francisco: Bua Luang Publishing Company.

Jackson, P. and Sullivan, G. (eds) (1999) *Lady Boys, Tom Boys, Rent Boys: Male and Female Homosexualities in Contemporary Thailand,* New York: Haworth Press.

—— (eds) (2001) *Gay and Lesbian Asia: Culture, Identity, Community,* New York: Harrington Park Press.

Jefferson, T. (2002) 'Subordinating hegemonic masculinity', *Theoretical Criminology* 6(1): 63–88.

Kenway, J., Kraack, A. and Hickey-Moody, A. (2006) *Masculinity beyond the Metropolis,* Basingstoke: Palgrave Macmillan.

Kimmel, M. S. (2005) 'Globalization and its mal(e)contents: the gendered moral and political economy of terrorism', in M. S. Kimmel, J. Hearn and R. W. Connell (eds), *Handbook of Studies on Men and Masculinities,* Thousand Oaks, CA: Sage, pp. 414–31.

Kimmel, M. S. and Messner, M. A. (eds) (1992) *Men's Lives,* New York: Macmillan.

Light, R. (2003) 'Sport and the construction of masculinity in the Japanese education system', in K. Louie and M. Low (eds), *Asian Masculinities: The Meaning and Practice of Manhood in China and Japan,* London: Routledge, pp. 100–17.

Light, R. and Kirk, D. (2000) 'High school rugby, the body and the reproduction of hegemonic masculinity', *Sport, Education and Society* 5(2): 163–76.

Lindsay, L. and Miescher, S. F. (eds) (2003) *Men and Masculinities in Modern Africa,* Portsmouth: Heinemann.

Louie, K. (2002) *Theorising Chinese Masculinity: Society and Gender in China,* Cambridge: Cambridge University Press.

—— (2003) 'Chinese, Japanese and global masculine identities', in K. Louie and M. Low (eds), *Asian Masculinities: The Meaning and Practice of Manhood in China and Japan*, London: Routledge, pp. 1–16.

Louie, K. and Low, M. (eds) (2003) *Asian Masculinities: The Meaning and Practice of Manhood in China and Japan,* London: Routledge.

Lusher, D. and Robins, G. (2009) 'Hegemonic and other masculinities in local social contexts', *Men and Masculinities* 11(4): 387–423.

Mac an Ghaill, M. (1996) 'Introduction', in M. Mac an Ghaill (ed.), *Understanding Masculinities: Social Relations and Cultural Arenas*, Buckingham: Open University Press.

Manderson, L. and Jolly, M. (eds) (1997) *Sites of Desire, Economies of Pleasure: Sexualities in Asia and the Pacific,* Chicago: University of Chicago Press.

Mohanty, C. T., Russo, A. and Torres, L. (eds) (1991) *Third World Women and the Politics of Feminism,* Bloomington: Indiana University Press.

Moller, M. (2007) 'Exploiting patterns: a critique of hegemonic masculinity', *Journal of Gender Studies* 16(3): 263–76.

Morrell, R and Swart, S. (2005) 'Men in the third world: postcolonial perspectives on masculinity', in M. S. Kimmel, J. Hearn and R. W. Connell (eds), *Handbook of Studies on Men and Masculinities*, Thousand Oaks, CA: Sage, pp. 90–113.

Nilan, P., Donaldson, M. and Howson, R. (2009) 'Indonesian Muslim masculinities in Australia', in M. Donaldson, R. Hibbins, R. Howson and B. Pease (eds), *Migrant Men: Critical Studies of Masculinities and the Migration Experience*, New York: Routledge, pp. 172–89.

Ong, A. and Peletz, M. G. (eds) (1995) *Bewitching Women, Pious Men: Gender and Body Politics in Southeast Asia,* Berkeley: University of California Press.

Osella, C. and Osella, F. (2006) *Men and Masculinities in South India,* London: Anthem Press.

Osella, F., Osella, C. and Chopra, R. (eds) (2004) *South Asian Masculinities: Context of Change, Sites of Continuity,* New Delhi: Women Unlimited.

Ouzgane, L. and Morrell, R. (eds) (2005) *African Masculinities: Men in Africa from the Late Nineteenth Century to the Present,* New York: Palgrave Macmillan.

Peletz, M. (1995) 'Neither reasonable nor responsible: contrasting representations of masculinity in a Malay society', in A. Ong and M. Peletz (eds), *Bewitching Women, Pious Men: Gender and Body Politics in Southeast Asia*, Berkeley and Los Angeles: University of California Press, pp. 76–123.

Pringle, R. (2005) 'Masculinities, sport, and power: a critical comparison of Gramscian and Foucauldian inspired theoretical tools', *Journal of Sport and Social Issues* 29(3): 256–78.

Roberson, J. and Suzuki, N. (eds) (2002) *Men and Masculinities in Contemporary Japan: Beyond the Urban Salaryman Model,* London and New York: Routledge.

Schiele, J. H. (2000) *Human Services and the Afrocentric Paradigm,* Binghamton: The Haworth Press.

Sedgwick, E. K. (1995) 'Gosh, Boy George, you must be awfully secure in your masculinity!', in M. Berger, B. Wallis and S. Watson (eds), *Constructing Masculinity*, New York: Routledge, pp. 11–20.

Segal, L. (2000) *Why Feminism?,* New York: Columbia University Press.

Sinha, M. (1999) 'Giving masculinity a history: some contributions from the historiography of colonial India', *Gender and History* 11(3): 445–60.

Srivastava, S. (2004) 'Introduction: semen, history, desire and theory', in S. Srivastava (ed.), *Sexual Sites, Seminal Attitudes: Sexualities, Masculinities and Culture in South Asia*, New Delhi: Sage, pp. 11–48.

Wang, Y. (2003) 'Mr Butterfly in *Defunct Capital*: "soft" masculinity and (mis)engendering China', in K. Louie and M. Low (eds), *Asian Masculinities: The Meaning and Practice of Manhood in China and Japan*, London: Routledge, pp. 41–58.

Wetherell, M. and Edley, N. (1999) 'Negotiating hegemonic masculinity: imaginary positions and psycho-discursive practices', *Feminism and Psychology* 9(3): 335–56.

1 Masculinities afloat

Filipino seafarers and the situational performance of manhood

Steven McKay and
Don Eliseo Lucero-Prisno III

Migrants from the Philippines have been central to the scholarship on both gender and migration. Yet few studies have focused on Filipino masculinity and almost none on one of the country's most dominant global occupational niches: merchant seafaring. Our research reveals that due to their work, remittances and growing visibility, Filipino seamen are often constructed – by themselves and by other Filipinos – as 'exemplars of masculinity' (Connell 1995). Nevertheless, they toil primarily at the lower rungs of an occupational and multinational hierarchy, and must grapple with both limited upward mobility and a reputation in the industry as merely 'good followers'. Drawing on interviews and extensive ethnographic field research conducted in the Philippines; in seaports in Europe, Asia and South America; and onboard five merchant ships with Filipino and mixed-nationality crews, this chapter focuses on the constructions and transnational performances of manhood among Filipino seafarers, tracing their strategies to compensate for their marginalization.[1] We argue that Filipino seafarers are caught in a 'masculine dialectic' between models of middle-class professionalism on the one hand, and working-class hyper-masculinity of adventure on the other.

Theoretically, we develop the notion of not only multiple but conflicting masculinities to better understand how the situational performance of competing masculinities are spatially practised. This account complicates Connell's (1995, 1998) extension of a single hegemonic masculinity at the global scale. With rising global economic interdependence and greater cross-border flows, Connell and Wood (2005) have argued that a certain 'transnational business masculinity' is becoming hegemonic over the local. Our focus on the workplace demonstrates how occupational and organizational structures influence both the class character of and power relations between different nationally grounded masculinities (Collinson and Hearn 2004; Ashcraft 2005), adding weight to assertions that there continues to be a diverse range of masculinities among regions and countries, and that it remains crucial to specify the constraints and contexts in which such masculinities are formed (Louie and Low 2003; Osella and Osella 2006; Gutmann 2007).

The chapter also captures the discursive and performative elements of masculinity and how men actually 'do masculinity' in multiple contexts (Fenstermaker and West 2002). Migratory workers in particular highlight such creative efforts, since there is a greater separation of workplace and home and migrant men are able to enact their masculine identities in a broader array of locations. The fact that these migrant working men operate in a transnational environment highlights how masculinities can conflict, particularly in interaction with other types of social difference, such as nation, race and ethnicity (Connell and Messerschmidt 2005), and the extent to which constructions of masculinities are both situational and performative (Paap 2006; Gutmann 2007). While facing considerable structural constraints, Filipino seafarers succeed in acting across a variety of stages to render this masculine dialectic both productive and creative. They resist a marginalized masculinity driven by workplace subordination and labour-market insecurity by combining a 'cautious masculinity' of self-control and competence on the job, an 'expressive hyper-masculinity' of compensation in port and among peers, and a 'breadwinner masculinity' of providership, sacrifice and responsible fatherhood at home.

Masculinity and work

A key arena in which masculinities are fashioned is the workplace, where central elements associated with hegemonic masculinity, such as competitiveness, autonomy, providership and risk-taking, are played out. One of the primary divisions between masculinities contrasts a dominant, 'civilized' middle-class masculinity of professional or managerial men against a subordinate or marginal 'primitive' masculinity of working-class men (Willis 1977; Ashcraft and Flores 2003). Of course, there is variation within each of these masculinities related to organizational or occupational specialization. Barrett (1996) demonstrates that while all the American naval officers in his study construct their masculinity against women and gay men, their occupational specialties mean that each highlights an element of hegemonic masculinity that sets his group apart – whether it is autonomy and risk-taking by pilots, competence under pressure by bridge officers, or technical rationality by supply officers. This strategic and variable approach is also evident among working-class men. As Paap (2006) has shown in the American context, working-class labourers often celebrate a masculine 'pigness' – coarse, physically tough and aggressively heterosexual – to set themselves apart from more refined, effete professionals who lack 'real' manhood. But since this strategic 'pigness' conflicts directly with managerial-class masculinities, it is used to justify the continued subordination of such working-class 'pigs'. Taking into account occupational and class relations highlights how men often struggle with a class-tinged 'masculine dialectic' between a more civilized model of middle-class manhood associated with professionalism and upward mobility, and a more physical, aggressive and hyper-masculine working-class model (Willis 1977; Ashcraft and Flores 2003).

Merchant seafaring has had a distinct masculine identity since its earliest years in the Mediterranean and in East and Southeast Asia (Hohman 1956; Reid 1993; Connell 1995). Because shipboard relations were modelled along military lines, merchant ships have also historically had an extremely hierarchical power structure. Thus, like other kinds of subordinate workers, sailors tend to construct their dangerous work as particularly masculine and even heroic, in part to help them survive exploitative relations (Willis 1977; Reid 1993; Kimmel 1996). Filipinos on Western merchant ships also have a long history, from forced labour aboard Spanish galleons from the sixteenth to the nineteenth century, to crew members on British trading and American whaling ships in the nineteenth century, to a brief stint as stewards in the American merchant marines in the early twentieth century (Melendy 1977; Borah 1995/1996; Aguilar 2003). In fact, Filipinos became so identified with crewing that the term *Manilamen* became an entire category for 'Asiatic' seafarers on Western ships, including Filipinos, Chinese, Malays, Pacific Islanders, South Asians and those of mixed race (Chappell 2004).

Changes in the modern shipping industry have altered the jobs and masculine image of the seafarer. With larger ships, smaller crews, and increased automation, there has been a marked push to professionalize both maritime education and the workforce (Alderton *et al.* 2004). For most seafarers – particularly those from developing countries like the Philippines – this means that even entry-level positions often require a post-secondary degree from an accredited maritime college. Such changes have also led to a contemporary occupational masculinity that embodies professional, military *and* working-class masculinities, depending on one's position onboard. At the top of the hierarchy, junior and senior officers support their claims to professionalism through their authority, education, licences and relatively high salaries. Yet they share with their unlicensed subordinates a workplace that is generally all-men, hierarchical, risky, and often dangerous and physically taxing. Taken together, seamen in many ways project an image of what Connell (1995: 185) calls 'exemplars of masculinity': heterosexual, competitive, adventurous, homosocial and able to dominate women as well as other men. But how different masculinities get constructed, and by whom, pivots on rank and nationality, markers that are often closely correlated.

Another important development in contemporary shipping has been the increasing dominance of multinational crews. Since the economic crisis of the mid-1970s, ship owners have begun hiring cheaper crews from the Philippines, South Korea, India and Indonesia (Turnbull 2000). From only 2,000 Filipinos on foreign ships in the 1960s, today there are over 275,000 and Filipinos are now by far the largest national group, making up 28.1 per cent of the global workforce (NSB 1982; Amante 2003; POEA 2007). Despite this influx, the seafaring labour market remains quite stratified as strong European and Japanese maritime unions have fought to protect their senior officers in exchange for allowing ship owners to hire junior officers and low-level 'ratings' (non-licensed deck, engine or catering crew) from other countries. As a result, Filipino seafarers' position within the occupational hierarchy has shifted only slowly. In the mid-1970s, 90 per cent of Filipinos sailed as lower-level ratings, and 10 per cent were junior officers (NSB 1976). In 2005 73 per cent of Filipinos were still sailing as lower-level crew, with 19 per cent as junior officers and 8 per cent as senior officers (POEA 2007).

The situational performance of conflicting masculinities

The limited scholarship on contemporary Filipino masculinities has generally situated its analysis in a colonial and/or international context. As Rafael (2000) and others note, the American colonial project from 1898 was racialized and gendered, with the masculinist imperial conquest aiming in part to 'rationalize and buttress the power of "civilized" white men' while simultaneously constructing Filipino colonial subjects as savage, child-like, feminized, unmanly and generally unfit for self-rule (Espiritu 2003: 50). Yet resistance to colonial conquest also created opportunities to exercise local notions of masculinity. For example, anti-colonial fighters were often mythologized as *magaling na lalaki*, literally 'good men', for their bravery, invincible bodies and indomitable spirit (Aguilar 1998: 53). These notions drew on older beliefs – shared across much of Southeast Asia – regarding ideal male qualities of *malakas* or strength, embodied in pre-colonial *datu* chiefs or 'Big Men' who combined bravery, physical strength, intelligence, eloquence and rapport with the spirit world to gain followers (Aguilar 1998: 29).

Colonization by Spain and the United States and the drawing of the Philippines into the modern capitalist system then led to a mixing of Western concepts of a 'civilized' and self-disciplined masculinity with local concepts of male power and potency focused on *kapangyarihan ng loob* or interior strength of will, physical prowess and invulnerability of the body (Rafael 2000; Tremlett 2006: 13). This mixing is evident in studies of contemporary Filipino masculinity. Pingol (2001), in her study of Illocano men whose wives work abroad, demonstrates that the Philippines' deep interconnection with the global economy has proven to be an enormous challenge for Filipino men facing norms of masculinity that centre on being 'good providers, virile sex partners, firm and strong fathers' (ibid.: 8). House-husbands left behind by migrating women actively refashioned their masculine identities, appealing to broader masculine ideologies of 'being in control' and 'maintaining autonomy'. Respect was earned through a man's self-discipline, independent earnings, leadership, endurance of suffering and ability to abstain sexually, while fear was maintained through physical domination, risk-taking, psychological coercion and publicly expressing the 'machismo of rogues and daredevils' (ibid.: 4). Margold (1995: 290) makes a similar argument, contrasting the masculine ideals of verbal eloquence, *galante* (gracefulness) and adventurousness among Illocanos with the 'aggressive control' over wives and children chosen by some 'failed' migrant men returning from the Middle East. Importantly, Margold points out the class associations of the two ends of the spectrum and how the exploitation and humiliation of low-paid, low-status labour can limit men's ability to construct a masculine identity from actions garnering respect rather than fear. At the same time, Parreñas (2005, 2008) argues that while migration tends to heighten gendered norms of conventional fatherhood around providing material support and projecting authority from afar at the expense of emotional attachment and shared child-centred parenting, when migrant fathers were home, they tended to do *more* housework and childcare than fathers in families whose wives worked abroad. This may demonstrate that being in the economic position to be a good provider can allow for a wider repertoire for enacting one's masculinity.

Masculinities onboard

As Gutmann (2007: 245) points out, '[M]en and women are presented with stages and scripts not of their own choosing. What they do creatively within these social and cultural constraints, and how originally they perform their roles, however, is not preordained.' The character of the maritime workplace and the stratification of the seafarer labour market are both key factors that influence the construction of Filipino masculinities and the ways Filipino seafarers act to develop meaningful masculine selves. This stratification is felt most directly onboard, where many Filipinos feel there is a national if not racial division of labour by rank. As one seafarer commented:

> There are mixed crews, with Europeans. But the Filipinos are only seconds [engineers or officers] and below. You'll never see a European crew under a Filipino captain – no way. Maybe someday in the future, but now, no way.

Another Filipino – who held a junior officer licence but was working as an Ordinary Seaman (the lowest-level position on deck) – observed bitterly that:

> Germans are prejudiced. Ukrainians are also a bit prejudiced. They would say that Filipinos have studied in school so long but onboard all we do is clean and remove rust. Unlike them, they just studied for a short period of time and still get promoted easily . . . The Ukrainians sometimes even call us slaves.

Such workplace segmentation in a hierarchical and homosocial environment can lead to a questioning of the masculinity of the lower ranked, especially in a multinational workforce, as demonstrated by a study aboard two cargo ships with Norwegian officers and Filipino crews, which concluded that the Norwegian sailors constructed a hegemonic masculinity in direct contrast to the subordinate masculinity of the lower-ranked Filipinos (Ostreng 2001: 7).

Filipinos vigorously resist this ascribed, subordinate masculinity by enacting their own combinations of professional and selective marginal strategies. On the one hand, many Filipino seamen, particularly of lower ranks, view their jobs in traditionally masculine terms, reinterpreting their exploitative and dangerous work as 'a heroic exercise of manly confrontation with the task' (Willis 1977). This is clear in the gender typing of the job's unique characteristics. As one seaman exclaimed:

> From the start, I knew that this is a man's job. Before, I read in comic magazines that if you are a seaman, you are macho. You have to be a real man [*lalakeng-lalake*] with tremendous endurance to survive staying for a long time at sea . . . When you are aboard a ship, the things you discuss are man's stuff [*usapang lalake*]. You would really feel like a man because work is really hard.

Yet on the other hand, many Filipino seamen also realize the class stigma of manual work and seek to cast their jobs in more professional terms, arguing that *all* Filipino seafarers should be considered 'professionals'. For example, a young Second Mate explained that, regardless of rank, Filipinos exhibited professionalism through their skill, competence and quality as attested to by the government accreditation they received before leaving the Philippines. As a result, he argued, even unlicensed lower-level crew members are 'professional in the sense that they are quality exports of the Philippines because they would not send you to other countries if you are not qualified, if you are not competent'. This observation reflects the fact that, since 90 per cent of Filipino seafarers do not have the authority of a master (captain) or chief engineer, many choose to emphasize occupational competence in their claims for professional status.

In part because many Filipinos have had long tenures without significant upward mobility, they tend to highlight their experience, ingenuity, and capacity for improvisation, which they say set them apart from 'educated' white officers. For example, one Filipino captain bragged about Filipinos' ability to repair machinery creatively:

> The Filipino, he can fix anything . . . Other nationalities, if they see there are no spare parts, they will say, 'OK, that's it, we'll wait 'til we're in port.' But Filipinos somehow will get it working again. They'll make a new part or fix one.

Many Filipino seamen also tried to project a more professional and self-disciplined masculine image by distancing themselves from what they described as the 'older' negative image of Filipino seamen from the 1970s and 1980s. One non-officer noted:

> Before, the Filipinos were known for . . . drinking and fighting but not anymore. Before, maybe they are just hiring anyone around Luneta [a city park in Manila, where seafarers congregate] asking 'Hey, do you want to be a seaman? OK, come on.' Like a market. Some of these guys were not so good. Now, almost all Filipino seamen are graduates [of maritime colleges], more professional. Most of us are also married, have families.

What is most interesting to note here is how the seamen use a variety of reference points – both at and beyond the workplace – to redefine what they consider 'professional'. Education, competence, skill and creativity, but also maturity, responsibility, self-control and discipline, are all areas in which Filipino seamen – regardless of rank – are seen to demonstrate a professional masculinity. In this sense, they reconstitute and borrow some elements of a working-class breadwinner masculinity to define their own notion of 'professionalism', yet downplay or reject those elements traditionally associated with seafarers, often associated with rough and 'macho' behaviour: drinking, womanizing and fighting (Pingol 2001).

By contrast, other elements often associated with a professional masculinity, such as aggressiveness, risk-taking, decisiveness or taking charge in dangerous or stressful situations are often not open to Filipino seafarers or are simply seen as too perilous (Barrett 1996). Many seamen noted that they try to avoid asserting themselves onboard in ways that might jeopardize their employment because there is a surplus of seafarers in the Philippines and increasing competition from seafarers from other low-wage countries. A non-licensed deck worker explained:

> You shouldn't complain too much or make too many reports. They will think you're a troublemaker and maybe you won't get a line-up [selected for possible hire] . . . If you get a bad report, it can be very bad for your career . . . The seaman really needs to work. His family needs it. His kids need it . . . So we Filipinos are very careful to think, think, think before we do anything.

Given their labour-market vulnerability, many of the Filipino seamen embrace this 'cautious masculinity' that plays down assertiveness and risk-taking and instead focuses on self-control and ability to do one's job. On ships with full Filipino crews, both officers and lower-ranking seamen understand the context of market vulnerability and accept 'cautiousness' as a sign of good judgment, restraint and professionalism.

Yet while industry leaders and many non-Filipino officers on mixed-nationality crews appreciate the discipline of Filipino seamen, they nevertheless interpret Filipino cautiousness as 'meekness' and an inability to take responsibility or lead – (masculine) qualities viewed as central for moving into senior officer positions. For example, a manager at a leading Japanese firm who found Filipinos to be excellent crew members explained why he nevertheless preferred Indian captains over Filipinos:

> One is the leadership qualities that an Indian displays as compared with a Filipino . . . If you tell him [a Filipino] what is to be done, it'll be done, you can sleep on it . . . But if you tell him, 'read this rule and implement it', that's where the Indian has an advantage. Of course there are shining examples [of Filipino captains] . . . and we've had excellent, excellent Filipinos – much better than some Indians we've had. But on average, [the Filipino] says, 'you chew the food, put it in my mouth and I'll swallow it' . . . I think it's an attitude . . . they're not an ambitious lot.

Thus the cautious competence that Filipino seamen display to defend their niche is often used by more powerful industry actors to reinforce the subordinate reputation of Filipinos as merely 'good followers'.

Despite their limited ability to construct a professional masculinity through work, Filipino seamen nonetheless resist their subordinate reputations and act in other ways to assert their masculinity while aboard ship. These expressive acts of masculine recovery are most often performed among their peers in the more power-neutral or leisure spaces onboard. For example, on one bulk carrier ship with a full Filipino crew, one way the lower-level seamen expressed their physical prowess and competitiveness was through games such as basketball. Here, on the crowded main deck at the emergency muster station, a makeshift court was set up in a space not marked by obvious workplace hierarchy. Officers and ratings took part in these regular afternoon games on deck, providing an opportunity for lower-ranked sailors to out-perform and physically dominate their superiors in ways that were not possible during the working day. Similar recreational outlets exist for mixed-nationality crews, though non-Filipino officers are often less likely to engage in such games with crew members of a different nationality and of a lower rank.

On both full Filipino and mixed-nationality crewed ships, lower-level Filipino seamen found other opportunities to express their masculinity in common social areas of the ship, such as the mess hall and the adjacent recreational area. In these off-duty moments, the Filipino crew, as well as some Filipino officers, spent much of their time playing cards, watching movies and, quite often, watching taped sporting events such as cockfight derbies from Manila, boxing matches and basketball games. In multiple ways, these moments re-created for many Filipinos the common male *barkada* or homosocial friend groups found throughout the Philippines. These feelings and solidarities were even further heightened during birthday parties or social occasions, during which the consumption of alcohol was openly allowed. These events – which almost always took place in the crew mess, a space clearly marked off as the 'turf' of the lower-ranking crew – provided another opportunity for lower-ranking men to publicly outdo their superiors and highlight another aspect of Filipino masculinity: verbal or vocal eloquence, performed in this case through Karaoke and competitive singing. As a way to foster better relations across the occupational hierarchy, while taking part, some officers, especially on full Filipino crews, were careful not to dominate events clearly initiated by the lower-ranking crew. Thus men of all ranks selected their favourite songs and competed, in a friendly and at times boisterous atmosphere, for high scores and the accolades of their peers. Such mixing, however, was less typical in mixed-nationality crews, where non-Filipino officers were less likely to frequent the crew mess, where the lower-ranking Filipinos congregated.

Masculinities in port

Expressive acts of masculinity are not confined to the ship. In fact, one of the primary locations where Filipino seamen most freely affirm their manhood is in port. During nine- to twelve-month contracts, port visits provide one of the few opportunities for the seamen to compensate for the lack of autonomy onboard. For many, port visits are used primarily as a break from monotony and a chance to shop and communicate with family back home. A majority of seafarers interviewed asserted that phone calls home were their top priority and the first thing they did when ashore. For many, the highlight of their calls home is their conversations with their kids. A 29-year-old Oiler (an unlicensed engine-room worker) summed up the feelings of many seamen as follows:

> I do not get to see my family often because we are on sea for nine months and are on vacation only for a few months. I feel that I am growing old but I am

> not growing old with them. I miss them. It feels like I am left out. They are all there, growing old together, and then I come home and see them and I feel like a part of me is missing.

Phone calls updating the seamen on important family matters, family celebrations, children's school performance, as well as family problems, help ease the stress, loneliness and isolation experienced onboard. In many ways, they represent an opportunity for the seamen to reconnect with family, but also to reassert their paternal – if physically distant – authority as responsible breadwinners, husbands and fathers.

However, port visits are also an opportunity to engage in risk-taking, in part because ports provide a liminal context between work and home, where one's actions can be performed for and witnessed by male peers but not by superiors or families. Depending on the port and time ashore, many seamen take the opportunity to visit local bars or seamen's clubs to relax, drink alcohol and/or meet local sex workers. Going ashore is a social event and many go in small groups. While seafarers of different nationalities tend to hang out at the same seamen's centres or bars, when present in sufficient numbers they tend to sit and drink with those of the same nationality who speak their language. This grouping may also reflect a division by rank, since rank and nationality are often closely correlated. At one large bar frequented by seamen and sex workers in Santos Brazil, seafarers will often request the DJs to play music or provide their own CDs of music from their country of origin. So the DJ may play Indian music to get the South Asian seafarers to dance, Middle Eastern music for Turkish seamen, or Tagalog pop songs to entice the Filipinos.

As noted above, virility and sexuality constitute a core element of Filipino masculinity. But as Pingol (2001: 232) suggests, 'sexuality pivots on the productive self' and masculinity can be threatened when men cannot fulfil normative expectations at work. While not all seafarers privilege sexual encounters, exhibitions of (hyper)sexuality in port can serve as both an outlet and as compensation when faced with being in subordinate positions onboard. A married, 31-year-old Able-Bodied Seaman (AB) commented:

> Being a seamen, there is lots of adventure. You have to survive the rough seas . . . of course, you meet a lot of girls. In every port. Sometimes, you don't even have to pay . . . Maybe they're looking for adventure too.

Filipino seamen compete against seamen of other nationalities in the realm of sexual performance and reputation. One way they do this is by asserting their national and sexual identities through a practice of penile enhancements or implants, known as *bolitas*, literally 'little balls'. The practice involves the insertion – usually onboard ship by a fellow seaman – of small metal, glass, jade or plastic balls under the skin along the shaft of the penis.[2] When asked why they go through such a dangerous and painful procedure, Alberto, a 33-year-old married seafarer, explained, 'Well, Americans and Europeans, you really don't need them, but we Filipinos – we need something extra.' His shipmate added, 'Yes, *bolitas* are the Filipino's secret weapon!' As this observation suggests, the Filipino seamen we encountered appear to have internalized a subordinate sexual identity that seems to be a direct expression of their subordinate occupational, national and ethnic identity onboard and in the global market. Thus these seafarers view *bolitas* as a way to compensate for their perceived disadvantage in the sexual marketplace by 'enhancing' their sexualized bodies to establish a distinct and positive national identity and self-image. This national competition is arbitrated by 'girls in port'. Alberto continued to explain, 'Filipino seamen are famous for [*bolitas*] . . . that's why they [women in port] like us, why they keep asking for us. When they hear that Filipinos are coming, they're happy.'

Yet at the same time that they assert their masculinity through their sexual adventures and body modification, Filipinos do not necessarily conform to 'hyper-masculine' ideals. As a Chief Officer boasted:

> The women prefer Filipinos because we treat them nicer, not like other nationalities. They think because they pay, they can treat them badly. Like the Koreans . . . But the Filipinos – we treat them like girlfriends. We pay too, but we're nice, we smile, we even court them. That's what makes the Filipino special, we're romantic.

Here, in the competitive context among men of different nationalities, the Filipino seamen profess a superior masculinity, not in terms of being able better to dominate women, but rather for being preferred by women for their kinder, more restrained behaviour.

Of course, not all (or even most) Filipino seamen have sex in port and some seafarers resent their reputation as sexual adventurers, particularly where they want to bolster their professional image. One way some senior officers are able to maintain their status and assert their professional masculinity off the ship is to provide spending money to lower crew, either providing cash advances or dipping into the captain's discretionary recreation fund. Under these circumstances, a captain might accompany other crew members to a bar or seamen's club, acting as a father figure by providing 'his' crew the means to enjoy themselves, while drinking little and abstaining from engaging a sex worker. Others distance themselves from commercial sexual activity to assert their more professional masculinity, even as they accompany their crewmates. This was particularly true among officers. As one Third Mate explained:

> Some crews also go to the girly bar [and] the purpose only is for drinking . . . and not for women . . . what to do when they are in the girly bar will depend also on the person . . . I mean, you are only responsible for your actions.

Another officer stressed a slightly different form of self-restraint, observing that:

> Sex is also a problem, when our ships dock in America, Bangkok, Europe, and Brazil – those places are seamen's paradise. Even if you don't do it with

them, nobody will believe that you don't have any women in any of the ports
. . .We really sometimes do it with others but not in all the ports we dock.

Here, the seaman makes clear his claim on virility but couples it with the notion
of sexual self-control to project a more 'respectable' masculinity that reinforces
his professionalism.

Masculinities at home

Just as ports and off-duty occasions provide key opportunities to express masculinity outside of work, other locations – such as within families and local communities – can broaden further the possibilities for multiple masculinities (Pessar
and Mahler 2003). This is particularly true for labour migrants, since migration
allows a greater divide between home and work, giving migrants more control over
their gender performances (Margold 1995). Studies of migrant men have shown
that, despite exploitative and even emasculating labour relations, migratory work
can provide the material and cultural capital to enact exemplary forms of
masculinity upon a migrant's return home through conspicuous consumption, tales
of adventure, and the ability to fulfil the social obligations of a high-status male
(Osella and Osella 2000; Brown 2006; Datta *et al.* 2008).

Filipino seafarers are able to augment their claims to professionalism when at
home where they assert a 'breadwinner masculinity' of middle-class providership,
fatherhood and endurance of hardship for their families. Seafaring represents one
of the few channels for Filipino men to work abroad and earn high salaries in US
dollars. In large part because seafarers must remit at least 80 per cent of their base
wages, seafarers collectively send home some US $2 billion each year (Amante
2003). Understandably, their earnings are a point of considerable pride. As a
42-year-old Oiler with three children boasted:

> The really big thing about being a seaman is the big salary. To be a seaman is
> to be well known. My family thinks highly of me because I am a seaman. My
> children are proud . . . my neighbours see me as someone who can afford things.
> . . . Filipinos think highly of seamen because we are earning dollars.

Providership, then, bolsters seamen's masculinity by combining the agency or independence gained through the command of significant resources with a reaffirmation
of men's patriarchal status (Osella and Osella 2006).

Once home, seafarers also try to convert their earnings into wider social status
through conspicuous consumption aimed at the wider community. As one of the
few surveys of Filipino seafarers shows, seamen come from primarily rural or
working-class backgrounds, with over 50 per cent from farming or fishing families
and only 2 per cent the children of professionals (Amante 2003). Thus being a
seafarer – whether an officer or a lower-ranked rating – represents a real potential
for class mobility. As a married Third Engineer explained:

People can see that seamen have money. In my town, lots of seamen, and they can build houses . . . Even an AB [Able-Bodied Seaman] or OS [Ordinary Seaman], they can already build a house. And you can always tell a seaman's house. They always put an anchor on the gate. An anchor, or a propeller if they are from the engine department. And maybe on their car or jeep, the name of their ship, so everybody knows they are a seaman.

Likewise, a Third Officer boasted:

You know, I'm always being asked to be a *Ninong* [baptism or wedding sponsor], or my wife a *Ninang* because they [relatives or friends] know later I can help them. My car is always being used for weddings. A seaman is always in demand in his hometown. I was even invited to be a judge at a beauty contest! Me and a town councillor, people like that.

By coming home and fulfilling both his family's material needs and his community obligations, the seaman is simultaneously able to conceal his exploitative working conditions and transform the fruits of his labour into recognizable trappings of masculine prestige.

Seamen, then, clearly cultivate a certain pride in their occupation and ability to provide. Yet many also recognize that, despite their high earnings, seamen are not viewed quite as highly as other professionals – such as physicians, lawyers or politicians – due in large part to their persistent and class-linked reputations as womanizers, drinkers and spendthrifts. To distance themselves from this image, many seamen stress the changing demographics in the industry and try to project a middle-class professionalism based on maturity, sacrifice, endurance and an ability to save for investment and the education of their children. As one seaman noted:

When you are in a ship, there is a high possibility that you might not be able to return home or, if you do get back, you may be disabled. This job also requires lots of patience in the sense that you have to bear being away from your family just to earn . . . They [neighbours] do not know the difficulty we go through especially when we are on vacation [and] there is no income coming in. That is why I invest my money in projects that will generate income.

This endurance of hardships highlights both the marginal masculinity of dangerous work and the professionalism of self-control and sacrifice for long-term investment.

At the same time, however, Filipino seamen reproduce their status as masculine exemplars through their narratives of adventure. Indeed, many of the seamen interviewed confessed that they themselves were drawn to the occupation in the first place by the stories of older relatives or community members about their adventures at sea and in port. As one seaman noted, discussing his conversations with his neighbours:

They have high regard for seamen because they know that they have high incomes. You try telling stories in your town; nobody would pay attention to you. But if you are a seaman, before you open your mouth to tell a story or joke, everybody would already be laughing. That means, *bilib sila sa iyo* [they believe you/have faith in you].

These kinds of story-telling allow seafarers to shape discourses regarding seafaring and to perform important elements of dominant Filipino masculinity beyond providership – in this case, verbal eloquence, risk-taking and adventurousness that enhance their hyper-masculine reputations as adventurers, womanizers (*babaeros*) and 'one-day millionaires', a reputation that helps elevate them as masculine exemplars, particularly in the eyes of non-migrating men. As another seaman claimed:

People in the neighbourhood in the province tend to idolize you because you always have many stories to tell, about certain experiences, women, etc. . . . For example, surviving a storm in the middle of a sea is a big thrill which you can share with other people . . . [neighbours] think that going abroad means being rich . . . that is why some seamen tend to be so proud.

However, many seamen choose to temper their occupational image as sexual adventurers with assertions of self-control. A Chief Officer noted:

If a girl at home knows you're a seaman, she'll want to be your girlfriend, even if she knows you're married. Because some seamen, you know, have two families. But I don't think that's fair to your children. I always think about my kids, and their future. I think it's OK to go to bar girls sometimes, even if you have a wife already, it's natural. But it's not good if you have a second wife.

In this way, they try to counter the negative class associations of seafaring and manage the sometimes difficult relations with their families by veering back towards claiming a more respectable, breadwinner masculinity.

A final key element of Filipino masculinity is fatherhood. Approximately 75 per cent of seafarers from the Philippines are married and 71 per cent have children (Amante 2003). In many ways, the seamen interviewed generally subscribe to Filipino gender norms of conventional fatherhood, performing their roles as familial authority figures to the best of their ability. Nearly all seamen with families interviewed commented on the difficulties of being separated from their children and on having to work outside the country in order to support them. An Able-Bodied Seaman lamented:

I like my job, but I hate it. You understand what I mean? I like it because I can provide for my family; my wife and kids. But I hate it because I'm away from them all the time. But what can you do? At home, you can't earn enough, so I do it only for my two kids. But my kids, they just say, 'Hi Papi.' That's it. You know, just 'Hi.' We're not really close. They don't know me.

A Second Officer with four children expressed a similar regret:

I remember, my second boy, I came home one time and he asks, 'Who are you?' He asked me that! I just tried to laugh and explain, then I turn away so he doesn't see me crying . . . It hurts very much, it really makes me cry, but I try to hide it. I try to have one thing I always say so they remember me when I call on the phone.

Thus although seamen held generally conventional views of fatherhood, these migrant fathers did not necessarily or simply accept an emotionally detached role, instead trying quite hard upon their return home to re-establish emotional bonds with their children.

As Parreñas (2008) speculates, it seems that seamen's ability to perform as the 'good provider' can make it possible for them to transgress other gender roles. In fact, many seamen break with gender role stereotypes and expand their household duties when they are on vacation in order to build closer, more intimate relations. Speaking about returning home, a married Bosun said:

I'll be the one to cook for my kids, go shopping, take them to school, stay home. I try to do the things my wife does for nine months, to give her a break and let her relax. I like to do those things for my kids.

A 45-year-old Second Mate with two children takes a similar approach in order to maintain his relevance in the lives of his children:

When I arrive they're excited, but if I'm staying for a long time, I'm like nobody here. That's why I make up for my absence. I wake up in the morning to prepare their breakfast and I personally give them their allowance and sometimes I approach them to tell their problems and be open with me.

As these examples suggest, gender role transgressions are not limited to emotionally distant tasks, and can include child-centred and emotionally caring activities that help the seaman reconnect with his children and be a 'good father' as well as a 'good provider'.

Conclusion

The case of Filipino seafarers makes clear the influence of workplace and labour-market structures on the formation of masculine identity in transnational, multi-ethnic yet homosocial contexts. While the dominant masculinity in seafaring is one of professional authority and control, few Filipinos are in positions to realize these ideals. As a result, building a professional identity at work means downplaying workplace autonomy and command, and instead emphasizing a 'cautious masculinity' of self-discipline, competence and endurance of hardship to reassert their sense of 'being in control' despite being in insecure and/or subordinate positions. But, as we have noted, such performances may be interpreted by their superiors not in terms of competence but as a lack of assertiveness, initiative and leadership – all qualities associated with both dominant masculinity and the top positions in the occupational hierarchy. The seamen thus engage in what we understand as a 'masculine dialectic' between a professional masculinity of command and a hyper-masculinity of protest. Faced with the limits to a professional masculinity, Filipino seamen often look to other locations, opportunities and occasions to express their masculine selves. As they cannot entirely escape their low occupational positions while still onboard and under contract, their off-duty performances tend towards an expressive hyper-masculinity of compensation.

In the liminal spaces of the crew mess, the port bar or seamen's club, the men often attempt to recover a masculine identity among their peers through physical dominance, gallantry and a competitive and risk-taking heterosexuality. Much like other men doing manual labour, then, Filipino seamen try to subvert or at least survive their subordination by embracing their dangerous, physically demanding work and defining it, along with their occupational culture, as 'truly masculine' (Paap 2006). However, the place where Filipino seamen are arguably best able to validate their masculinity and fuse the tensions between professional and hyper-masculine strategies is back home in their local communities (Brown 2006). Here, the toiling migrant workers can return as *both* successful family breadwinners *and* overseas adventurers, able to shroud the conditions under which their wealth was created, while also projecting an image as 'new heroes' of the nation (Peletz 1995; Osella and Osella 2000).

Others have argued that the core elements of manhood in the Philippines consist of being 'good providers, virile sex partners, and responsible fathers' (Pingol 2001: 223). The Filipino seamen in our study do not contradict these general findings. However, as we have shown, achieving these goals is by no means straightforward, often requiring the threading of multiple strategies to achieve meaningful masculine identities. Through their occupational competence, self-sacrifice, endurance, control over savings and investment, and attempts to reconnect emotionally with their children, they demonstrate their *choice* to act as responsible providers, partners and fathers. But at the same time they feed their hyper-masculine reputations through conspicuous consumption and narratives of workplace hardship and sexual adventure, as seamen signal to others their *ability* (and occasional willingness) to act as sexual risk-takers, one-day millionaires and hyper-masculine exemplars through their tales of hardship and adventure. What elevates them to exemplary masculine status, then, is not their ultimate embrace of a middle-class, professional masculinity but rather their power to 'be in control' of their own gender performances. In this way, Filipino seafarers strategically locate themselves 'betwixt and between' the professional and hyper-masculine categories in large part because they can and because it allows them to out-compete other men for the label of 'masculine exemplars' (Paap 2006; Gutmann 2007). The case of the Filipino seafarers thus helps illustrate the difficulties of discerning a singular 'Filipino masculinity' or any national masculinity given the complexities of organizational and economic contexts and increased transnational flows. What is clear, then, is that the multiple, relational and sometimes conflicting character of masculinities requires a deep investigation into both the contextual conditions and the wide array of performative strategies any group of men may use to secure and construct their identities as men.

Notes

1 Data for this chapter were collected through interviews with approximately 100 seafarers in Manila in 2003, and participant observations conducted by the authors with Filipino and other crew members while onboard five merchant vessels in 2005 and 2006. Research trips lasted from 16 to 19 days onboard and 1 to 7 days in port. Crews consisted of 20 to 21 seamen, aged from 27 to 61, both single and married. We sailed with a full Filipino crew, and mixed-nationality crews that were predominantly Filipino, with up to three senior officers from India, Japan and/or Korea. Interviews were conducted in Tagalog, Cebuano/Visayan and English.
2 The practice, which seems to have originated in and been unique to Southeast Asia, actually goes back at least as far as the sixteenth century, when Magellan's chronicler, Pigafetta, described a similar activity in what is now the southern Philippines and Borneo (Reid 1988). It is unknown if the practice has been continuous, but it is clearly quite prevalent among contemporary seafarers, primarily Filipinos. In one of the very few studies on this topic, Estrella-Gust *et al.* (1998) randomly interviewed some 314 Filipino seamen in Manila, 180 or over 57 per cent of whom admitted to having *bolitas*.

References

Aguilar, Filomeno (1998) *Clash of Spirits: The History of Power and Sugar Planter Hegemony on a Visayan Island*, Honolulu: University of Hawaii Press.
—— (2003) 'Global migrations, old forms of labor, and new transborder class relations', *Southeast Asian Studies* 41(2): 137–61.
Alderton, T., Blorr, M., Kahveci, E., Lane, T., Sampson, H., Thomas, M., Winchester, M., Wu, B. and Zhao, M. (2004) *The Global Seafarer: Living and Working Conditions in a Globalized Industry*, Geneva: International Labour Organization.
Amante, M. (2003) 'Filipino global seafarers: a profile', draft report, Cardiff: Seafarer International Research Centre, Cardiff University.
Ashcraft, K. (2005) 'Resistance through consent? Occupational identity, organizational form, and the maintenance of masculinity among commercial airline pilots', *Management Communication Quarterly* 19(1): 67–90.
Ashcraft, K. and Flores, L. (2003) '"Slaves with white collars": persistent performances of masculinity in crisis', *Text and Performance Quarterly* 23(1): 1–29.
Barrett, F. (1996) 'The organizational construction of hegemonic masculinity: the case of the U.S. Navy', *Gender, Work and Organization* 3(3): 129–42.
Borah, E. G. (1995/1996) 'Filipinos in Unamuno's California Expedition of 1587', *Amerasia Journal* 21(3): 175–83.
Brown, C. (2006) 'Race and the construction of working-class masculinity in the Nigerian coal industry: the initial phase, 1914–30', *International Labour and Working-Class History* 69: 35–56.

Chappell, D. (2004) 'Ahab's Boat: non-European seamen in Western ships of exploration and commerce', in B. Klein and G. Mackenthun (eds), *Sea Changes: Historicizing the Ocean*, New York: Routledge, pp. 75–90.

Collinson, D. and Hearn, J. (2004) 'Men and masculinities in work, organizations and management', in M. Kimmel, J. Hearn and R. W. Connell (eds), *Handbook of Studies on Men and Masculinities*, London and New Delhi: Sage, pp. 289–310.

Connell, R. W. (1995) *Masculinities*, Berkeley: University of California Press.

—— (1998) 'Masculinities and globalization', *Men and Masculinities* 1(1): 3–23.

Connell, R. W. and Messerschmidt, J. (2005) 'Hegemonic masculinity: rethinking the concept', *Gender & Society* 19(6): 829–59.

Connell, R.W. and Wood, J. (2005) 'Globalization and business masculinities', *Men and Masculinities* 7(4): 347–64.

Datta, K., McIlwaine, C., Herbert, J., Evans, Y. and Wills, J. (2008) 'Mobile masculinities: men, migration and low paid work in London', Working Paper, Department of Geography, Queen Mary University of London.

Espiritu, Y. L. (2003) *Home Bound: Filipino Lives across Cultures, Communities and Countries,* Berkeley: University of California Press.

Estrella-Gust, D., Tecson, A., Busque, A., Ricon, F. and Javines, J. (1998) 'Assessing the need for preventative action against STD/HIV/AIDS among Filipino seafarers', unpublished report, Occupational Safety and Health Center, Department of Labor and Employment, The Philippines.

Fenstermaker, S. and West, C. (eds) (2002) *Doing Gender, Doing Difference: Social Inequality, Power, and Resistance*, New York: Routledge.

Gutmann, M. (2007) *The Meaning of Macho: Being a Man in Mexico City*, Berkeley: University of California Press.

Hohman, E. P. (1956) *History of American Merchant Seamen*, Hamden: Shoe String Press.

Kimmel, M. (1996) *Manhood in America: A Cultural History*, New York: The Free Press.

Louie, K. and Low, M. (eds) (2003) *Asian Masculinities: The Meaning and Practice of Manhood in China and Japan,* London: Routledge.

Margold, J. (1995) 'Narratives of masculinity and transnational migration: Filipino workers in the Middle East', in A. Ong and M. Peletz (eds), *Bewitching Women, Pious Men*, Berkeley: University of California Press, pp. 274–98.

Melendy, H. (1977) *Asians in America: Filipinos, Koreans and East Indians*, Boston: Twayne Publishers.

National Seamen Board (NSB) (1976) *Annual Report*, Department of Labor, Republic of the Philippines.

—— (1982) *Annual Report*, Department of Labor, Republic of the Philippines.

Osella, F. and Osella, C. (2000) 'Migration, money and masculinity in Kerala', *Journal of the Royal Anthropological Institute* 6: 117–33.

—— (2006) *Men and Masculinities in South Asia*, London, New York and Delhi: Anthem Press.

Ostreng, D. (2001) 'Does togetherness make friends? Stereotypes and intergroup contact on multiethnic-crewed ships', Paper 2, Vestfold College Publication Series, Tonsberg, Norway: Vestfold College.

Paap, K. (2006) *Working Construction: Why White Working-class Men Put Themselves – and the Labor Movement – in Harm's Way*, Ithaca: Cornell University/ILR Press.

Parreñas, R. S. (2005) *Children of Global Migration: Transnational Families and Gendered Woes*, Stanford: Stanford University Press.

—— (2008) 'Transnational fathering: gendered conflicts, distant disciplining and emotional gaps', *Journal of Ethnic and Migration Studies* 34(7): 1057–72.

Peletz, M. (1995) 'Neither reasonable nor responsible: contrasting representations of masculinity in a Malay society', in A. Ong and M. Peletz (eds), *Bewitching Women, Pious Men*, Berkeley: University of California Press, pp. 76–123.

Pessar, P. and Mahler, S. (2003) 'Transnational migration: bringing gender in', *International Migration Review* 37(3): 812–46.

Philippine Overseas Employment Administration (POEA) (2007) 'Overseas employment statistics'. Online document. Available at www.poea.gov.ph/html/statistics.html (accessed 8 November 2008).

Pingol, A. T. (2001) *Remaking Masculinities: Identity, Power and Gender Dynamics in Families with Migrant Wives and Househusbands*, Quezon City: University Center for Women's Studies/University of the Philippines.

Rafael, V. (2000) *White Love and Other Events in Filipino History*, Durham, NC: Duke University Press.

Reid, A. (1988) *Southeast Asia in the Age of Commerce 1450–1680: Volume One: The Lands below the Winds,* New Haven: Yale University Press.

—— (1993) *Southeast Asia in the Age of Commerce 1450–1680: Volume Two: Expansion and Crisis,* New Haven: Yale University Press.

Tremlett, P. (2006) 'Power, invulnerability, beauty: producing and transforming male bodies in the lowland Christianized Philippines', Occasional Papers in Gender Theory and the Study of Religion, School of Oriental and African Studies, University of London.

Turnbull, P. (2000) 'Contesting globalization on the waterfront', *Politics & Society* 28(3): 367–92.

Willis, P. (1977) *Learning to Labour: How Working Class Kids Get Working Class Jobs*, New York: Columbia University Press.

2 Masculine intent and migrant manhood

Thai workmen talking sex

Pattana Kitiarsa

The social lives of migrant workers are situated within the intertwining discourses of social marginalization, ethnocultural foreignness and transnational labour migration. In her discussion of Filipino workers in the Middle East, Margold claims that masculine identities are transfigured by the act of migrating across borders for work, arguing that 'the sense of manhood that develops locally may be partially disassembled when the migrant is incorporated into the lowest ranks of the global labor force' (Margold 1995: 276). However, the masculine identities of overseas migrant workers are not always dismantled, in part or in whole, by their experiences of transnational labour. A migrant workman's sense of manhood incorporates both personal and emotional standpoints that are embedded in living narratives of everyday life performance, and there are at least some areas where migrant workmen retain or successfully renegotiate their sense of manhood.

Margold emphasizes the partial disassemblage of migrant manhood in a transnational labour setting. But overseas foreign workers persistently seek to maintain 'masculine domination' (Bourdieu 2001) through their 'poetics of manhood' (Herzfeld 1985) in the realm of sexual desire and intimacy. A transnational labour setting does not necessarily suppress or dismantle the masculine manhood of foreign workmen. There are multiple forms of male gender identity negotiation and complication, and their agency and pattern of reaction and engagement with the transnational work and life environment needs closer consideration. I argue that the social life of migrant workmen away from home has become a space that can stimulate and harbour patterns of hegemonic masculine ideology, which they have possessed and carried with them from home.

Sexual intimacy forms a core part of migrant men's subjectivity as transnational actors. Male foreign workers actively engage in patterns of sexual intimacy despite strict control and regulation of their work and social life by their employers and authorities. Their status as foreign migrant workers may be highly marginalized in their work and contacts with the host society but they express dominant modes of masculine desire for sexual intimacy and sexual behaviour. When it comes to sexual desire and intimacy, migrant workmen constantly make emotional and financial investments in order to fulfil their sense of masculine pride. In this chapter, I explore the intersections between desire, sexuality and masculinity through the narratives of Thai migrant workers in Singapore. Although sexual intimacy is an intensely private aspect of migrant subjectivity, it is possible to unveil aspects of migrant sexual desire and practice through complex narratives of migrant labour sojourning. I suggest that understanding male migrant manhood must begin first and foremost with the fact that workmen are actors with purposeful intent, especially in their pursuit of everyday romance and sexual intimacy away from home. Despite their marginal and relatively powerless social position in the host society, migrant workmen are knowledgeable and resourceful social actors. As Giddens (1984: xxiii) observes, 'human agents or actors . . . have the capacity to understand what they do while they do it. The reflexive capacities of the human actor are characteristically involved in a continuous manner with the flow of day-to-day conduct in the contexts of social activity.' Such reflexive capabilities are best captured through an interpretation of individuals' own purposeful conduct and words. The stories that heterosexual Thai workmen tell about their sexual lives provide insights into the ways in which such men redefine their masculine intention and manhood away from home. These narratives of sexual life reveal the humanly intimate, personal aspects of transnational working-class labour. Tracing these stories of sexual intimacy through the men's own words and deeply personalized viewpoints, I disclose Thai workmen's naked masculine pleasure in their new-found freedom and anonymity, beyond family responsibilities and the surveillance of the Singapore state. My aim in writing about intimate encounters between transient working-class men and women in a highly regulated international labour market is to portray a nuanced interpretation of transnational migrant life.

Data discussed in this chapter are drawn from a four-hour focus group discussion carried out with twelve Thai construction workers in Singapore in 2006.[1] The average age of the participants was 38 years. The oldest was 48 and the youngest was 28. All participants were Thai-Lao (Isan)-speaking Buddhists from the northeastern Thai provinces (Isan, hereafter) – the area from which the majority of Thai migrant workers in Singapore come (see Wong 2000: 60).[2] Five of them had finished Year 12, three of whom held certificates of technical vocation (*po. wo. cho*) and two of whom held high school certificates (*matthayom 6*); one had finished Year 9 (*matthayom 3*); and six had completed either six or four years of compulsory education (*prathom 6* or *prathom 4*). Seven were married, two were divorcees and three were single. All of the men were experienced workers, with an average of ten years of employment in Singapore. The longest-serving worker had spent twenty-two years working in Singapore and the most recent arrival had been there for five years. They had all passed Singapore's standard skills tests for construction workers, and possessed skills and knowledge in a range of construction areas (e.g. electricity, concrete works and carpentry). Five were employed as supervisors or foremen. Their average monthly earnings were 22,750 THB (600 USD) – the highest was 35,000 THB (923 USD) and the lowest was 10,000 THB (263 USD).[3] All participants remitted almost 60 per cent of their income to their families on a regular basis. Their average monthly remittance was 13,000 THB (343 USD).

The chapter begins with a brief description of how Singapore manages its foreign migrant workforce, which provides the backdrop against which I portray the Thai workmen's personal narratives about sexual desire and intimacy during their stay in Singapore. These stories reveal how migrant manhood is crafted in a socio-economic and cultural context where the men are marginal foreign subjects. In the following sections, I describe relationships between Thai workmen and their female migrant partners from Thailand and other Southeast Asian countries. The chapter ends with a discussion of how Thai workmen's migrant masculinities are articulated and reaffirmed through patterns of sexually intimate experiences. This discussion reveals what it means to be both transnational labour migrants and sexually active men.

Disciplining the foreign migrant workforce in Singapore

Although the Singapore state has expressed a strong interest in managing the sexuality of its 620,000 foreign workers, written policy or legislation aimed at explicitly regulating the sexual behaviour of its foreign worker population is rare (Hui 1997; Ofori n.d.; Rahman 2006; Toh 1993; Yeh 1995; Yeoh 2004).[4] The Employment of Foreign Workers Act treats foreign workers as economic assets, while the Immigration Act regulates the legal flows of people in and out of the country. A complex system of work permits has been developed to manage the unskilled and low-skilled foreign workforce. Migrant workers are expected to work in Singapore on a short-term basis and must leave the country at the end of their contracts. They are not permitted to bring their families with them, and are prohibited from marrying Singaporean citizens or permanent residents. Furthermore, Chapter 91A of the Employment of Foreign Workers Act states that:

> [T]he foreign worker shall not go through any form of marriage or apply to marry under any law, religion, custom or usage with a Singapore Citizen or Permanent Resident in or outside Singapore . . . If the foreign worker is a female foreign worker, the foreign worker shall not become pregnant or deliver any child in Singapore during the validity of her Work Permit/Visit Pass. The foreign worker shall not indulge or be involved in any illegal, immoral or undesirable activities, including breaking up families in Singapore.
>
> (Ministry of Manpower 2008)

Every foreign worker must pass a medical check-up (which includes testing for HIV/AIDS) prior to obtaining a work permit. Once in Singapore, the sexuality of female migrant workers is regulated more closely than that of male migrant workers. Female domestic workers are required to complete a bi-annual medical examination. As Iyer *et al.* (2004: 26) point out:

> [T]he examinations were targeted at catching pregnancy or detecting an infectious disease. During the examinations, the bodies of FDWs [foreign domestic workers] are constructed as being sites of 'danger' in two ways: in terms of their sexuality and as potential transmitters of various infectious diseases.

These medical check-ups aim to trace the unwanted outcomes of possible sexual encounters during the period of their employment in Singapore and are 'symptomatic of the deep-seated discomfort with, and perhaps fear of, the migrant other' (Iyer *et al.* 2004: 10).

Migrant sexuality in Singapore is also conditioned by the politics of organized public spaces which are designed to separate foreign workers from the local population. A number of 'ethnocultural enclaves' (Rahman and Lian 2005; Yeoh 2004) accommodate the presence of foreign workers, namely dormitories, hostels or living quarters in designated areas separate from local communities; new housing developments specifically tailored for foreign workers within established residential communities (Hui 1997: 109); and red-light districts such as Geylang and Orchard Towers.[5] The Singaporean authorities carefully organize where and how the populations of foreign migrant workers are housed. First and foremost, they must not be placed too close to the local population. For migrant workers, however, these ethnocultural enclaves are places of opportunity that allow them to be with people like themselves. They spend time in these places, organizing a range of social activities, and inscribing meaning on to the places they inhabit. In the case of Thai workmen, their social activities include partying, drinking and engaging in sexual encounters.

Various state agencies involved in regulating workers and their environments (such as the Urban Redevelopment Authority and the Ministry of Manpower) may not necessarily share the same view about the appropriateness of these activities. In addition to these regulatory frameworks, a number of organizations have attempted to curb the sexual behaviour of migrant workers through public health and sex education campaigns (Brazil 2004). These campaigns are conducted by the Singapore authorities, foreign embassies, local and international non-governmental organizations (NGOs) and some charity organizations. For example, Singapore's Health Promotion Board distributed a comic book in Thai promoting safe sex among Thai construction workers (Singapore Health Promotion Board 2003). The Royal Thai Embassy and the Office of Thai Labour Affairs in Singapore have also sponsored a series of healthcare and educational activities for Thai workers at the Golden Mile Complex for many years.

Migrant sexual intimacy and ethnographies of desire

In their conversations about sex, the men revealed a number of established patterns of intimacy, including paid sexual encounters and one-night stands, as well as short- and long-term relationships. It is common practice among Thai workmen to use the services of a foreign sex worker in Geylang when they are under the influence of alcohol. In Geylang's brothels or lanes, they are able to choose women of different nationalities and ages and with different physical attributes. The fees range from 35 SGD up to 200 SGD per night including a hotel room rental charge.[6] Sometimes, usually after their pay-day, the men purchase sex from bar girls or entertainers in the Golden Mile Complex. Thawon, 29, insists that 'Younger guys pay lots of money for sex. They usually do it when they are drunk.' Songwut agrees, adding that 'Alcohol stimulates sexual lust. When you are drunk, an ordinary looking girl becomes a sex diva. You are ready to take her to bed at all costs. Sometimes they fight over girls.'

It is also not uncommon for the men to take an Indonesian or Filipina domestic worker (FDW) on a date and then end up in a rented hotel room in Geylang. Many couples terminate their relationship after the first few sexual encounters. The men insist that their FDW friends are not prostitutes, commenting, 'It would definitely disappoint her, if you offer her money after sex.' However, it takes time to establish longer-term relationships with Indonesian or Filipina domestic workers. SMS-messaging and daily chats are very important if one wants to get to know one's partner more closely. Songwut says:

> I use many phone cards per month. I had to make phone calls to my [Filipina] girlfriend every day before our first date that eventually led to sex. SMS-messaging helped me save money as it is a much cheaper way to communicate. We talked about our daily life and what each of us had been up to. She shared with me her work situation and how her employers treated her. I also told her my story. We felt connected. Our daily chitchats always lifted our spirits. We got to know each other more and more as we began to trust each other. In the later stages of our relationship, we decided to go out with each other on Sunday. We went to Lucky Plaza, movie houses or tourist spots. Of course, we ended up at love motels in Geylang many times.

Weera, who has had a number of foreign girlfriends, says that honesty is important in these relationships:

> Besides common issues like employment and other personal particulars, the most commonly asked question is whether you are married. In my early days in Singapore, I simply told the girls a lie. No, I was still single. I was quite lonely in Singapore and was looking for a girlfriend. I wanted somebody I could talk to at the end of my laborious day. I wanted somebody to lift my spirit. I can do that because I was much younger than I am now. Nowadays, I am getting older. I respond to the same question differently. When I am asked if I am married, my answer is: 'Yes, I am married, but I am still available for a girlfriend in Singapore. My wife is in Thailand, not here.' I want to keep it straight. I have found it quite effective. Many Indonesian and Filipino girls are in the same situation. Most are married, but, like us, they wish to have sexual partners or foreign boyfriends. They too have their husbands and children back home. If we are mature, we have to be open and straight.

These relationships usually last just a few months because romance is difficult to sustain. Weera explained that the lovers break up for a number of reasons:

> [T]hey argue over things like the girl going out with another man or vice versa. The couple has had enough of each other sexually. Money is not a big deal

because each side has separate incomes. Many women, like men, have more than one potential partner. Some girls I went out with just sent me a message to thank me, said good bye, and wished me luck. I did not feel any heartbreak because I knew that was the nature of our relationship. Sometimes one of us was sent home if our employer terminated our contract and therefore our romance automatically ended. Sometimes, if either party failed to respond to SMS-messaging or phone calls, we had no way to continue our romance. Breaking up the relationship is quite easy. We all understand that our relationships in Singapore are just temporary and make-shift. We can't get too serious with girls here.

Lovers inevitably part ways given their non-resident, transient status as contract migrant workers in Singapore. The men accept that their relationships with foreign girlfriends will gradually come to an end after spending time together over a period of several months. In fact, many of the men were keen to keep their relationships short-lived. For them, migrant romance is fun (*sanuk*), exotic, new (*prasopkan mai*) and temporary (*chau khrao*).

In this context, any relationship between a Thai workman and foreign woman in Singapore that extends beyond a year can be regarded as a long-term commitment. Longer relationships are considered unusual for foreigners who make their living in transit. Very few couples entered into international or inter-racial marriages. Even where they are possible, they are not necessarily desired. Thawon found it would be possible for him to marry an Indonesian domestic worker. His Singaporean employer promised to sponsor the marriage because he wanted to keep a model worker like Thawon in his company. However, Thawon refused.

The girl is quite good-looking and has worked in Singapore for three or four years. I liked her a lot, but she is Muslim. I am Buddhist. She does not speak Thai. I do not speak Indonesian. I do not think my marriage would be a happy one. We are quite different.

Long-term relationships are more likely to develop between Thai workmen and Thai women who work as cashiers, store clerks, bar girls or sex workers, or who are divorced or estranged housewives in Singapore. The single participants explained that, ultimately, they would marry Thai women. As Chaiwat, 28, says:

I am rather serious with love and life. I think my realistic choice of future bride is a Thai woman. Filipina, Indonesian or Singaporean girls are not for me. They are good and pretty, but I know where I stand. We are quite different.

For the men interviewed for this study, sex with migrant women in Singapore is never regarded as a product of serious romantic love. Instead, when discussing these encounters, the focus group participants described their sexuality in terms of erotic desire as well as engagement in sexual intercourse. The participants believed that sex was a necessary part of their lives, whether they were single or married. It is thus a part of their 'labour-selling' life (*chiwit khai raeng*) abroad. Many participants repeatedly used the phrases 'men's business' (*ruang khong phuchai*) and 'things that all men know by heart' (*khong baep ni phuchai thuk khon ru kan*) when they referred to issues of sex and their sexual urges. Sex is commonly assumed among them to be a psychological and biological need and they believe that all healthy men possess sexual fantasies, desires and urges. Sommai, 48, bluntly stated, 'Taking a look at some good sensual female figures on the street, I wished I could have sex with them. These young ladies' figures are damn sexy. Their busts and bottoms are so killable (*pen ta kha thae*).'

The term 'killing' is Thai masculine slang for a man's desire to have sex with a female object of his fantasy. It is a term that objectifies women as desirable sexual beings. In this sense, a woman is dehumanized and reduced to a non-human object of men's sexual desire (*khong*). The same term – *khong* (thing) – is also generally used to refer to desirable, feminine bodies and also a woman's vagina. Women who are identified as *khong* are usually sex workers, call girls or bar girls. For most Thai men, to have sex with women of their choice is equivalent to releasing their sexual desire to 'kill things'. The Thai workmen I spoke to expressed a strong desire to have sex with women of other nationalities. For them, having sex with foreign women was one of the most rewarding aspects of their transient migrant life in Singapore.[7] Songwut, 46, acknowledged that 'It is always in the back of every work-man's mind. It is a man's profit in life (*kamrai chiwit*) to have sexual encounters with girls from another country.' Sex is fundamental in their transient, mostly short-term intimacies. Weera, who regards himself as a true playboy or a womanizer (*suea phuying*), commented, 'I have lost count of how many Filipina and Indonesian partners I had sex with in my seven-year employment in Singapore.' Anon, 43, also confirmed that having sex with women from other nationalities was a 'good experience but we cannot take the relationships seriously because we are married. We have wives and kids back home.'

Among the different national groups preferred by the men were Chinese Singaporeans, Mainland Chinese, Indonesians, Filipinas, Malays, Indians and Thais. Sommai liked Chinese girls' 'good figures and fair skins' but also Indian and Malay girls' 'larger breasts', whereas Chatchai desired 'Indian girls' fair skins, pretty dreamy eyes, and large chest' but their 'rather strong body odour' turned him off. Chinese Singaporean women were the object of the men's fantasies rather than realistic sexual partners. Weera, 37, revealed that:

[W]e prefer them because of their fair skin and curvy figures. However, it is almost impossible to have sex with the Chinese Singaporean women. We know from their look that they regard foreign workmen very low. We are dirt in their eyes. They look down upon us. Besides, it is against Singapore's law for foreign workers to establish relationships with local women. If the women report sexual molestation, harassment or rape to the police, we are in danger. Singapore police always protect their citizens and the law here is very strict. We will easily be put in jail or deported. It is too risky for us. We have to be extremely careful dealing with Singaporeans. We sometimes have to restrain ourselves from gazing or looking at them too obviously.

Chatchai, 41, who had spent years as a factory worker in Taiwan before coming to Singapore, agreed:

> Singaporean women look down on us, unlike the Taiwanese girls who are friendlier to foreign workmen. I was upset when I offered them my seat on the bus or the MRT and they ignored my hospitality. I know they look down on us, but failing to acknowledge our goodwill is rather painful for us. They are too suspicious of us and regarding themselves to be above us.

Women from mainland China who work as sex workers in the red-light district of Geylang are more realistic partners of Thai workmen. They are preferred because they are young and have good figures and thus fit an idealized image of beauty shared by men in contemporary Thailand, namely 'fair skinned, pretty, Chinese-looking and busty' (*khao, suai, muai, uem*). The downside of approaching Chinese girls for sex is that they demand higher fees for their services (80 SGD to 120 SGD per night). To them, sex is business. By contrast, women from Indonesia, the Philippines or Thailand provide intimate companionship and friendship without the expectation of payment.

The majority of participants agreed that Indonesian and Filipina domestic workers were their most realistic and approachable choices as sexual partners in Singapore. Jetsada, 43, prefers Indonesian and Filipina women because they have strong legs and compact breasts. Songwut, who has already had four Filipina and two Indonesian domestic workers as lovers in Singapore, commented that:

> They are by far most similar to Thai girls both in their appearances and manners. They have good hearts and are ready to embrace us as lovers and friends. They are not sex workers. They do not demand money. We are more comfortable to have relationships with them.

Like most of the men in the study, Songwut has another incentive for engaging in relationships with Indonesian and Filipina girls. He loves practising his spoken English with them. Bunmee, 32, says his English has improved dramatically since he began seeing his Filipina girlfriend: 'She taught me a lot and I have expanded my grammatical and conversational skills.' Bunmee's efforts to improve his English have paid off: he was one of the top students in my evening English classes for Thai workers, housekeepers and housewives. Chaiwat, 28, who studied English with me briefly, has since consulted me (mostly via telephone) when he has problems understanding the English-language text messages (SMS) he receives on his mobile phone from his Malaysian and Indonesian girlfriends.

Thai workmen regard Filipina or Indonesian domestic workers as ideal sex partners despite their ethno-religious and cultural differences. The men believe that migrant women share their sexual fantasies and urges. They consider foreign domestic workers to be mature and sexually active women who are removed from their husbands and lovers. As live-in domestic workers, they are closely supervised by their employers. Their work seems endless and more tiring than

outdoor construction work. Songwut, who has had relationships with several
Filipina domestic workers, sympathizes with his female counterparts' private and
social life in Singapore:

> They earn a very low monthly income.[8] Some maids have to work from early
> morning until almost midnight. Some are not given enough food to eat or no
> day-off at all. As they are isolated from their fellow maids, they need someone
> to talk to. They need friends. They talk and make friends via SMS-messaging
> or hand phones. When they are allowed to go out on Sunday, it is common to
> see them hanging out with friends or boyfriends.

Weera is bold enough to insist that:

> Female workers want to have sex just like us. Sometimes they are more sexually
> active than us. They work very hard and need somebody to share their
> frustrations, loneliness and hardship. Sex is a common part of their life when
> they are off duty. I can interpret their inner feelings from the ways they look
> at men.

Weera described his sexual encounters with domestic workers from these two
countries as follows:

> Although both are generally open and easy-going in carrying out their relation-
> ships with Thai workmen, the Indonesians are more sincere and committed as
> lovers in comparison with the Filipinas. The Indonesians say, 'You may
> undress me, even if you do not pay me' (*mai chai ko kae*). Money does not
> mean anything to her. Love, sincerity and loyalty mean more to her. For the
> Filipina, money comes first: 'Show me the money, or you can never undress
> me' (*mai chai, mai kae*).

Most Thai women the men encounter in Singapore are sex workers (*phuying ha
ngoen*) in the Golden Mile Complex or Geylang, or are women who travel to
Singapore on social visit passes to 'sell sex' (*khai borikan thang phet*) in the mobile,
jungle brothels near the men's dormitories. Women who come to work in Geylang
brothels legally as entertainers are known as 'home-stationed girls' (*dek ban*). Some
women who come to Singapore on a short-visit pass are 'tradeswomen' (*mae kha*)
who are ready to offer sexual services to workmen. Many young women also work
in the beer bars and karaoke pubs as waitresses (*dek soep* or *sao cheer beer*) with
the real intention of making money from temporary sex work.

When the men spoke about their sexual liaisons with Thai women, there was no
excitement or admiration in their voices or eyes. Perhaps they are too familiar,
and remind the men of their wives or girlfriends back home. One notable exception
to this lack of interest in Thai women was Pornchai, 39, who came to Singapore
as a divorcee and has had many Thai girlfriends in the past seven years away from
home. He maintains that:

I always love and wish to preserve my Thai-ness (*anurak khwam pen Thai*). I think Thai women are the best for me. We come from similar cultural background. We get along with each other well. I have rarely looked at foreign girls.

None of the participants mentioned having sexual relationships with girls from South Asian countries such as Bangladesh, India or Sri Lanka, who are regarded as *khaek* women – *khaek* being a Thai racialized and ethnocultural construction of the people of Persian, Middle Eastern, Indo-Malay and South Asian origins (i.e. *Khaek Persia*, *Khaek India* or *Khaek Khao*, meaning white *Khaek*) but also a term sometimes used with some implications of religious otherness, such as *Khaek Muslim*, *Khaek Sikh* or *Khaek Hindu*.[9] Although there are some sex workers from these countries in Geylang, they were not selected by the Thai workmen because they prefer women with fairer skin colour, skinnier shape and more familiar body odour. Totally absent also from the participants' list of sexual partners are Caucasian women (*sao farang* or *phuying farang*). Although there are some white women, mainly from Eastern European countries, who provide sex-for-sale services in Singapore (Lim 2004), they mostly target customers with high purchasing power, and never foreign construction workers. The men's marginalized lifestyles and work patterns, along with linguistic barriers, make it impossible for them to have social encounters with Caucasian women.

Establishing intimate migrant relationships

Thai workmen employ complex friendship networks to get to know their sexual partners. They use a number of different channels to meet each other: SMS-messaging networks; telephone conversations; meeting in person via friends or acquaintances on Sunday and during social events; and meeting in workplaces or places where migrants gather, such as construction sites (for construction workmen), residential areas (for domestic workers), or places such as Little India, Lucky Plaza and the Golden Mile Complex. Most friendships between foreign workers begin with one partner introducing himself or herself and stating his/her friendly purpose. 'I want to be your friend' and 'I need someone to talk to' are among the most popular expressions used by migrant workers in their first-time conversations. Some participants used the term 'courting' (*chip sao*) to describe their interactions with migrant women.

Meeting women depended on a combination of factors including the location of the men's workplace, free time, appearance, courage and luck. The men who worked in residential areas were more likely to get to know domestic workers working in the same building complex, while men in supervisory roles had a better chance of moving around and had more spare time to chat with girls. For example, Anon took advantage of his position as a supervisor to attract the attention of foreign domestic workers. When he rode his bicycle between construction sites to oversee the workmen under him, he would talk to domestic workers who took their employers' children to playgrounds or who ran errands for their employers at the neighbourhood supermarket. He liked the person-to-person approach and gradually established friendships with women through these meetings. According to Anon, the neighbourhood supermarket is one of the best spots to meet foreign domestic workers, who shop on a daily basis. 'You can help her carrying baskets or push the shopping cart, while engaging her in conversation. If the girl is interested in you, she will respond to you positively. You can ask her out when she has a day off.'

Despite their limited English and the regulations that govern their mobility, the men had a number of common 'tricks' that they used to attract the attention of women they fancied. Songwut revealed the secret of his success in approaching Indonesian or Filipina domestic workers:

> I become overtly friendly to the girl I am interested in as I try to befriend her. The most important thing is to get to know her name and hand-phone number. In some situations, I used to write my number on a small piece of paper and dropped it her way. I've seen workmen and their girls exchange phone numbers via hand-signals from a distance, for example from different buildings or floors. A hand-phone number is the best way to get to know a girl.

With the girl's hand-phone number in hand, the men pursue their target. The men claimed that they had to talk to or correspond with the women via SMS several times a day. They had to maintain contact on a regular basis in order to show their genuine interest in establishing a friendly or romantic relationship. The workmen tried their best to attract the women's attention despite the obvious language barriers. As Chaiwat explained, it was quite common for Filipina and Indonesian domestic workers to exchange the hand-phone numbers of male workers:

> They begin with SMS-messaging. If the correspondence goes well and both sides like each other, they will follow up with the chats on their hand-phones. SMS is used intensively because it is cheaper than making phone calls. Everything begins from there.

However, some older Thai workers explained that they do not enjoy using SMS-messaging because their written English skills are limited. They prefer phone conversations in which they can hear the woman's voice and simultaneously react to her. One of them commented, 'It is a totally different feeling. I feel better to talk to the girl I am interested in. It is much better than composing, sending, or responding to mere messages.'

Weera described the intensive use of his hand-phone to court women as 'courtship through media' (*chip sao phan sue*). However, migrant romance and sexuality require an investment of money as well as a fun-loving attitude. Some men spent over a hundred dollars on phone cards every month. For many, the hand-phone is their lifeline, allowing them to talk to their families back home and to maintain networks with fellow workmen, but also to talk to their target girls on a daily basis. In recognition of this fact, the men are willing to spend money to top up their girlfriends' pre-paid hand-phones. Songwut says:

The girl usually asks for one or two phone cards from us. We have to understand that she earns less than us. Besides, giving her hand-phone cards shows our willingness to be her friend and our generosity. You cannot be stingy, if you wish to win over a girl. We can give her the card's PIN number via our daily chats. Or you can give it to her in person when you go out together. I think giving phone cards to the girl of your choice is a worthy investment. Normally, the girls from Indonesia or the Philippines whom I went out with do not ask for anything else. They do not have sex with us for money. You have to respect them and treat them well. They are your girlfriends, not prostitutes.

The third step in establishing their relationship is going out together. The men usually took their girlfriends to popular migrant spots such as the Golden Mile, Little India or Lucky Plaza, or Singaporean tourist attractions such as Sentosa Island or the Orchard Road shopping malls and movie houses. Many women preferred to go out in a group on their first date. Group dates had the added advantage of being able to introduce more couples to each other.

The fourth step in the courtship ritual is initiating sexual relations. After all, as the men all clearly state, sex is the prime reason for having a foreign girlfriend. Generally, couples do not have sex on their first date. Chaiwat, for example, exchanged messages and chatted with his Indonesian girlfriend for weeks before meeting her in person. They finally met at Eunos MRT station and later ended up in a Geylang hotel room. Although they have talked on the phone many times since, they have never managed to get together again. The rules also vary from girlfriend to girlfriend. Weera reveals that:

No sex on the first date is the rule for Filipina partners. It usually applies to the Indonesian girls too. Guys have to be patient, especially when your date is an inexperienced young girl. I had sex with two virgins from the Philippines. In each case, it took me over a year. You have to build trust. The Filipina girls are rather romantic and serious about love. However, each relationship is different. Each girl I date has her own personality. I have had sex with many girls after just a few outings together. Some look forward to long-term engagements, others just want to have fun.

As Chaiwat's experience suggests, the chance to have sex is also subject to a confluence of circumstances. Indeed, as Bunmee pointed out, 'sex is possible, if the couple find themselves the right opportunity (*okat*), place (*sathanthi*) and time (*wela*)'. The men use a variety of places as temporary love nests, including the homes of their girlfriends' employers. Songwut took his Filipina lover to a dark corner of the neighbourhood park for their night-time dates. However, most participants admitted that Geylang's numerous and cheap hotels, where rooms can be rented by the hour for 10 to 15 SGD, were their most popular destinations. Some hotels offered a special rate of 20 SGD for three hours. For those able to stay overnight, the cost ranges from 30 up to 45 or 48 SGD per room, depending on the room's condition and facilities. Chatchai confirms that 'If you have money, you can stay in a luxury, air-con room with proper towels, soap, shampoo and purified drinking water. Beware of bedbugs, lice or mosquitoes, if you prefer the cheap one.'

Experienced lovers such as Anon, Thawon, Songwut and Weera agreed that men should know when, where and how to act when they take their girlfriends to a Geylang hotel. In particular, they should show some sign that they are unfamiliar with the place. Instead of taking the lead, they should allow the girl to reveal what she knows. According to Songwut:

> You should show some signs that you too are a rather innocent guy. I sometimes pretend I do not know how to use the electronic card/key to open the door and ask my girlfriend for help. However, every guy should always have condoms handy. This will save both sides. Sex without using a condom is very harmful. Your girlfriend could get pregnant. Both of you might contact some disease. Using condoms also shows that you are willing to save her and honour the relationship with her.

All participants, except Bunmee, regularly used condoms when they had sexual intercourse with their girlfriends. Bunmee says it is uncomfortable to use a condom but if his girlfriend insists then he has no choice but to acquiesce. The men felt that it was important that the man impresses his lover during their first sexual encounter. A good lover has to be careful and has to handle the relationship smoothly. Weera reveals that:

> Most Indonesian and Filipina girls I slept with cried after our first sexual encounter. Some said, 'I should not have slept with you. Our relationship went too far. We are more than friends now. I was not an easy girl, who always had sex with men I went out with.' From my side, I gave her my best, sweet hug and said, 'Calm down. Don't cry. Don't be sad. I am a gentleman and responsible for what I did. You can trust me.' I know it is girls' touching side. I have to show her my side, too. I assure her that I am a gentleman as well as a good lover.

At the same time, Weera claims that men should be prepared to satisfy their sexual partners:

> In bed, young, single and married women are quite different. I prefer experienced, mature women as they know how to satisfy their lover. They are very good. A virgin girl is not tasty (*bo saep*) despite the fact that she is in a better shape. Men have to be aware that women tend to be ready for multiple orgasms. They can be ready for the next round, while most men tend to finish after the first shot. A good lover should be careful enough to satisfy and care for his partner. You cannot just finish your business quickly, and then proceed to take a bath and dress up to get ready to leave after intercourse. Your girlfriend wants to be held or caressed. She loves to have your attention and wants to stay in bed with you for a while.

Masculine intent and reassertion of migrant manhood

This discussion shows that working and living in economically and ethnoculturally marginalized transnational contexts does not necessarily damage a worker's sense of manhood. Thai workmen's masculinity may be suppressed in their workplace and in the presence of authority figures such as supervisors, employers, police or immigration officials. However, in private spaces and during leisure time, they are first and foremost sexually active men.

The narratives of sexual intimacy among Thai workmen in Singapore remind us that there are 'sexual scripts' (Britten 1989: 60–61) in which maleness is instantly constructed and represented especially when they are off-duty. One of the major functions of these sexual scripts among workers is to communicate their sexual intent and desire. In discussing or sharing sexual narratives, 'men come to believe in the reality of their sexuality; they know that their desires are urgent and powerful, demanding instant release and gratification' (Britten 1989: 60). Thai workmen show their articulated 'masculine intent' through their migrant sexual desire and intimacy. By masculine intent, I refer to conscious commitment, effort and investment by men in order to actualize their ideal norm of being a man. Thai workmen in Singapore demonstrate their masculine intent away from home through patterns and paths of migrant sexual practice, with its particular characteristics and patterns, which are different from other forms of transient sexual intimacies, such as tourist and high-class sex-for-sale. The stories that Thai workmen in Singapore share show that male and female migrant workers view sex not as a reproductive mechanism, but as something completely removed from the domestic domains of family and home. Transnational migrant sexual encounters must be understood outside the sphere of reproduction because marriage and the starting of families among foreign migrant workers are legally prohibited. Rather, it is a case of intimacy-seeking in which men and women develop social and emotional bonds.

Thai workmen's sense of manhood is best understood in relation to their heteronormative engagements with their female counterparts. In this context, 'women have been made "Other" to men' (Bach 1993: 49), a process of power relations, in which workmen as masculine performers and storytellers have assumed the ultimate subjective role of 'I'. Migrant manhood is modelled after the dominant version of masculine culture which foreign workers carry with them from home. Viewing sexualized female partners as a 'thing' or 'object' but also treasuring sexual experiences with a foreign or Thai woman other than one's wife as a 'profit' in life are common masculine traits among Thai men in Thailand. These ideas are also widely held among Thai migrant workmen in Singapore, who transfer and translate their perceived model of Thai manhood into practice in their everyday migrant life. In short, Thai workmen subscribe to a hegemonic mode of masculinity which is the cultural norm in their home country.

Through their stories, Thai workmen accentuate patterns of how to behave sexually as a man whose life has been entangled in transnational migrant encounters. Thai workmen insist that having intimate relationships is part of the ideology and set of practices associated with migrant masculinity, which serve to comfort and console them and inspire them to become men and not just workers. When Thai workmen talk and discuss their sexual desires and experiences, the sense of socio-economic inferiority is consciously removed from their masculine migrant selfhood. They position themselves as successful tricksters, lovers or womanizers, who 'somehow anticipate the coming freedom' (Foucault 1980: 6). Stories are fun to tell, especially when it involves their fellow workers or somebody else's affairs. Embarrassment and shame are turned into jokes, which generate laughter. Success and failure are converted into lessons and wisdom. Of course, joyful emotion is shared with pride. In other words, migrant sexuality constitutes a channel to express masculine sensitivity which is strangely meaningful in the laborious and back-breaking context of everyday life.

At the same time, however, male domination and sensibility sometimes mean different thing to different people. There is always room for individual interpretation of what are ideal roles for men. Masculinity is complicated by an ideology of gentlemanly behaviour, especially when it involves romance, love and emotional attachments. For example, Jetsada is married and faithful to his wife. His fellow workers accuse him of not being 'man enough' to have a foreign girlfriend. Jetsada has not been immune to approaches, but these have failed to alter his resolve:

> There was an Indonesian girl working in an apartment near my worksite. She expressed interest in me and sent me some signals by giving me her hand-phone number via a friend. One day, she came to see me at a building corner. I cannot speak English well, but she really wanted to go out with me. She even held me tight and kissed me in the mouth. I simply couldn't respond to her. She left, disappointed. I had to run away and I threw up. My mind is always with my wife and family. I can't betray them.

Jetsada's narrative shows how he values love for his wife and family. It suggests alternative practices of masculine culture in a transnational setting beyond acts which dominate or oppress woman.

Conclusion

Stories of migrant sexual desire and practice as told by Thai construction workers in Singapore illustrate two major points concerning the private sexual life of foreign workers. First, they demonstrate how migrant workmen deal with their sexual desire and intimacy. Second, the Thai men's vocabularies and narratives about their sexual intimacy show how the workmen have refused to surrender their maleness and seek to negotiate and reassert their masculine intent in the context of the transnational labour migrant community in Singapore. In his compelling account of a Balinese cockfight, Geertz (1973: 448) reminds us that the cockfight not only shows Balinese men's masculine passion, but 'is a Balinese experience, a story they tell themselves about themselves'. Thai workers in Singapore may be less sophisticated in their storytelling art, but their stories are textually rich and their intimate experiences, especially with fellow migrant women from Indonesia and the Philippines, are more than metaphorical. Although their lives are conditioned by their transient employment and migrant livelihood situations in Singapore, their commitment to masculine pride as male sexual performers is always enunciated. Their stories confirm their intention that during their time working abroad they take it as their personal priority to become 'manly men' as much as 'dutiful workmen'. They insist that migrant sexual encounters must begin with the fact that working-age migrant men (and women) are sexual beings.

Sex for Thai workmen is a form of migrant sociability. For the men in my study, sex constitutes an important aspect of their private life as border-crossers. It is primarily considered a pleasure-oriented activity with certain degrees of freedom from moral, religious or familial restraints. Their responsibilities as married men are to work hard to earn and send money back home and keep in touch with their families via regular phone calls. They believe that as mature men in a transient situation they are entitled to go out and have fun. Migrant sex is one of the many activities open to them during their leisure time. Migrant sexuality is a highly mutual and reciprocal enterprise, in which migrant men and women are both potentially active sex-seekers. The workmen's narratives show that men and women are willing to establish relationships and pursue sexual pleasure with the partners of their choice. They are aware of immigration, legal and economic regulations which Singapore's authorities and employers impose on them. However, they have learned to adjust and live within the limited freedom and rights, and to make use of the resources they are allowed to possess. The intensive use of hand-phones and their improvised abilities with the English language are everyday strategies which the workers employ to pursue sexual intimacy in Singapore.

Like many other migrant groups, Thai workmen in Singapore are articulate in their efforts to redefine their migrant manhood and other aspects of their ethnocultural identities. These self-narrated stories from a group of experienced Thai workmen demonstrate how active the men are in pursuing their heterosexual engagements with fellow female migrant workers, but also how insistent the men are in their statements of masculine intent. They are purposeful and knowledgeable agents who actively craft their migrant selfhood, who seek to have their hegemonic masculine position reaffirmed in the new foreign environment. Instead of being disassembled, their migrant masculinity is strongly accentuated in the realm of sexual intimacy, where they demonstrate that they are men with a desire to perform their manliness. In their marginal migrant situations away from home, they wish to express their culturally defined domination over other migrant women and men. In Singapore, these Thai workmen express their desire for sexual intimacy through heterosexual encounters with migrants from neighbouring countries of close ethnocultural proximity. Such intent and performance provoke hegemonic masculine sensitivities. For them, migrant sexuality collapses the private–public distinctions of their social life away from home.

Notes

1   Five of the participants were either students in my evening English-language classes for Thai workers in Singapore or worker-volunteers at the Friends of Thai Workers Association (FTWA). The other seven were invited participants, who had been working as foreign construction workers in Singapore for at least five years. My interview and focus group study were conducted by using Central and Northeast-Thai (i.e. Isan) dialects. All stories presented in extended quotations were translated from the original accounts which were recorded in my fieldnotes. Pseudonyms are used throughout the chapter in order to protect the informants' privacy and identity.

2   More specifically, informants came from Nong Khai, Khon Kaen, Udon Thani, Buriram, Phetchabun, Sakon Nakhon and Surin. I consider Phetchabun to be an extended part of the northeastern region due to its close geographical and ethnocultural connections to the other nineteen Thai-Lao-dominated northeastern Thai provinces.

3   In 2006 the currency exchange rate was 1 USD for 37.88 THB.

4   The Singapore government rarely releases data on the nationalities, visa types and occupations of the country's large foreign workforce. Rahman (2006) reports that, of the 620,000 foreign workers reported in the local press, 540,000 are work permit holders and the remaining 80,000 are employment pass holders. Low (1995: 746) points out that 'Singapore is particularly secretive about its population movement statistics. Not even the number and source of foreign workers are officially released due to political sensitivities.'

5   Despite the Singapore state's strict screening and monitoring of migrant workers, it is impossible to shut the door completely to the flows of people across international borders. Women from countries such as China, Indonesia, the Philippines and Thailand, many of whom are professional or opportunistic sex workers, enter Singapore on social and business visit passes and work illegally in brothels and other venues.

6   In 2006 the currency exchange rate was 1 USD for 1.58 SGD.

7   Only one of the men in the focus group discussion insisted that he has never had an interest in going out with foreign women.

8   At the time, wages were 250 SGD to 300 SGD for Indonesians and 300 SGD to 350 SGD for Filipinas.

9   Another separate meaning of this term is a 'visitor', 'stranger' or 'sojourner' to the land or home of the Thais.

References

Bach, M. (1993) 'Uncovering the institutionalized masculine: notes for a sociology of masculinity', in T. Haddad (ed.), *Men and Masculinities: A Critical Anthology*, Toronto: Canadian Scholars' Press, pp. 37–55.

Bourdieu, P. (2001) *Masculine Domination,* Stanford: Stanford University Press.

Brazil, D. (2004) *No Money, No Honey: A Candid Look at Sex-for-Sale in Singapore*, Singapore: Angsana Books.

Britten, A. (1989) *Masculinity and Power,* Oxford: Basil Blackwell.

Foucault, M. (1980) *The History of Sexuality, Volume I: An Introduction*, R. Hurley (trans.), New York: Vintage Books.

Geertz, C. (1973) *The Interpretation of Cultures: Selected Essays*, New York: Basic Books.

Giddens, A. (1984) *The Constitution of Society: Outline of the Theory of Structuration*, Berkeley: University of California Press.

Herzfeld, M. (1985) *The Poetics of Manhood: Contest and Identity in a Cretan Mountain Village*, Princeton: Princeton University Press.

Hui, W.-T. (1997) 'Regionalization, economic restructuring and labour migration in Singapore', *International Migration* 35: 100–20.

Iyer, A., Devasahayam, T. W. and Yeoh, B. S. A. (2004) 'A clean bill of health: Filipinas as domestic workers in Singapore', *Asian and Pacific Migration Journal* 13: 11–38.

Lim, Gerrie (2004) *Invisible Trade: High-Class Sex for Sale in Singapore*, Singapore: Monsoon Books.

Low, L. (1995) 'Population movement in the Asia Pacific region: Singapore perspective', *International Migration Review* 29: 745–64.

Margold, J. A. (1995) 'Narratives of masculinity and transnational migration: Filipino workers in the Middle East', in A. Ong and M. G. Peletz (eds), *Bewitching Women, Pious Men: Gender and Body Politics in Southeast Asia*, Berkeley: University of California Press, pp. 274–98.

Ministry of Manpower (2008) Employment of Foreign Workers Act (Chapter 91A). Singapore: Ministry of Manpower (1 January). Online. Available at www.mom.gov. sg/NR/rdonlyres/ 2F03CDE4–3B1A-43DE-8933–34ABC638A5458/7612/WPSPass Conditions. pdf (accessed 26 June 2006).

Ofori, G. (n.d.) 'Foreign construction workers in Singapore' unpublished manuscript.

Rahman, M. M. (2006) 'Foreign manpower in Singapore: classes, policies and management', Asia Research Institute Working Paper Series No. 57 (February) www.nus.ari.edu.sg/ pub/wps.htm (accessed 10 October 2006).

Rahman, M. M and Lian, K.F. (2005) 'Bangladeshi migrant workers in Singapore: the view from inside', *Asia-Pacific Population Journal* 20: 63–89.

Singapore Health Promotion Board (2003) *The Manual for Foreign Workers in Singapore,* Singapore: Health Promotion Board.

Toh, R. (1993) *Foreign Workers in Singapore*, SILS Information Series, Singapore: Singapore Institute of Labour Studies.

Wong, D. (2000) 'Men who built Singapore: Thai workers in the construction industry', in S. Chantavanich, A. Germershausen and A. Beesey (eds), *Thai Migrant Workers in East and Southeast Asia 1996–1997*, Bangkok: Asia Research Center for Migration, Institute of Asian Studies, Chulalongkorn University, pp. 58–107.

Yeh, C. (1995) *Foreign Workers in Singapore*, SILS Information Series, Singapore: Singapore Institute of Labour Studies.

Yeoh, B. S. A. (2004) 'Migration, international labour and multicultural policies in Singapore', Asia Research Institute Working Paper Series No. 19 (February) www. ari.nus.sg/ pub/ wps.htm (accessed 10 October 2006).

3 Low-wage Vietnamese immigrants, social class and masculinity in the homeland

Hung Cam Thai

This chapter examines the complex transnational dimensions and trajectories of Vietnamese low-wage immigrant men and reflects on the ways in which return visits to their homeland alter or highlight these men's sense of masculinity and social class. Although scholars continue to debate the relative importance of class versus gender, I underscore the intersecting or 'interlocking' nature of these categories for low-wage immigrant men in the United States (Andersen and Collins 2001; Collins *et al.* 1995). In my interviews with low-wage immigrant men, there is a consistent theme demonstrating that these men view their class identity as central to their sense of being a man.

A number of studies have pointed to how immigrant men assert their manhood by their socio-economic status as they return to the homeland and take on transnational activities (Goldring 1998; Smith 2006). A central point I make in this chapter is that the intersecting categories of social class and masculinity need to be expanded globally because much of what we know about both concepts in the West is still nation-specific (Connell 1995; Wright 1997), despite the enormous increase in transnational flows of capital and people in recent years. Globally expanding research on the related concepts of social class and masculinity is particularly relevant to the lives of immigrants whose low wages take on different social and economic meanings when they make visits to their homeland in developing countries. For men, whose wages and labour-market positions carry meanings significant to their manhood, this is especially worthy of exploration.

For some immigrants, as Waters (1999: 102) succinctly points out, 'their sense of self is tied to the status system in the home country'. That status system is often reworked in complex ways as immigrants take on transnational lives. This transnational focus is particularly important because some immigrants continue to work in the lowest sectors of the US formal and informal labour markets (Chiswick 1982). Vietnamese American men earn on average 30 per cent less than their white counterparts, and they are one of the lowest-income-earning ethnic groups in the United States (Yamane 2001). The issue of social class and gender among low-wage Vietnamese immigrant men is also worthy of exploration because, unlike the general population, research has shown that among Asian American immigrants in the low-wage labour market, especially in California, women tend to get jobs more easily, work longer hours and earn more money than men (Espiritu 1999). A number of studies in the United States have pointed out that men in general, and working class and minority men in particular, define themselves as men by the nature of their work and wage-earning power (Ehrenreich 1983; Hochschild and Machung 1989; Rubin 1976, 1994). I examine this point globally by examining the situation of low-wage Vietnamese immigrant men who return to visit their home country.

Except for a few men who worked in ethnic enterprises such as nail salons, where average hourly wages range from $8 to $12 per hour, the Vietnamese American low-wage men in this study earned on average between $6 and $8 per hour. These men usually worked in hourly wage, secondary labour-market jobs that offered them little stability (Sakamoto and Chen 1991). For the most part, they worked long hours for low pay. Their yearly salaries ranged between $8,000 and $24,000, and many of them fell below the US poverty level at the time I conducted fieldwork (Dalaker 2001). For many of these men, as I have pointed out elsewhere (Thai 2008), low-wage status frequently translated into low marriageability, which is directly related to their sense of masculinity. Many of the men in this study pointed out that lack of financial resources in Vietnamese migrant communities made them less desirable marriage partners, and therefore less desirable men to the women in their marriage markets. Moreover, many of them also talked about their low-wage jobs as unrespectable, which they felt was connected to their sense of being a man. My findings reflect other findings that have shown how men are more likely than women to view their work lives as the most central aspect to their gender identity (Lamont 1992, 2000; Rubin 1976).

At the most basic level of cultural ideology, masculinity is a 'personal and collective project', which often assumes an association between breadwinning and manhood (Donaldson 1993: 645). In the mid-1980s, a 'new sociology of masculinity' (Carrigan *et al.* 1985) was proposed in order to critically examine power relations among men and between men and women. Since that frame-work was introduced, much of the scholarly work on the topic invokes the plural *masculinities* to account for the diverse range of men's experiences (see the Introduction to this book). Although most scholars agree that masculinity does not constitute a singular ideology or practice, it is clustered around what Connell (1995) calls 'hegemonic masculinity' which 'asserts the naturalness of male domination, based on solidarities between men as well as on the subordination of women' (Jackson 1991: 201). While the notion of hegemonic masculinity is directly linked to the institution of male dominance, few men actually embody it, although most men 'benefit from the patriarchal dividend of dominance over women' (Kendall 2000: 261). And although hegemonic masculinity operates across the spectrum, most scholars agree that it often marginalizes working-class men, while excluding men of colour and gay men. As Ford and Lyons point out (Introduction), a number of scholars have argued that the concept of hegemonic masculinity is of limited value in non-Western contexts. Yet, I call attention to the transnational dimension of masculinities in a new 'world gender order' (Connell 2005). An analysis of a new world gender order involving transnational migrants must, in my view, account for meanings of social class across international borders. As Donaldson (1993) points out, an under-studied aspect of research on contemporary manhood is the relationship between social class and masculinity. This focus is important because class privilege, for some men, sometimes makes up for other kinds of marginality (such as racial marginality). Here, I view masculinity as a process, rather than an outcome, for low-wage Vietnamese immigrant men. Return activities, even if they are temporary, are important moments of redefining manhood.

Studying low-wage immigrant men who are beginning to build and sustain transnational ties to their homeland may shed light on the effects of global and transnational forces on gender relations in immigrant communities and the homeland. This task is a particularly important one because immigrants are more frequently turning to their home countries for social, economic and political activities (Espiritu 2003; Goldring 2003; Portes 1996; Portes *et al.* 1999). The narratives of the men involved in this study reveal how low-wage immigrant men construct their manhood given that their lives are placed 'at the intersection and interstices of vast systems of power: patriarchy, racism, colonialism, and capitalism, to name a few' (Chen 1999: 589). As Smith (2006: 13) argues, immigrant men 'are seen to want to return home or to imagine themselves returning, whereas women want to settle or imagine themselves settling, because men lose status and power in the United States and women gain them'. Indeed, the Vietnamese immigrant men I spoke to talked about the importance of the homeland to their sense of being a man much more than Vietnamese immigrant women draw on the homeland as defining their womanhood. In short, the homeland enhances immigrant men's socio-economic worth in ways that help to redefine their masculinity.

In this chapter, I tell the stories of men whom I met in the course of conducting a larger study on the emergence of a transnational marriage market linking women in Vietnam and Vietnamese men living and working in Vietnamese immigrant communities in the United States (Thai 2008). During fourteen months of fieldwork conducted at distinct intervals in Vietnam and in the United States from 1997 to 2001, I got to know of a total of sixty-nine transpacific marriages in the Vietnamese diaspora. In this distinct and emergent global marriage market, immigrant Vietnamese men typically go to Vietnam to marry through arrangement, subsequently returning to their places of residence (most are from the United States, Canada, France and Australia) to initiate paperwork to sponsor their wives. During this waiting period, I came to know the brides in Vietnam and later the US-based grooms (Thai 2008). In the process of these marital arrangements, most of the grooms had returned to Vietnam for the first time since their emigration from Vietnam. That is, the first time they met their wives was also the first time that many of them returned to their home country after some years of being away. The focus of this chapter, therefore, is on the homeland return visits that immigrant men make to Vietnam. At the outset, I note that I am only providing the perspectives of the men in this chapter, although the larger project also focuses on their wives.

This chapter examines how return visits alter men's sense of manhood, especially in relation to their socio-economic status. Return visits are key to transnational activities among Vietnamese immigrants because return migration in order to resettle in the homeland is rare for the overseas Vietnamese population (Long 2004). Most post-war Vietnamese immigrants left Vietnam as political refugees over the last quarter of the twentieth century, and, for many of these former refugees, returning to settle is difficult because the Vietnamese government has not yet fully implemented legal policies for incorporating overseas Vietnamese into the homeland. Return visits, therefore, are important for overseas Vietnamese to sustain transnational family ties. In fact, return visits have only been made possible due to recent changes in national policies by the Vietnamese government and to recent international diplomatic relations among nation-states, particularly between the United States and Vietnam. Historically, the Vietnamese represented the core group of refugees who fled Southeast Asia shortly after the withdrawal of American troops from Vietnam and the fall of Saigon on 30 April 1975. In 1986, after having no contact with most of the outside world for over a decade, the government of Vietnam adopted a socio-economic policy called *Doi Moi* (renovation) which did not end state ownership or central planning, but moved the country from complete state-sponsored socialism to partial free market capitalism (Ebashi 1997; Morley and Nishihara 1997). The normalization of economic and social ties by 1995, the year that US President Bill Clinton established full diplomatic relations with the country (Morley and Nishihara 1997), gradually increased the number of individuals from the Vietnamese diaspora who returned to Vietnam to visit family members or to vacation. The Vietnamese government estimates that there are currently more than 300,000 overseas Vietnamese who return to visit annually, a dramatic increase from 8,000 in 1988 and 87,000 in 1992 (Carruthers 2008; Thomas 1999).

The analysis in this chapter is based on the first return visit to Vietnam that the men took to meet their future wives as well as subsequent trips they took while their wives waited in Vietnam for paper clearance to migrate. Espiritu (2003: 15) notes in her study of Filipino transnational communities that the idealization of the home

> becomes problematic when it elicits a nostalgia for a glorious past that never was, a nostalgia that elides exclusion, power relations, and difference or when it elicits a desire to replicate these inequities as a means to buttress lost status and identities in the adopted country.

The fact that men in my study returned to Vietnam for a spouse is a telling story about gender relations in their transnational journey from Vietnam to the West and back to their homeland. In my interviews with informants about their transnational networks and in more than twenty-five trips to Vietnam to do fieldwork since 1997, I was always told by respondents that return visits were made generally first by men, followed by women and children in later return visits. In general, however, single men are some of the first groups of people who return to Vietnam, some for the sole purpose of finding a wife.

In what follows, I consider intersecting aspects of these Vietnamese low-wage immigrant men's lives that precede and follow their return visits to their communities of origin. For analytical clarity, I supply narratives of two men – Chanh and Loc – to show two related patterns in which these men take on, redefine or challenge meanings of masculinity as they move from the categories of refugees to immigrants to transmigrants through return visits to their homeland. These different patterns include how these men 'achieve' masculinity and how they 'restore' masculinity. Both patterns show how men redefine their socio-economic status, affecting their sense of masculinity. In this study, twenty-one of the sixty-nine men in my sample migrated when they were under the age of 18; in addition, only eleven of these men could be considered as part of the 'new' second generation, that is, those post-1965 immigrants who migrated at or before the age of 12 (Kibria 2002). On the one hand, for the men who migrated as children, returning to the homeland and taking on transnational activities allowed them to achieve masculinity, perhaps for the first time in their adulthood. On the other hand, the vast majority – 70 per cent – of the men in this study migrated to the West after having come of age in their homeland. It was for these men that, through return visits, restoring masculinity was made possible by developing transnational ties to their homeland. I use the term 'restore' to capture an experience of social class that is directly linked to masculinity which was lost due to migration, and perhaps regained upon making return visits to the homeland. Examining the interview data revealed these distinct patterns among Vietnamese immigrant men who are just beginning to develop transnational identities. I note that some men experience only one of these two patterns, while others undergo multiple, sometimes overlapping, patterns of change.

Achieving masculinity

The story of Chanh Tran, a 32-year-old jewellery repairman who lived near Seattle when I met him, illustrates how return visits allow some men to remake social class in order to 'achieve' masculinity as they take up transnational identities. Among men who achieve masculinity through return visits, most were minors at the point of their migration overseas and generally did not have experiences with the labour market prior to their emigration from Vietnam. As children, these men had a mixture of socio-economic backgrounds, but for the most part they were low-wage working adults. Because these men entered adulthood in the West as immigrants in low-wage work, many felt that they were unmarriageable men in their immigrant contexts. Return visits to their homeland offered these men, both temporarily and in the long term, an opportunity to achieve masculinity by trading in their low wages for seemingly high wages in Vietnam. This is because many men asserted their sense of being a man through the power of earning money and spending it in the homeland. When I asked Chanh, for instance, how he felt the first time he made a return visit to Vietnam, he quickly explained to me, 'As soon as the plane touched the airport, I knew there was something there for me. I definitely had the feeling that I was home.' One of the ways in which class identity becomes so poignantly significant for the men in this study is the way in which they talk about the affordability of consumption in Vietnam, an indicator of how their low economic status took on different meanings as they returned to Vietnam. As a case in point, when

I asked Chanh why he felt there was 'something there' for him when the plane touched the ground, he explained how much of the leisure economy in Saigon caters to men. For example, he told me that the café culture, massage parlours, night clubs and karaoke bars were mainly focused on catering to men:

> Before I decided to come to Vietnam, I wanted to know what to expect, and so I talked to some of my friends who had gone, and to my cousin who made visits to Vietnam. Most of the men told me how everything in Saigon is catered to men, that everywhere you go, it's really cheap and you can have a good time without having much money, and everyone treats you very nicely.

Chanh's family migrated to the United States when he was 7, being part of the first large group of Vietnamese refugees who were evacuated directly out of Vietnam a few days before the fall of Saigon. Chanh came of age in a suburban town two hours outside of Seattle in a family of four. His father worked on the assembly line at a factory when they arrived in the United States, eventually becoming a manager of the plant, while his mother took on nursing as an occupation. Chanh said he was an ambitious student in high school, excelling in maths and sports. He wanted to 'confess', as he framed it, that he was enamoured early in his life by the idea of having money because one of his uncles owned a lucrative jewellery store near where they lived. 'I wanted to earn as much money as I could, to help my parents, and to provide for my future family', he explained.

Many of the immigrant men I spoke to in this study made strong links between making money and providing for their families, including their wives and parents, as significant to their identity as men. For this reason and although he graduated in the top ten of his high school class, Chanh decided not to attend college immediately after high school, but instead took on an apprenticeship with his prosperous uncle. Chanh earned more than his friends after high school, but over time his income stagnated as his friends who went on to college eventually earned more than he did. When I met him, Chanh had not been able to open up his own jewellery store as he had hoped, and he was still earning by the hour working for his uncle. This experience of coming of age and working in low-wage work defined Chanh's sense of being a man. Reflecting on his choice of work, Chanh told me he had strong regrets for not having gone to college. He said he felt extremely marginal in his circle of friends, especially in the Vietnamese communities and networks in which he and his family were embedded:

> I definitely think that there is a stigma for not having a college degree, and most people in the Vietnamese community I know who came to the United States the same time I did went to college. I regret not having gone to college because it definitely gave me less status in the community. At the time that I decided on not going [to college], I thought that I would eventually open a jewellery store like my uncle and would make a lot of money.

Some scholars have argued that the homeland is sometimes experienced only in the imagination, that homeland is not just 'a physical place that immigrants return to for temporary and intermittent visits, but also a concept and a desire' (Espiritu 2003: 10). I contend that it is precisely the physical movements through return visits that allow some immigrants to realize their social status and to take on their economic privilege relative to the people remaining in their homeland. For instance, when I asked Chanh to elaborate on the moment his plane landed when he took his first visit in 1998, he explained:

> When we landed, the moment we stepped outside the airport and got a taxi to drive to my uncle's house, everything was cheap. I could afford to pay for taxis and other things that I couldn't pay in the US. The rest of the trip was awesome because I was able to pay for many of the times we went out.

Chanh's assertion that he could pay for the times he went out in Vietnam indicates how his lack of economic resources and the inability to spend money in the United States made him feel less of a man because he was unable to pay for many consumptive activities in Seattle. In contrast, by returning to Vietnam to visit, he experienced a different socio-economic identity, which elevated his sense of being a man. As he said, 'In Seattle, very few women pay attention to me because I can't afford to buy them fancy stuff. Even the Vietnamese women in Seattle I know, they wouldn't want a man like me because I don't make that much money in America.'

Restoring masculinity

Men who restore masculinity as they visit their homeland experienced tremendous downward mobility when they migrated overseas as adults. The migratory downward mobility of these men affected how they defined their potential of providing for their future families, which was a central concern in the lives of the Vietnamese immigrant men I interviewed. Men who restore masculinity differed from men who achieve masculinity primarily because the former group had reached adulthood prior to emigration and had either entered or finished secondary education before they left Vietnam; many of them had already entered the labour market prior to migrating abroad. Moreover, many of them were unable to translate their skills or social status once they migrated to the West. In some ways, the men who restored masculinity had already 'achieved' it in their homeland before they migrated because they had already defined their economic power prior to migration.

The story of 44-year-old Loc Phan highlights how, rather than increasing one's status, migration could in fact bring substantial loss to one's sense of status, especially when the homeland is drawn upon as the reference point for understanding one's position in the Vietnamese transnational status system. As part of the urban middle-class in Saigon, Loc aspired to become a doctor after he graduated from high school in 1974, but his parents told him that he could not attend college because they wanted to prepare for leaving Vietnam when the war ended. His father had connections in the Mekong Delta with someone who organized boat trips for potential refugees to go to another Southeast Asian country so they could be 'processed' by various Western countries as refugees. Eventually, Loc's family became boat refugees and arrived in a suburb of Orange County where his parents had family ties. At the time that I met him, Loc was working for minimum wage in the produce department at a large ethnic supermarket near the enclave of Little Saigon in Orange County. He had been working there for nearly fifteen years, after a number of odd jobs in various ethnic enterprises, and had been living with his parents in government subsidized housing since 1979, when they arrived in the United States after spending a few years in a refugee camp in Malaysia. Loc had hoped that, over time, he could start his own business. But low-wage work meant that he could not save enough capital to start any kind of business.

In talking about the pre-migration years, Loc disclosed that his childhood was one of privilege by any global measure – he grew up in a household with successful parents who owned a factory that produced office furniture for the domestic market. As an adolescent, Loc had luxuries he never encountered as a young adult: domestic servants, chauffeurs and the best education available in his context. It was this affluence that shaped how Loc understood his social standing as a young man coming of age in Vietnam. As a high school graduate in 1974, near the end of the war in Vietnam, Loc had already formed a romantic relationship with a classmate, to whom he had promised marriage prior to his family's migration. When I asked him what happened to that first romantic relationship, Loc explained:

> Well, of course, I told her that I would return in a few years and marry her. But that didn't happen. The bad part of it is that I couldn't afford to go back there until two years ago, and of course I don't expect her to wait for me for that long. I thought I would be sad, but when I came back to Vietnam for the first time, there were so many people I met, so many old friends. So I wanted to make new relationships, meet new people, maybe find a wife on that trip.

For men like Loc, restoring masculinity was possible most often because they were able to return to the homeland – to a familiar community of people who recognized their economic privilege from the West, even if they were low-wage workers. The effect was that such men were able to restore masculinity upon their return to the homeland precisely because of the economic divide between their homeland and their immigrant communities that offered them the opportunity to 'convert' their low wages from the West to high wages as they made return visits to Vietnam (Thai 2005). Partly because of the lack of knowledge about life in the United States, Loc's relatives and friends in Vietnam frequently thought of migration as desirable, which enormously enhanced his status when he returned home. As Loc explained:

> I saw many people of my youth. Some of them became very successful in Saigon, but they did not judge me for what I do in the United States. Some really wanted to find ways to go to the United States. I don't know why they want to. I think they have much better lives in Saigon. But they always think the United States is a land of opportunity. They don't know that it's hard to make money unless you have a lot of money.

Yet it is precisely this perception of the United States among locals in Vietnam and Loc's ability to convert low wages to high wages upon returning to the homeland that offered him the opportunity to remake notions of social class in the context of a transnational status system. In this way, men who restored masculinity also achieved it by returning home and by redefining their sense of being a man through their class identity. But the ones who restored their sense of manhood were those who came of age in Vietnam and had already built a community there prior to their migration. Such men also had some sense of economic privilege, which greatly enhanced their sense of manhood, prior to migration. When I asked Loc to recount how he felt during the first visit back, he described his feelings:

> When I returned to Vietnam for the first time, I didn't know for sure if I was going to tell people that I worked at the supermarket all these years. But when I went there, I remember not feeling as poor as I do in America! So even for many people I knew in Saigon, my job at the supermarket was a dream job. I remember this very clearly because the first time I went back in 1998, they opened up one of the first Western style supermarkets in Saigon and I took some of my friends there and I told them with this feeling of shame that I work at one of those places in the United States. And some of them told me they thought it was a great job! [laughs] I didn't feel like I was this poor man like I do in the United States working in a job that no one cares about.

The complex intersection of class identity and experiences of masculinity is often reframed among men who have been dislocated along class lines because of migration. As I have shown, the homeland provides a pivotal social space in which some men are able to redefine their sense of manhood relative to their country of settlement and country of return.

Remaking class and masculinity through return visits and transnational ties

The return of Vietnamese immigrant men to the homeland produces extraordinary moments in which they experience contradictory class positions across international borders. These experiences have an enormous influence on their constructions of manhood. These homeland visits are not just based on nostalgic notions such as 'home' and 'roots'. They have powerful implications for destabilizing and altering myriad social relations in the community of origin, including producing new social hierarchies along class and gender lines as well as restoring traditions that have been seemingly abolished over time. For example, I have found that low-wage immigrants in the West are often able to assert 'high status' when they return to Vietnam to visit because of their foreign passports, even when they live in dire conditions in the West. This is because their low wage in the West takes on different economic meanings when they return to Vietnam. A fundamental concern here is the question of how transnational migration and transnational mobility can simultaneously challenge as well as reinforce patriarchy. 'Instead of being a social equalizer that empowers all migrants alike', as Guarnizo (1997: 281) argues, 'transnational migration tends to reproduce and even exacerbate class, gender, and regional inequalities'.

This chapter shows that return visits are powerful moments for low-wage immigrant men in the Vietnamese diaspora, potentially transforming how the social construction of gender and class can be reworked in transnational contexts. Return visits to Vietnam have the potential of eliciting enormous emotions and a strong sense of belonging to the homeland. I suggest that return visits produce and fashion such emotions in ways that remake class and masculinity in the context of transnational ties. Social class and gender relations are particularly enmeshed as men take on new class identities across international borders, especially among men who potentially have more to benefit from returning to their homeland. A number of prominent scholars have made it clear that migration powerfully reshapes gender relations in post-migrant communities (Espiritu 1997; Hondagneu-Sotelo 1994, 2003; Kibria 1993). But few have studied how return visits to the homeland can alter or amplify gender relations during the post-migration years. Return visits build and sustain transnational ties, offering an important geographical space for taking on and challenging class positionings in the immigrant's adopted country. This is especially important because immigrant men are more likely than immigrant women to return to the homeland for various activities and to turn to the home country for valorizing social status (Smith 2006).

References

Andersen, Margaret L. and Collins, Patricia Hill (2001) *Race, Class, and Gender: An Anthology*, Belmost, CA: Wadsworth.

Carrigan, Tim, Connell, Bob and Lee, John (1985) 'Toward a new sociology of masculinity', *Theory and Society* 14: 551–604.

Carruthers, Ashley (2008) 'Saigon from the diaspora', *Singapore Journal of Tropical Geography* 29: 68–86.

Chen, Anthony S. (1999) 'Lives at the center of the periphery, lives at the periphery of the center', *Gender & Society* 13: 584–607.

Chiswick, Barry R. (1982) 'Immigrants in the U.S. labor market', *Annals of the American Academy of Political and Social Science* March: 64–72.

Collins, Patricia Hill, Maldonado, Lionel A., Takagi, Dana Y., Thorne, Barrie, Weber, Lynn and Winant, Howard (1995) 'Doing difference', *Gender and Society* 9: 491–506.

Connell, R. W. (1995) *Masculinities*, Berkeley: University of California Press.

—— (2005) 'Globalization, imperialism, and masculinities', in M. S. Kimmel, J. Hearn and R. W. Connell (eds), *Handbook of Studies on Men and Masculinities*, Thousand Oaks, CA: Sage, pp. 71–89.

Dalaker, Joseph (2001) 'Poverty in the United States: 2000', US Census Bureau, Current Population Reports, Series P60–214, Washington, DC: US Government Printing Office.

Donaldson, Michael (1993) 'What is hegemonic masculinity?', *Theory & Society* 22: 643–57.

Ebashi, Masahiko (1997) 'The economic take-off', in J. Morley and M. Nishihara (eds), *Vietnam Joins the World*, Armonk, NY: M.E. Press, pp. 37–65.

Ehrenreich, Barbara (1983) *The Hearts of Men: American Dreams and the Flight from Commitment*, New York: Doubleday.

Espiritu, Yen Le (1997) *Asian American Women and Men: Labor, Laws and Love*, Thousand Oaks, CA: Sage.

—— (1999) 'Gender and labor in Asian immigrant families', *American Behavioral Scientist* 42: 628–47.

—— (2003) *Home Bound: Filipino American Lives across Cultures, Communities, and Countries*, Berkeley: University of California Press.

Goldring, Luin (1998) 'The power of status in transnational social fields', in M. P. Smith and L. E. Guarnizo (eds), *Transnationalism from Below*, New Brunswick, NJ: Transaction, pp. 165–95.

—— (2003) 'Gender, status, and the state in transnational spaces', in P. Hondagneu-Sotelo (ed.), *Gender and U.S. Immigration: Contemporary Trends*, Berkeley: University of California Press, pp. 341–58.

Guarnizo, Luis E. (1997) 'The emergence of a transnational social formation and the mirage of return migration among Dominican transmigrants', *Identities: Global Studies in Culture and Power* 4: 281–322.

Hochschild, Arlie Russell and Machung, Anne (1989) *The Second Shift: Working Parents and the Revolution at Home*, New York: Viking.

Hondagneu-Sotelo, Pierrette (1994) *Gendered Transitions: Mexican Experiences of Immigration*, Berkeley: University of California Press.

—— (2003) *Gender and U.S. Immigration: Contemporary Trends*, Berkeley: University of California Press.

Jackson, Peter (1991) 'The cultural politics of masculinity: towards a social geography', *Transactions of the Institute of British Geographers* 16: 199–213.

Kendall, Lori (2000) '"Oh no! I'm a nerd!": hegemonic masculinity on an online forum', *Gender and Society* 14: 256–74.

Kibria, Nazli (1993) *Family Tightrope: The Changing Lives of Vietnamese Americans*, Princeton: Princeton University Press.

—— (2002) *Becoming Asian-American: Second Generation Chinese and Korean American Identities*, Baltimore: Johns Hopkins University Press.

Lamont, Michele (1992) *Money, Morals, & Manners: The Culture of the French and the American Upper-Middle Class*, Chicago: University of Chicago Press.

—— (2000) *The Dignity of Working Men: Morality and the Boundaries of Race, Class, and Immigration*, New York: Russell Sage Foundation.

Long, Lynellyn D. (2004) 'Viet Kieu on a fast track back', in E. Oxfeld and L. D. Long (eds), *Coming Home? Refugees, Migrants, and Those Who Stayed Behind*, Philadelphia: University of Pennsylvania Press, pp. 65–89.

Morley, James W. and Nishihara, Masashi (1997) 'Vietnam joins the world', in J. W. Morley and M. Nishihara (eds), *Vietnam Joins the World*, Armonk, NY: M.E. Press, pp. 3–14.

Portes, Alejandro (1996) 'Global villagers: the rise of transnational communities', *American Prospect* 25: 74–8.

Portes, Alejandro, Guarnizo, Luis E. and Landolt, Patricia (1999) 'The study of transnationalism: pitfalls and promise of an emergent research field', *Ethnic and Racial Studies* 22: 217–37.

Rubin, Lillian Breslow (1976) *Worlds of Pain: Life in the Working-Class Family*, New York: Basic Books.

—— (1994) *Families on the Fault Line: America's Working Class Speaks about the Family, the Economy, Race, and Ethnicity*, New York: Harper Perennial.

Sakamoto, Arthur and Chen, Meichu D. (1991) 'Inequality and attainment in a dual labor market', *American Sociological Review* 56: 295–308.

Smith, Robert Courtney (2006) *Mexican New York: Transnational Lives of New Immigrants*, Berkeley: University of California Press.

Thai, Hung Cam (2005) 'Globalization as a gender strategy: respectability, masculinity, and convertibility across the Vietnamese diaspora', in R. P. Appelbaum and W. I. Robinson (eds), *Critical Globalization Studies*, New York: Routledge, pp. 76–92.

—— (2008) *For Better or for Worse: Vietnamese International Marriages in the New Global Economy*, Rutgers, NJ and London: Rutgers University Press.

Thomas, Mandy (1999) *Dreams in the Shadows: Vietnamese-Australian Lives in Transition*, Sydney: Allen and Unwin

Waters, Mary C. (1999) *Black Identities: West Indian Immigrant Dreams and American Realities*, Cambridge, MA: Harvard University Press.

Wright, Eric Olin (1997) *Class Counts: Comparative Studies in Class Analysis,* Cambridge: Cambridge University Press,

Yamane, Linus (2001) 'The labor market status of foreign born Vietnamese Americans', unpublished manuscript.

4 Homosociality and desire

Charting Chinese Singaporean sex tourists' online conversations

Sophie Williams, Lenore Lyons and Michele Ford

Questions pertaining to heterosexual men's consumption of sex tourism have only recently come into focus in a literature that engages primarily with the narratives and experiences of Western male sex tourists (see Kruhse-Mountburton 1995; O'Connell Davidson 1995; Frank 2003). A glaring problem in much of this litera-ture is the use of an almost universal categorization of 'man', a categorization that leaves little room for cultural and locational specificity. This has led Louie (2003: 1) to argue that the move towards a global analysis is premature, especially in terms of the lack of understanding of Asian masculinities.

In this chapter, we examine the interrelationship between hegemonic masculin-ities (see Connell 1995), which are always at once both culturally and historically contingent, and Chinese Singaporean men's localized practices in a sex tourist space spanning the online and offline worlds. Our focus in on men who visit the island of Batam, located in the Riau Archipelago of Indonesia, just kilometres south of Singapore.[1] Middle-class tourism has been targeted as a key growth industry for the island. The journey by high-speed ferry takes less than one hour, and Singaporean passport holders can stay for up to thirty days without a visa. But although some parts of Batam attract middle-class Singaporeans in search of sun, sand and pampering, most Singaporean tourists who come to the islands are working-class men in search of sex.[2] Demand for the sex industry is fuelled by the comparative cost of the sexual encounter, but men visiting Batam also enjoy the added benefits of cheap food, gambling, shopping and other forms of entertainment during their visits (Ford and Lyons 2008).

Although we know that Chinese Singaporeans constitute the overwhelming majority of sex tourists to Batam and neighbouring islands, we know very little about their motivations and understandings of sex tourism. Clients are notoriously difficult to contact and our knowledge of the behaviours and practices of male clients globally is often inferred from the statements of sex workers rather than from the men themselves (see Perkins 1994; McKeganey and Barnard 1996; Brewis and Linstead 2000; Law 2000; Sanders 2005b). Observation of online sexual communities can provide one means for researchers directly to access clients.[3] As Sanders (2005a: 70) argues:

> Previously, buyers and sellers of sex communicated on only a private and individual basis whereas now, through CMC [computer mediated communica-

tion], these interactions have entered the public domain. Observing relationships between those who buy and those who sell sex has been practically
impossible before the advent of CMC . . . Through the Internet the researcher
can now be privy to other aspects of sexual behaviour that have been hidden
and largely clandestine.

As cyberspace interactions are embedded within normative discourses of gender,
race and sexuality, we should expect that sex tourism websites reflect (and
contribute to) wider networks of meaning that intersect with discourses about male
dominance and solidarity, as well as female sexuality.[4] This is not to deny the greater
potential for more fluid constructions of identity within cyberspace, especially in
the realm of gendered and sexualized identity. In the Singaporean context, Ho
et al. (2002) have written about the use of the Internet as a site of resistance to
normative state–society relations through the production of non-state-friendly
sexualities. However, as Slater (2002) points out, these are not the only forms of
sexuality to be performed online. Within the online world of Singaporean sex
tourists we witness both a reinscription of normative constructions of masculinity
and some potential for transgression to be realized.

Williams' (2006) work on constructions of hegemonic Chinese Singaporean
masculinity demonstrates that career and marital, reproductive and financial success
are key elements of what it means to be 'a man' in contemporary Singapore. Many
working-class men fail to meet these social expectations about employment and
income, and some face difficulties in finding marriage partners (Lyons and Ford
2008). Men's conversations about their plans for and experiences of sex tourism
in Batam provide one means to examine how such Singaporean men engage with
and negotiate hegemonic masculinities. Through the analysis of such sites we
are able to better articulate both normative and potentially idealized notions of
masculinity and heterosexuality, regardless of whether or not they are materially
practised and thus representative of the 'truth' of men's experiences.

The Sammyboy Times

'Women need a reason to have sex. Men just need a Place.'[5] The Sammyboy Times,
self-proclaimed as Singapore's 'premier sex site', provides a virtual space within
which Singaporean men are able to discuss the finer details of commercial sexual
relations.[6] The site's homepage banner proclaims that Sammyboy publishes 'Real
Singapore News – Warts and All. We publish what the Straits Times [Singapore's
main English daily newspaper] leaves out.' As this suggests, the site caters for a
variety of discussion topics, ranging from local politics to press censorship to racism
to public housing. For example, the Coffeeshop provides a space dedicated to the
discussion of Singaporean politics. However, Singapore's self-declared 'virtual sex
hub' is primarily a site about sex. As its forum page declares, 'Sam's Sex Forum
IS the definitive guide for those who want to get more bang for their buck in the
Commercial Sex Scene around the World!'[7]

Most of the Sammyboy site is publicly accessible but individuals must become
members to post text and upload pictures. Thus, although membership is the

preferred way to become a fully fledged Sammyboy netizen it is by no means essential in order to participate in the Sammyboy online community. The multiple spaces contained within the website indicate also that the wider Sammyboy cybercommunity is not an exclusively male one, although graphic, sexualized photographs of Asian women on its homepage mark it as primarily a male space. Although there is no way to restrict access to the Sex Forum to men only, the sexualized and gendered nature of the forum pages are one way in which a preferred male audience is constructed. Visual and textual clues clearly signal that men are the perceived, and intended, audience. At the top of each page of each thread is a banner incorporating a picture of an opened mangosteen, the 'queen of fruits', suggesting eroticism and bodily flesh. Underneath this, images of partially undressed women sit alongside written text that provides phone-sex numbers and other websites offering online sex. However, these advertisements play a secondary role to the primary function of this space, which is to provide a place where 'experienced fornicators' can come together as a community to discuss their sexual experiences at home and abroad.[8]

The most active thread within the Talk Sex forum is the International Field Report thread which contains sub-threads related to different sex tourism destinations. Some Internet scholars suggest that cyberspace is situated in a physically 'spaceless' context 'where the social production of space, place, and self is not dependent or contingent on what is "physically real", nor are such productions necessarily grounded in that which is empirically veritable' (Waskul and Douglass 1997: 381). This assertion overlooks not only the diverse forms of CMC but also the ways in which cyberspaces emerge in particular localized forms. The Sammyboy forum is not a 'geographic location without physical presence' (i.e. a 'place' without a 'space') (cf. Waskul and Douglass 1997: 394), but a space within which place is constantly inscribed. The nature and content of the communication within the forum is entirely dependent on place and space; sex tourism destinations provide the *raison d'être* for Sammyboy. In the context of Sammyboy members, the online and offline worlds are not separate spaces detached from each other, but rather are dialectically defined by their rich and complex connections. This is apparent in the ways in which the content of the forum postings is structured – members are able to pose questions before they travel overseas and to post detailed 'field reports' on their return, creating a constant process of exchange between the online and offline worlds.

The Batam Info Thread sits within the International Field Reports. Its stated purpose is to share information about the structure of the sex industry on the island in order to assist 'newbies' (men who have yet to visit Batam for sex and/or those men with limited experience as sex clients) and provide 'old hands' with the latest up-to-date information on events, prices and venues. In this way, the site functions as an arena for social experience, a space where men can lurk to find out more about language, culture and behaviour. Ross (2005: 344), who looks at cybersex, describes the Internet as 'a space between fantasy and action' and argues that the 'importance of the Internet as a sexual medium is its placement as an intermediate step between private fantasy and actual behaviour. It provides a gap between thinking, doing and being – and especially, an opportunity to do and not be, or to type and not do.' The

Sammyboy site certainly performs such a role – men who have never engaged the services of a sex worker as well as men who have never been to Batam can learn 'how' to be a sex client.

However, Sammyboy's role in the performance of sex tourism is not limited to participants' discursive strategies in cyberspace. The site enables more than simply the creation of fantasies or the exchange of information between these two worlds – it is a forum which facilitates sex travel through organized trips involving members. Members use the space to contact each other much like email or Internet Relay Chat (IRC) – posting short questions and responses about dates and times of meetings. While not all members participate in these organized groups, and some express an aversion to travelling together, the forum functions as a space whereby fraternal relations can be both imagined and extended from the offline to the online world and back again: even where they go alone, members clearly compile their sex tourism field reports with their virtual community in mind.

Sammyboy as a fraternal space

The Sammyboy website is decidedly Singaporean in its visual and textual constructions, something that is accentuated by the use of the term 'hub' in the banner that flies across the top of each thread,[9] and the visual representation of a durian on the homepage. Members have developed their own unique terms and phrases that emphasize its exclusive character. Their use of language also works to designate the thread as a 'Singaporean space'. The men use a combination of English, Singlish,[10] Malay, Chinese pinyin and transliterated Chinese dialect and local references (e.g. locations and cultural events) in their postings. The most notable of the new words developed by members is 'cheong', a term that means 'to charge, or go out for happening stuff'.[11] In the context of the Batam thread it refers to the practice of travelling to Batam for commercial sex. Although this term is defined in the Frequently Asked Questions (FAQ) glossary, provided to assist newcomers with the process of translating postings into colloquial English, there is a tacit understanding that the members of the forum will have knowledge of both the term and the practices it signifies. The term varies in its usage throughout the forum for both the act of sex and the act of going to Batam.

Kiesling (2005: 721) notes North American use of the term 'dude' amongst members of a college fraternity (and men in general) as a 'cool' stance that allows for the 'expression of homosocial desire without the speaker's coming across as "too earnest" in his desire'. This male form of familial address works to exclude women at the same time that it inscribes fraternal bonds between the men. Members of the forum refer to themselves as 'cheongsters' or 'samsters' (after Sammyboy) – terms that create a similar community of belonging amongst members. The language of fraternity is also present in the use of the term 'bro' (brother) to address each other. The site is also infused with militaristic language that resonates with the men's experiences of National Service.[12] The language of 'field reports' and the structure of many of the postings, which often use 24-hour time to report on the sequence of events in 15–30 minute intervals, are suggestive of military briefings. Many of the terms and phrases used by the men make reference to military spaces, or at least military language and sexual innuendo, as the following glossary suggests:

Phrase	Meaning
I salute you	To be commended for a particularly unusual sex act
Will not fight war without a helmet	Will not have sex without a condom
Shots	Orgasm
Loaded	Ejaculation
SOP (Standard Operating Procedure)	Standard Orgasm Procedure
Fire hand gun	Masturbation
Go on tour	Denotes tourism, but also 'tour of duty'
Happy hunting	Looking for girls

Previous research demonstrates the ways in which masculinity and femininity are inscribed in patriarchal militarism (Enloe 2000). Female subordination is central to the functioning of male domination within the military, which actively uses sexualized gender stereotypes to describe women and a range of male 'others', including ethnic and sexual minorities (D'Amico and Weinstein 1999). The use of sexualized and gendered language is one element of this performance of hegemonic masculinity within military and non-military contexts.

Members of the Batam Info Thread actively inscribe a militarized masculinity into their online personas. Without physical presence, screen names are an important means of communicating qualities of selfhood; they are an essential means of establishing a 'cyberself' (Waskul and Douglass 1997). Although names can change over time, individuals usually choose their screen name carefully and continue to use it over time. In her discussion of chat rooms, Danet (1996) describes nicks (online nicknames) as masks that serve two purposes – they provide camouflage on the one hand and are a form of conspicuous marking on the other. The screen names chosen by members of the Batam Info Thread reinforce that this is a sexualized, masculine space. Members use names that reflect a debasing of women's bodies (Meatlover); the link between sex and the night (Nightcrawllerr); sex and violence (Bangbangman; v.killers [virgin killers]); a link between sexual prowess and military armaments (Snipeshot08); cheating (Xdeception); and masculine control of technology (Logitek).

Members of the Sammyboy Talk Sex forum can also attach a visual icon next to their name, and a signature that is included at the bottom of each posting. Visual icons and signatures, when combined with a screen name, allow members to disseminate as much information as possible about themselves to transient audiences. The specificities of the visual icons and signatures used in the Batam Info Thread are also noteworthy in what they reveal about the localized production of masculinity and fraternity in the Sammyboy site. Snipeshot08 has a picture of a target next to his name; Ronsee is an innocent-looking toy holding a gun; and technofreak is the face of a woman's corpse with blood streaming from her eyes and mouth. Such visual clues point to the way in which the Batam Info space is constructed as a masculine space, with the fraternal bonds of National Service being replicated online through the use of militaristic visual imagery.

The link between the construction of a cyberidentity and militarized violence should not, however, be overemphasized in the case of the Batam Info Thread. In addition to screen names that reflect this link, members also use names associated with geographical places (Btm man [Batam Man]); hobbies (Blackjack_king); and ethnic identifiers (Vincentlim81). Although it is difficult to determine whether Sammyboy is an ethnically exclusive space, members use other textual clues to their ethnicity, including the use of Chinese characters in signature files and the frequent use of Chinese pinyin or dialect in postings. These signifiers of gender and ethnicity serve to demarcate the boundaries between members and non-members, and thus mark out the space of fraternity. Members also declare their allegiance to the brotherhood of samsters through their signature files. Popiah signs off by declaring he is 'a member of BOSS Club (Bros of Share Share)' and the member known as 'no-go' states: 'if I have a million dollars . . . then I will cheong, cheong, cheong'.

The combination of icon, screen name and signature allows members to produce a consistent cyberself to non-members and members who enter different threads and shift between different parts of the site over time. As in everyday life, however, this cyberself is 'continually presented, negotiated, and validated through inter-action with others' (Waskul and Douglass 1997: 387). Members who post more frequently establish their online presence in a number of ways: they reveal information about their personal preferences and 'sexploits', as well as potentially more revealing information about age, marital status, employment and education. Significantly for the study of fraternity, each member is provided with an online 'reputation' made up of 'power' and 'points' that establishes their position within a hierarchy of brothers, as described in the discussion below.

Performance of fraternity in the Batam Info Thread

The Batam Info Thread provides the latest information about various tourist commodities in Batam, ranging from an overnight booking with a girl to a taxi ride from the ferry terminal to the hotel.[13] A key element of this information sharing involves detailed accounts of the different types of women available, including physical characteristics such as skin colour, breast size and appearance, as well as other attributes such as hygiene, attitude, experience and performance. But above all, the site is a means for men to ensure that they receive value for money during their visits to Batam. A typical posting at the end of a field report reflects both these elements:

Damages:

Ferry: $34

Taxi: $2.50–$3.30 (Rp. 15,000–20,000 the most)

Hotel: $45 (or Rp. 275,000)

Ger [Girl]: $42 (Rp. 250,000)

Makan [Food]: Ard [Around] $80 (total 12 persons) + beer & drinks

* beer there is only ard S$1.00, damn cheap sia.

Total damages ard $180–200

Ger Looks: 7/10

Age: 25

Body: 6.5/10

BBBJ [Bareback Barrel Blow Job]: 8.5/10 (mind blowing & hardworking)

Fuck: 9/10 (damn responsive & wet especially doggy)

Gf [Girlfriend]: 8.5/10 (treat u well & very gf feelings, shower for u etc) Shiok [Great]

Total Shots [Orgasms]: 2 nia. 😊

RTF [Return To Fuck]: sure, y not, kinda of miss her rite nw.

SonicGear 18.04.2007, 10:42 am.

As this posting indicates, it is possible to construct a very detailed account of Singaporean male sex tourism to Batam from the reports and conversations contained in the Batam Info Thread. But since 'men's sexual storytelling is shaped by homosocial masculine cultures' (Flood 2008: 342), their conversations also provide us with insights into the ways in which this particular group of Singaporean men establish and perform fraternity through their experiences of sex outside Singapore.

Bonding through sex

Studies of homosociality in Western contexts draw our attention to the 'male homosocial double bind' born of the tension between male solidarity and compulsory/ requisite heterosexuality:

> In the former men are supposed to form a close bond, but in the latter they are supposed to refrain from intimacy . . . Because heterosexuality is such a strong discourse, the men must present their emotional intimacy as clearly nonsexual, since sexual and emotional intimacy are often bound up with each other.
>
> (Kiesling 2005: 711)

In other words, men seek to establish connections with each other (i.e. express homosocial desire) without direct expressions of homosocial feelings. In his study of an American college fraternity, Kiesling (2005) argues that men adopt linguistic and social strategies of indirectness to create and display homosocial desire. This desire is not expressed individually but it is effectively created and communicated through their language and behaviour. Kiesling identifies three kinds of indirectness through which men seek to achieve intimacy in the North American context. Social indirectness refers to situations in which men perform conflict to form connections, while addressee indirectness involves conversations in which the real target is within earshot but is not the interlocutor. A third kind of indirectness is topic indirectness, which refers to the development of intimacy through discussions of topics not related to self (Kiesling 2005: 696, 703). The role of indirectness in the construction of homosociality is supported by Flood's (2008) study of an Australian military academy, where 'the boys' constitute 'an imagined audience for [a] man's sexual achievements, their collective male gaze informing the meaning of his sexual relations' (ibid.: 348).

Like Flood's Australian military academy students, the participants in the Batam Info Thread use talk about sex as a means through which to deflect desirability 'to a non personal domain' (Kiesling 2005: 711). Flood notes that, like the American subjects of research by Bird (1996) and Boswell and Spade (1996), Australian students' stories of their sexual exploits are 'an important part of homosocial male banter and represent competition in internal "pecking orders"' (Flood 2008: 353). In contrast, the conversations that men have in the explicitly sexual domain of the Batam Info Thread are remarkably devoid of boasting about their sexual exploits or explicit competition. As discussed below, the Batam cheongsters use strategies of addressee indirectness and social indirectness to create hierarchies of fraternity within the thread's homosocial space. But while they build fraternal relationships through their talk about sex and sex tourism, they are almost completely silent on their own – or others' – performance of heterosexual sex.

This silence is most glaringly evident in the substantial field reports that comprise a significant proportion of the postings. These reports, which as noted earlier provide a blow-by-blow account of men's visits to Batam with often military precision, include little or no information about the sex act itself. For example, in a 334-word field report contributed by Nitecrawllerr on 27 July 2007, only thirty-four words described the time he spent in his room with the sex worker:

> Very friendly GF [girlfriend] feeling and very horny too. Sleeping time would hug u till next morning. Middle of the nite woke her up for kongkek [fuck] and she obliged. Not many cewek [girls] would do that.
>
> Nitecrawllerr, 27.07.2007, 8:37 pm

Nitecrawller's final assessment of the performance this 30-year-old 'mother I'd like to fuck' (milf) at the bottom of his report provides us with a few more hints concerning the technical details of their sexual encounter. The sex worker, called 'Angel', scored 7/10 for her all-over 'catbath'; 8/10 for the 'bareback barrel blow job' (BBBJ), and 8/10 for her 'fuck job' (FJ), which took place with a condom. He did not ask for an 'ass rim' (AR), and suggests that that an ordinary blow job (BJ) would have been a better option than the BBBJ. There is no suggestion at all in the account of how he himself performed.

In DexDJ's 827-word field report of 5 May 2007, only twenty-four words describe the two incidences of sexual 'action' that took place during his three-day two-night trip. During the first:

> Action was ok only but she wasn't like a dead fish or giving me a 'when-the-fuck-are-you-cumming?' kinda look..no rush..7/10
>
> DexDJ, 05.05.2007, 5:26 pm

His description of the second sexual encounter is limited to noting that he went back to the hotel to 'bang again'. At the end of his report, DexDJ provides a detailed summary of the costs of the trip, but the report contains no additional assessment of the appearance or sexual prowess of his 'girl', beyond noting the fact that she was 'short, cute and looks Chinese'. What he does provide is a more lengthy description of the sex worker's treatment of him before 'the action began', suggesting that, like many of his comrades, DexDJ values the 'girlfriend experience':

> Went back to hotel and my girl literally treated my like a KING lah..gave me a massage, brought me the hotel's slippers, pour me water, wet a face towel to wipe my face and hands..then we watched the tele abit then we went shower together. Again, she washed every part of me cleanly..with a scrub too.
>
> DexDJ, 05.05.2007, 5:26 pm

Like the vast majority of other field reports written during the period examined, there is no mention of DexDJ's own performance or prowess.

These narratives suggest that for this group of Singaporean sex tourists topic indirectness emphasizes comradeship rather than the competition generated around sexual prowess and boasting more generally associated with men's talk about sex. However, this should not be confused with a sense of egalitarianism between members, as there is a definite hierarchy involved in the organization of the Batam Info community, which works to strengthen the fraternal paradigm within which it is located.

Hierarchy and desire

Many scholars have noted the centrality of hierarchy to the construction of heteronormative masculinities. Campbell's work on 'pub(lic) masculinity' in a New Zealand pub demonstrates that the public performance of drinking was intensely competitive and created distinct hierarchies amongst the men. These hierarchies were created and reinscribed through 'continual conversational cockfighting, during which other drinkers scrutinized men's performance. At these times, hierarchies of knowledge, historical embeddedness, and legitimacy were established' (Campbell

2000: 569). Sammyboy's sex forum explicitly establishes hierarchy through two means: induction processes for 'newbies' (newly joined thread members) and rankings of members. Traditionally fraternities have operated as a site of education and initiation rites into manhood for young men, with sexuality playing a pivotal role. The initiation rite within the Batam Info Thread of Sammyboy is set up explicitly by the structure of the site (in which newbies' postings are initially monitored for a time and a member's length of affiliation with the site is reflected in their 'power' rating) and by the internal structure of members' interactions. The forum inducts newbies in the sense of providing them with information about Batam, but also through the more subtle process of initiating them into the cultural mores and language of the Singapore sex client community. More established members improve their reputation by providing the knowledge that allows newbies to leave Singapore on future visits with a keen sense of knowledge of the island's physical and sexual geography.

Homosocial desire is created in American 'rushes' in the process of being recruited into fraternities through 'a kind of addressee indirectness in which a desirable camaraderie was displayed among the members of the fraternity but excluded a rush' (Kiesling 2005: 695). In the same way, Batam Info Thread newbies are the targets of addressee indirectness, where the more established members engage in banter between themselves in a way which signals that while newbies have entered the fraternal (homosocial) space of the forum, they are not yet part of the fraternity proper. Individual members' standing within the fraternal space of the Batam Info Thread depends on their 'reputation'. This measure of one's cyberself is the product of a hierarchical system of 'points' and 'power'. As suggested earlier, a member's power rating correlates closely with his length of association with the site, while points are awarded by other members on the basis of their postings. Points are not granted freely or easily, as indicated by statements such as 'Newbies DON'T REQUEST ME' (dreammare (06.05.2007) 5:45 pm).

Distinctions are created between newbies and 'bros' through this hierarchically organized system of points and power. The former are permitted into the fraternal space of the forum, but only the latter are fully fledged members of the online fraternity. Progression to full membership of the fraternity requires a demonstration of knowledge not only of Batam but also of the culture of the thread. It also demands recognition of and respect for seniority, reflected in other forum members' reputations. Newbies are required to master a series of terms specific to Sammyboy (provided for them in a glossary) and to accept advice gratefully from more senior forum members. The different status of 'newbies' and 'bros' is reflected in the speech acts of both groups. For example, on 23 October 2007, Rub&Buah, a forum member with three years' experience, congratulated the even more established Ronsee on his detailed list of 'experiences and pointers' posted on the previous day:

> Well said bro.way to go.Newbies must print this as ur 'secret little book of dos & dun abt cewek [girls]' & bring it with u when wanna go cheong batam.
> Rub&Buah, 23.10.2007, 5:12 am

This short posting, ostensibly about supporting Ronsee's effort to provide information to newbies, establishes Rub&Buah's membership of the brotherhood through both his use of the term 'bro' and his identification of the newbies as other. As Ronsee has many more points than Rub&Buah, in addition to his eleven months' seniority, Rub&Buah may also be attempting to leverage the status of Ronsee's better reputation. Batam Man, whose power and points ratings do not reflect his status since he had to rejoin the forum after his old account failed, offers us another example. He claims membership of the brotherhood through demonstration of his knowledge of both Batam and the online space of the Batam Info Thread and his implicit positioning of himself as a fully fledged brother. These strategies are demonstrated in his posting of 27 February 2007 through his complaint about repetitiveness, his use of forum-specific terms such as 'cheonging' and 'FRs' (field reports), and his claims to have the authority to direct another 'old hand' to post a field report on a recent visit to Batam:

> It's good to see a Batam only related thread, without mixing up with the other 'wonderland' (islands) [Bintan and Karimun].
>
> But I really hope we don't get people asking questions like, where got nice n cheap CB [chee bye, lit. vagina], nice n cheap hotel, nice n cheap KTV ect ect. All those had already been answered MANY times in other Batam threads.
>
> I think all die hard Batam lau chiaos [old hands] will try their cheonging best to answer questions related to Batam to help the newbies, and also post their juicy FRs here?
>
> First to start with, – > MeatLover < –, your FR on last weekend cheonging session please . . .
>
>   BtmMan, 27.02.2007, 9:27 am

Newbies too signal their outsider status in regard to the brotherhood, conforming to the clearly stated expectations of the fraternity by displaying linguistic badges of newness and inferiority. For example, Bangbangman, who wrote in one of his very first postings:

> Hi guys . . . I'm a newbie here . . . Thinking of going this Thursday . . . Is it safe to go alone? Me small size scared kerna [get] robbed or raped leh . . .
>
>   Bangbangman, 04.06.2007, 10.30 am

These linguistic badges of newbie status can be worn in a number of different ways. However, not all newbies fully perform their outsider status. Postings suggest that newbie subversion may be ignored by the Batam Info Thread's more established brothers as a form of naïve enthusiasm, or may draw social sanction for the disruption of the thread's internal hierarchy. Sexual taunts are sometimes used to discipline newbies who have overstepped the mark. This is demonstrated in a series of postings in August 2007 that begin when taka77, a Batam Info Thread newbie, both chastises Batam Man for being impatient with newbies and claims friendship with a much more established cheongster:

> BM [Batam Man] u walking dictionary leh . . . dun get angry . . . 🐷 so when my gd fren [good friend] Ah-Pui going to visit u again? haha
> taka77, 24.08.2007, 9.28 pm

Taka77's lack of respect quickly draws a flurry of postings from the brothers, which start with a friendly rejection of his claim to friendship, followed by a questioning of his geographical knowledge of Batam, and concluding with insinuations that he lacked sexual know-how. Batam Man then enters the conversation, shifting the focus of the banter from geographical taunts to sexual ones, casting aspersions on the sexuality of both apui and taka77:

> Go Batam also must need people to bring?
>
> Then kio kway [get a prostitute, lit. calling or getting chickens] must need people to bonk on your behalf?
>
> Apui can do the job anot leh?
> BtmMan, 28.08.2007, 03.25 pm

> Ya need ppl to take off pants . . . hahahahaha
> taka77, 28.08.2007, 05.08 pm

> Take off your own pants?
>
> You so jia lak, tng koh also dunno meh?! [are you so stupid that you don't even know how to take off your pants?] 😨
> BtmMan, 28.08.2007, 05.17 pm

A friendly tone is maintained through the use of emoticons in this exchange.[14] It is clear that taka77's subversive interjection is not considered to be too serious. At the same time, however, his newbie status is underscored: unlike the homophobic sexual banter between brothers described below, these jibes are directed at taka77's heterosexual competence – a rare target in the Batam Info Thread.

Intimacy through conflict?

Batam Info Thread members, like their Western counterparts, use strategies of social indirectness in their online conversations to manage the homosocial 'double bind' (Kiesling 2005: 711). In the online space of the forum, social indirectness focuses almost exclusively on homophobic banter. This 'conflict' – which is initiated and managed by the forum's well-established 'old hands' – takes the form of gentle jibes rather than flaming or other techniques associated with online aggression.[15]

The lack of flaming reflects the way that the brotherhood actively engages in the protection of its members. Within the fraternal space of the Batam Info Thread, individual identity is subsumed by the communal, collective sense of self, and, extending from this, to flame would be to ostracize oneself from the fraternity. Individual social capital is only made possible through acceptance into the fraternity, a pursuit which is always in process rather than achieved. The example below demonstrates this process. It involves Meatlover, a long-standing member with a power rating of 6, Batam Man, whose low power rating belies his long involvement, and Apui, a member with a power rating of 4:

> NBzzzz [newbies], FR [field report] on last weekend you took your darling cewek for 2 nites wan [fun] lah . . . share share abit here leh . . . 🙂
>
> BtmMan, 27.02.2007, 3:59 pm

> I thought we were together for 2 nights? You mean you = my darling? 😳
>
> Meatlover, 27.02.2007, 04.10 pm

> FUCK YOU ok!!!

> Any GAY kakis [buddies] got any questions can ask ML [Meatlover] the GAY ong [king]. 😊
>
> BtmMan, 27.02.2007, 04.18 pm

> wah!! 😳

> u mean u book him for two nites arh!!
>
> Apui, 27.02.2007, 04.30 pm

Homophobic taunts and teasing serve to distinguish the homosocial intimacy that operates within the fraternity from other, more sexual, forms of desire. Unlike the response to taka77 described earlier, these jibes emphasize each of these three participants' heterosexual masculinity and establish their non-sexual homosocial desire and the 'tightness' of the inner circle.

Newbies are seldom permitted to engage directly in these kinds of exchanges, although in-jokes about long-standing members' sexuality are sometimes incorporated into responses to newbies' questions. This suggests a kind of reverse audience indirectness where the ratified 'over-hearer' is the inner circle of brothers rather than the newbie to whom the response is ostensibly addressed. For example when newbie Intellkk asks:

> Where to look for lady boy [transsexual] in batam?
>
> Intellkk, 22.08.2007, 08.27 pm

DNAT, the forum member with the highest reputation – a power rating of six and over 1,100 points – continues the in-joke about Batam Man's dubious sexuality:

Ask Batam Man.

DNAT, 23.08.2007, 08.49 am

Direct expression of homosocial intimacy is averted through the use of both homophobic joking and the creation of hierarchy. This hierarchy is effective in its regulation of the online community, as it simultaneously constrains and permits entrée of members into the inner core of the Batam Info Thread. That is, while the use of a hierarchical membership enables newbies to identify who the core members of the fraternity are, this place of strength at the centre remains an ever elusive one, as it is the members of the core alone who effectively monitor processes of exclusion and inclusion in the cyber-clique.

Conclusion

Research suggests that for many Western men, sexual performance, potency and experience principally function as a normative requirement for hegemonic masculinity. By distancing themselves from homosexual desire and from any display of homoeroticism, the members of the Batam Info Thread use their conversations about sex textually and discursively to construct a strictly heterosexual self. Current debates about the sexualities of fraternal settings suggest that the performance of (hetero)sexuality must be active and explicit (Flood 2008). Within the Batam Info Thread, too, markers of sexual experience in Batam are crucial to the construction of hierarchy.

However, findings from our research point to the need for greater attention to be paid to the specificities of the performance of normative discourses of heterosexual masculinity in different cultural contexts. The hegemonic masculinity of this cyber 'space' is constructed through conversations about sex that render the sex act almost invisible. This means that Batam Info Thread members must demonstrate their sexual capability and experience – and through it, their masculinity – without actually describing their own performance. The lack of candid sexual detail does not diminish the men's sense of manliness. Rather it works to strengthen and reproduce a sense of hegemonic masculinity through the performance of fraternal bonds. These differences highlight the specific ways in which sexuality and masculinity intersect in the Singaporean context to generate an online hegemonic masculinity that is premised on common experiences of sex tourism, yet marked by fraternity rather than sex itself.

We have demonstrated in this chapter that the study of fraternity provides an important means to examine how cultural discourses legitimize men's privilege and dominance; in other words, it provides a means to examine how hegemony is reinforced and re-created through social practices. Our analysis of the Sammyboy Times demonstrates that the Singaporean men who use this site construct its homosocial space in a particular way. Cyberspace offers these men a space in which to perform a particular kind of heterosexual masculinity in the (assumed) company of like-minded men, thus constituting a fraternal community in the online world.

However, fraternity is not established simply by joining or even participating in the thread. Within their online community, the men repeatedly engage in the process of 'becoming' a brother through the reproduction of the textual signifiers of the hegemonic masculinity preferred within the Batam Info Thread space. In this sense, the active engagement of gendered identity construction through CMC enables a production of gender fluidity. In some ways this construction of masculinity resists certain aspects of Singaporean normative discourses about the relationship between sexuality and masculinity, but it does not wholly transgress offline heteropatriarchal norms. Instead the possibilities of an online masculinity reaffirm spatially contingent notions of hegemonic masculinity, embedding themselves within both online and offline identities and practices.

Notes

1   The research on which this chapter is based was funded by an Australian Research Council (ARC) Discovery Project grant, In the Shadow of Singapore: The Limits of Transnationalism in Insular Riau (DP0557368). Sophie Williams would also like to acknowledge fieldwork funding support provided by CAPSTRANS and the Faculty of Arts at the University of Wollongong.
2   The sex industry in the Riau Islands relies heavily on its Singaporean clients, over a million of whom visited in 2003 (BPS Kota Batam 2004). Singaporean sex clients are typically identified as 'old men' (*apek-apek*) and 'uncles' (Williams 2007; Ford and Lyons 2008). However, observation conducted within sex tourism venues (particularly discos and KTV lounges) in Batam supports the results of a survey conducted by the Singaporean NGO Action for AIDS, which showed that 35 per cent of sex clients interviewed at the ferry terminal to Batam were under the age of 40 (Action for AIDS Singapore 2006).
3   There is a growing literature on research methodology involving the web. See for example Danet 1996, 1998; King 1996; Kendall 1999; Sharf 1999; Anderson and Kanuka 2003; Hewson *et al.* 2003; Guimaraes 2005; Hine 2005. For a discussion of the difficulties of conducting academic research on sensitive Internet-based topics, see Lyons *et al.* 2010.
4   For discussions of sex and sex tourism on the web, see, for example, Mills 1998; Toomey and Rothenberg 2000; Griffiths 2001; Daneback *et al.* 2005; Chow-White 2006.
5   Quotation taken from the top banner of The Sammyboy Times, Singapore Asian Values Forum pages.
6   The Sammyboy Times is available at www.sammyboy.com. The postings used in this article are all taken from the publicly accessible pages of the January to October 2007 postings on the Batam Info Thread. Although a number of online forums have been created to meet the needs of sex tourists, The Sammyboy Times is the only site that currently identifies itself as a Singaporean site catering to the interests of Singaporean men. It therefore provides an important space to examine the performance of online 'Singaporean' sex tourist masculinities.
7   The Singapore government has sought to regulate Internet content through a range of measures, including censorship of websites and the introduction of rules pertaining to the publication of pornographic and violent material. Lee (2001, 2003) suggests that auto-regulation of Internet use is the most active and effective form of censorship operative in Singapore at present.

8 The FAQs on the site state that, although welcome elsewhere on the site, 'Non sexual topics are NOT to be discussed at Sam's sex forum'.

9 The term 'hub' has become a buzzword in Singapore in recent years. It is used to designate spatial areas within the city that the government seeks to develop for particular purposes – education hub, arts hub, science hub. Sammyboy's status as 'Singapore Virtual Sex Hub' is a tongue-in-cheek reference to these developments.

10 Singapore-English – a local creole.

11 Sammyboy Frequently Asked Questions (FAQ).

12 National Service of two years is compulsory for all male citizens and permanent residents of Singapore, and men continue to be called up for active reservist training until the age of 40 or 50 depending on rank. See Chapter 8 in this volume.

13 The postings contained within the Batam Info Thread vary in length from short questions (one to two sentences in length) to detailed field reports that last for several pages.

14 Waskul and Douglass (1997: 384) note that emoticons provide a 'mechanism for communicating contextual and emotional cues to others and hence validate them as experientially real in a social context'.

15 Danet (2002) defines flaming as 'sudden, often extended flare-ups of anger, profanity and insult'.

References

Action for AIDS Singapore (2006) *Profile of Singapore Male Travelers to the Riau-islands: Demographic, Travel Behavior & Safer Sex Practices*, Singapore: Action for AIDS Singapore.

Anderson, T. and Kanuka, H. (2003) *e-Research: Methods, Strategies and Issues*, Boston: Pearson Education.

Balsamo, A. (1996) *Technologies of the Gendered Body: Reading Cyborg Women*, Durham, NC and London: Duke University Press.

Bird, S. R. (1996) 'Welcome to the men's club: homosociality and the maintenance of hegemonic masculinity', *The Journal of Sex Research* 37(2): 161–8.

Boswell, A. and Spade, J. Z. (1996) 'Fraternities and collegiate rape culture: why are some fraternities more dangerous places for women?' *Gender & Society* 10: 133–47.

BPS Kota Batam (2004) *Batam Dalam Angka 2003 (Batam in Figures)*, Batam: Badan Perencanaan Penelitian dan Pengembangan Kota Batam.

Brewis, J. and Linstead, S. (2000) *Sex, Work and Sex Work: Eroticizing Organization*, London: Routledge.

Campbell, H. (2000) 'The glass phallus: pub(lic) masculinity and drinking in rural New Zealand', *Rural Sociology* 65(4): 562–81.

Chow-White, A. (2006) 'Race, gender and sex on the net: semantic networks of selling and storytelling sex tourism', *Media, Culture & Society* 28(6): 883–905.

Connell, R. W. (1995) *Masculinities*, Berkeley: University of California Press.

Connell, R. W. and Dowsett, G. W. (eds) (1992) *Rethinking Sex: Social Theory and Sexuality Research*, Melbourne: Melbourne University Press.

D'Amico, F. and Weinstein, L. (eds) (1999) *Gender Camouflage: Women and the U.S. Military*, New York: New York University Press.

Daneback, K., Cooper, A. and Mansson, S. (2005) 'An internet study of cybersex participants', *Archives of Sexual Behavior* 34(3): 321–8.

Danet, B. (1996) 'Text as mask: gender and identity on the Internet', paper presented at 'Masquerade and Gender Identity', Venice, Italy, 21–24 February.

—— (1998) 'Text as mask: gender, play, and performance on the Internet', in S. G. Jones (ed.), *Cybersociety 2.0: Revisiting Computer-Mediated Communication and Community*, Thousand Oaks, CA: Sage Publications, pp. 129–58.

—— (2002) 'Flaming', in P. Bouissac (ed.), *Garland Encyclopedia of Semiotics*, New York: Garland, pp. 1–4.

Enloe, C. (2000) *Maneuvers: The International Politics of Militarizing Women's Lives*, Berkeley: University of California Press.

Flood, M. (2008) 'Men, sex, and homosociality: how bonds between men shape their sexual relations with women', *Men and Masculinities* 10(3): 339–59.

Ford, M. and Lyons, L. (2008) 'Making the best of what you've got: sex work and class mobility in the Riau Islands', in M. Ford and L. Parker (eds), *Women and Work in Indonesia*, London: Routledge, pp. 173–94.

Frank, K. (2003) '"Just trying to relax": masculinity, masculinizing practices, and strip club regulars', *Journal of Sex Research* 40(1): 61–75.

Griffiths, M. (2001) 'Sex on the internet: observations and implications for internet sex addiction', *Journal of Sex Research* 38(4): 333–42.

Guimaraes, M. J. L. (2005) 'Doing anthropology in cyberspace: fieldwork boundaries and social environments', in C. Hine (ed.), *Virtual Methods: Issues in Social Research on the Internet*, Oxford and New York: Berg, pp. 141–56.

Hewson, C., Yule, P., Laurent, D. and Vogel, C. (2003) *Internet Research Methods: A Practical Guide for the Social and Behavioural Sciences*, London: Sage.

Hine, C. (ed.) (2005) *Virtual Methods: Issues in Social Research on the Internet*, Oxford: Berg.

Ho, K. C., Baber, Z. and Khondker, H. (2002) '"Sites" of resistance: alternative websites and state-society relations', *British Journal of Sociology* 53(1): 127–48.

Kendall, L. (1999) 'Recontextualizing "cyberspace": methodological considerations for on-line research', in S. G. Jones (ed.), *Doing Internet Research: Critical Issues and Methods for Examining the Net*, Thousand Oaks, CA: Sage Publications, pp. 57–74.

Kiesling, S. F. (2005) 'Homosocial desire in men's talk: balancing and re-creating cultural discourses of masculinity', *Language in Society* 34(5): 695–726.

King, S. A. (1996) 'Researching internet communities: proposed ethical guidelines for the reporting of results', *The Information Society* 12: 119–27.

Kruhse-Mountburton, S. (1995) 'Sex tourism and traditional Australian male identity', in M.-F. Lanfant, J. B. Allcock and E. M. Bruner (eds), *International Tourism: Identity and Change*, London: Sage Publications, pp. 192–204.

Law, L. (2000) *Sex Work in Southeast Asia: The Place of Desire in a Time of AIDS*, London: Routledge.

Lee, T. (2001) 'Auto-regulating new media: strategies from Singapore's internet policy', *Australian Journal of Communication* 28(1): 43–56.

—— (2003) 'Internet use in Singapore: politics and policy implications', *Media International Australia Incorporating Culture and Policy* 107: 75–88.

Louie, K. (2003) 'Chinese, Japanese and global masculine identities', in K. Louie and M. Low (eds), *Asian Masculinities: The Meaning and Practice of Manhood in China and Japan*, London: Routledge, pp. 1–16.

Lyons, L. and Ford, M. (2008) 'Love, sex and the spaces in-between: Kepri wives and their cross-border husbands', *Citizenship Studies* 12(1): 55–72.

Lyons, L., Ford, M. and Williams, S. (2010) 'Legal issues associated with the study of sexual content on the internet in Australia', *Australian Feminist Law Journal* 33: 143–59.

McKeganey, N. P. and Barnard, M. (1996) *Sex Work on the Streets: Prostitutes and their Clients*, Buckingham: Open University Press.

Mills, R. (1998) 'Cyber: sexual chat on the internet', *Journal of Popular Culture* 32(3): 31–46.

O'Connell Davidson, J. (1995) 'British sex tourists in Thailand', in M. Maynard and J. Purvis (eds), *(Hetero)sexual Politics*, London: Taylor & Francis, pp. 42–64.

Perkins, R. (1994) 'Female prostitution', in R. Perkins, G. Prestage, R. Sharp and F. Lovejoy (eds), *Sex Work and Sex Workers in Australia*, Sydney: UNSW Press, pp. 143–73.

Ramazanoglu, C. (1995) 'Back to basics: heterosexuality, biology and why men stay on top', in M Maynard and J. Purvis (eds), *(Hetero)sexual Politics*, London: Taylor & Francis, pp. 27–41.

Ross, M. W. (2005) 'Typing, doing, and being: sexuality and the internet', *Journal of Sex Research* 42(4): 342–52.

Sanders, T. (2005a) 'Researching the online sex work community', in C. Hine (ed.), *Virtual Methods: Issues in Social Research on the Internet*, Oxford: Berg, pp. 67–79.

—— (2005b) *Sex Work: A Risky Business*, Cullompton: Willan Publishing.

Sharf, B. F. (1999) 'Beyond netiquette: the ethics of doing naturalistic discourse research on the internet', in S. Jones (ed.), *Doing Internet Research: Critical Issues and Methods for Examining the Net*, Thousand Oaks, CA: Sage, pp. 243–56.

Slater, D. (2002) 'Making things real: ethics and order on the internet', *Theory, Culture & Society* 19(5/6): 227–45.

Toomey, K. E. and Rothenberg, R. B. (2000) 'Sex and cyberspace: virtual networks leading to high-risk sex', *Journal of the American Medical Association* 284(4): 485–7.

Turkle, S. (1995) *Life on the Screen: Identity in the Age of the Internet*, New York: Simon & Schuster.

Waskul, D. and Douglass, M. (1997) 'Cyberself: the emergence of self in on-line chat', *The Information Society* 13: 375–97.

Williams, S. (2006) 'Sex tourism and virtual communities: Chinese-Singaporean men and online sexual spaces', paper presented at 'Media: Policies, Cultures and Futures in the Asia Pacific Region', Curtin University of Technology, Perth, 27–29 November.

—— (2007) 'Sex, seafood and singing: sex tourism and Singaporean Chinese men in Batam', paper presented at 'Cultural and Social Research Seminar', Department of Geography, National University of Singapore, 31 October.

5 Being *broh*

The good, the bad and the successful man in Cambodia

Trude Jacobsen

> Like Rith, most of the friends in his social group are also military men. They go for sex once a week or once every two weeks; however, when he was single, he used to go for sex every single night. When Rith wants to go for a night of drinking and sex, he sometimes has to strategize to make sure his friend can come with him . . . 'Now that we are drunk, we should go find a girl to release our feeling.' Most of Rith's friends always agree to go.
>
> (PSI 2008: 9)

This excerpt, taken from a report on public health in Cambodia, is a standard representation of a typical *neak broh* or 'man' in Cambodia. According to most non-governmental organizations and the local media, men's purported lack of self-control, patronage of the sex sector and commitment to their (male) friends are responsible for myriad social issues, including child rape, sex trafficking, domestic violence, corruption and HIV/AIDS. This view, which reflects the view of men prevalent in the wider Cambodian society, is a far cry from the erstwhile ideal of Cambodian manhood extolled in traditional literature, in which men are portrayed as compassionate, hard-working and, above all, accepting of their lot in life. That men buy sex, rape young girls and set fire to their wives is well known; the reasoning behind these acts is rarely considered by ordinary Cambodians.

There has been very little research into notions of Cambodian manliness and how these impact upon or reflect male behavioural trends. In fact, organizational reports such as the one cited above are the sole genre of published work that even mentions masculinity, and then not as a category for analysis but as an explanation for behaviour. This has not been viewed as a serious omission by scholars who work on social issues in Cambodia. The corpus of work on gender issues, particularly on sex work and domestic violence, has largely focused upon women, as victims and survivors; the (male) perpetrators and facilitators have tended to remain shadowy figures, referred to as a generic collective 'men'. However, like women, Cambodian men are beset with conflicting messages as to what they are, how they should act and to what they should aspire.

This confusion has led to a crisis of identity as Cambodian society moves from a collectivist culture to one that is individualist, particularly for poorer men from rural areas who migrate to the cities in search of work. Exposure to ways of living that privilege the individual and their needs, rather than those of the family or group, place additional pressures upon seasonal migrants as they attempt to negotiate identities in an unfamiliar urban environment. As has occurred elsewhere, concepts of masculinity are affected by notions of class in Cambodia (Fenstermaker and West 2002), and any negative behaviour that arises as a result of the performance of maleness is legitimized (Doyle 2002).

This chapter begins by comparing 'traditional' paradigms of Cambodian masculinity with those now dominant in Cambodia. The inspiration for this analysis came from a comment made to me in 2003 when I was interviewing Cambodian sex workers on their attitudes towards their customers. Walking along the riverside in Phnom Penh, a group of sex workers were making ribald remarks about men when the eldest of the women observed, 'When you see them come in, you know right away if they are going to be a good or bad man. And sometimes if I am lucky they can be a successful man.' At the time, I was intrigued by the notion that 'good' men could patronize brothels and that a 'successful' man was not necessarily one who was good, but it was not until 2006 that I turned my attention to investigating these categories.

Over the next two years, I conducted interviews with fifty-two men and thirty-four women in Phnom Penh in which I asked people to describe different types of men. Informants commonly responded to my question by observing that there were 'good and bad men'. They then proceeded to explain first what an ideal (good) man was like and then elaborated on other types of men, all of which conformed to variations of the categories 'good' and 'bad'.[1] I then introduced the notion of the 'successful' man in order to determine whether success was synonymous with, say, Buddhist piety, wealth or some other criterion. Where possible, I referenced pre-colonial models of behaviour in order to ascertain the relevance of these to the informants.

Historical and contemporary ideals

Historical perspectives are crucial for understanding more recent notions of masculinity (Connell 2005; Gilmore 1990). Models sourced from pre-colonial, elite-authored literature continue to be the yardstick against which Cambodian men and women are measured (see Jacobsen 2008; Ledgerwood 1990, 1996), yet there is also an expectation that people be *samay* (modern) if they wish to demonstrate elite status or indicate prowess to their peers. Characteristics of being *samay* include familiarity with technology, particularly mobile phones and the Internet; wearing Western-inspired fashions; and speaking English. That *samay* behaviour is often at odds with traditional models is not commented upon, or when it is, it is assumed to be acceptable for elite Cambodians (high-ranking members of the government and armed forces and their families, members of the royal family, and the very rich), who are largely able to behave with impunity in any circumstance.

The Cambodian past is replete with models of courageous kings. One has only to look at the temple complexes of Angkor to see a dizzying array of images commissioned between the ninth and fourteenth centuries, their purpose to make plain the connection between these men and a particular Brahmanical god, for example Vishnu at the temple of Angkor Wat. The inscriptions that accompany these images emphasize the heroism of kings in battle:

> There was a king with lotus eyes, who became, because of his heroism, king above all other kings, who with no other support from his own people aside from himself, inflamed by the goddess Lakshmi, from the point of failure, brought about the ruin of his enemies.
>
> (Cœdès 1937–66: K.854 verse 2)

Rulers were charismatic. One of the key characteristics of a king was that he was endowed with the gift of eloquence, usually described as having the goddess Sarasvati 'dwelling in his mouth' (Cœdès 1937–66: K.661 verse 13). An essential component of kingship was fealty, both amongst his own courtiers and from those at the periphery of his territory. This was usually demonstrated by the sending of daughters and sisters to serve the king by living in the palace. Thus, sanctioned by the people they ruled, courts would maintain large numbers of women of diverse backgrounds. Not all of these women were expected to perform sexual services;[2] yet their presence certainly enhanced the meritorious prestige (*baramei*) of the king they served. For example, it was said of Suryavarman I that he 'bore on his body the marks of amorous games with his women' and that he was so handsome that women could not 'conduct themselves in a virtuous manner when he gave them a glance' (Cœdès 1937–66: K.218 verse 10). The ability of a king to provide for and control large numbers of women – ostensibly through satisfying their material and sexual desires – was thus an inherent aspect of Cambodian elite masculinity in the past.[3]

It is hardly surprising, therefore, to find the first hero of Cambodian literature, Ream, was not only an incarnation of the god Vishnu but also a brave warrior:

> A hero, he had the mark of *cakra* on his hands; he possessed an arrow which could fly back after hitting the target. A warrior, he was only equalled by Arjuna and Indra. In this respect, he became logically a model for Angkorian kings.
>
> (Pou 2005: 126)

The earliest extant text of the Cambodian *Ramayana*, known as the *Reamkr*, dates to the sixteenth century, although according to epigraphic evidence the tale was certainly known to Cambodians as early as the tenth century. We can deduce from this that for at least six centuries the ideal of Cambodian manhood was heroic, virile and eloquent. A further requirement was that a king be physically perfect; no deformity was permitted. For this reason, princes often blinded or amputated the limbs of their brothers in order to prevent them from usurping the throne (Zhou Daguan 1992: 72).

Clearly, these models were strictly for elite men. No lowly rice farmer could ever aspire to model himself upon Vishnu or Ream; his duty (*dharma*) lay in the paddies, not the battlefields. He may have been called upon to provide corvée labour in order to build monuments glorifying the manliness of his king, but he was very much aware of his place in society and could never aspire to more lofty ambitions. His life revolved around the seasonal planting and harvesting of rice, the festivals that punctuated the year and the everyday concerns of marriage, birth and death.

The advent of Theravada Buddhism as the religion of the elite sometime after the move away from Angkor in the fourteenth century further bolstered the acceptance of one's lot rather than social mobility. The *cbpab*, didactic codes authored by learned (and therefore elite) men, explained very clearly that one should be philosophical about the life to which one had been born, and not attempt to change the course of destiny (Ebihara 1984). These codes also spelled out, in no uncertain terms, the behaviour required of their respective audiences. Thus the *Cbpab Srei,* the 'Code of Conduct for Women', exhorted women to obey their husbands, not to draw attention to themselves, and to maintain the respectability of the family at all costs (Minh Mai 2001).[4] Domestic violence is legitimized in Minh Mai's *Cbpab Srei*, which text tells women that they should accept any behaviour from their husbands:

> If your husband speaks harshly to you, if in anger reproaches you and
> wounds you,
> If his anger gets worse and inflames him without respite nor wavering
> because his heart is full of irritation,
> If he goes on without ceasing with insults and reproaches, because of his
> rancour,
> my daughter dear, you must be patient and wait for it to pass.
> . . .
> Do not protest or respond sarcastically to excite his anger,
> Do not persist, do not look at him with stony eyes, do not provoke a quarrel
> with your lack of respect.
> Do not address him in a way that will prolong the argument and cause
> discord.
> Do not be like dogs and cats, holding forth with things that wound the heart
> of your husband,
> Do not upset things you touch, knocking them over, and breaking them.
> . . .
> If your husband upsets you, my daughter, go away to your room and reflect.
> When you come out, speak to him with soft words to smooth over the rift.
> If your husband gives you advice, keep it, my daughter, and guard it in your
> spirit.

(Minh Mai 2001: verses 66–77)

Women are thus warned against fighting back or telling anyone that they are abused, as admitting that their behaviour has led to their husband having to 'correct' them will bring shame upon the family. At the same time, however, the Code of Conduct for Men (*Cbpab Broh*), which was written around the same time as one version of the *Cbpab Srei*, clearly stated that men should act towards their inferiors with kindness and compassion. In fact, seventy-eight of the eighty-six descriptions of a 'good' man included some reference to being gentle or non-violent, or 'respecting wife's rights'.

This text, authored by Minh Mai at the turn of the nineteenth century, also engaged explicitly with questions of sexuality, warning against women, intoxication and 'silly games' (cited in Jennar and Pou 1976: 328). After enumerating the dangers of gambling with Chinese merchants, the courtier provided a lengthy and salacious description of the pitfalls of sexual congress with women. 'Do not throw yourselves into sensual pleasure as it will always enslave you . . . it always brings sadness', Minh Mai warned (cited in Jennar and Pou 1976: 323). Yet this clearly contradicted one of the main tenets of manliness, at least for would-be kings. How could they avoid women, when (sexual) access to large numbers of them was a requirement of the prestige necessary to be considered a king amongst men?

The answer lies in the fact that the Cambodian elite have never held themselves to the same yardstick as the common people. The educated may have penned the guidelines to which the masses were expected to conform but their own behaviour would never be held up to scrutiny. This division between elite and non-elite, in terms of societal norms, has continued to the modern day, where it is especially apparent with regard to the expectations placed upon men.

The 'good' man

Past traditions – or practices that are believed to reflect a Cambodia free from external cultural interference – have immense relevance in modern Cambodian society. This is understandable. On no fewer than three occasions in the twentieth century, Cambodian culture underwent severe modification: French colonialism (until 1954); the Khmer Rouge regime (1975–79), which sought to return Cambodia to an exclusively agrarian, completely conformist socialist state; and the People's Republic of Kampuchea (1979–90), during which time Vietnam superintended the reconstruction of Cambodia and insisted upon a high degree of Vietnamization of the culture and people in return. Once again free of outside cultural influence, since the 1993 elections Cambodians have clung tenaciously to the models and ideals that have been resurrected in a search for a culturally 'pure' Cambodia. A lack of willingness to disengage from models of behaviour that are believed to represent a true Cambodian society is logical given the context but cannot reasonably be achieved given the competing forces of globalization that are present in Cambodia today.

When asked to describe a 'good' man (*broh l'or*), informants ranked morality (*sel*) high on the list of desirable attributes. Ratana, a first-year university student, said that a good man 'always practises or observes the five precepts' and 'has *sel*'. According to his sister Malis, only monks could be good men as they were the only ones who had *sel*: 'He can only be a monk, a *chao adthika* [chief monk], who practises *dhamm*, and so gives all society advantage.' This statement is significant in that it expresses the underlying belief common to most Cambodians: the individual is not the smallest social unit. The family or the group – in this case, society as a whole – is seen as the beneficiary in all social transactions, be they positive or negative. An individual's *sel* benefits the larger community. Similarly, actions that detract from a community's reputation will affect everyone, not simply the individual performing them. Thi, a seamstress, observed that only monks were good men, as other men were not sincere in practising *dhamm*: 'Men rarely exert themselves to make offerings like women during ceremonies, because from observation men go to join ceremonies for drinking alcohol or dancing only.'

Although not as rigorous as the obligations placed upon women in Cambodia, there are clear expectations placed upon men. To some extent, Gilmore's (1990: 223) 'ubiquitous male' standard holds true in Cambodian society, wherein all men have basic tasks that they are expected to perform. Cambodian men are expected to father children, protect their immediate families, and ensure the wellbeing of the extended family and others within their *khsae* network, a kind of 'prestige structure' (Keyes 1986: 67). As businessman Sokha observed, a man 'should work hard to earn money to support his family'. And meeting these obligations – particularly those of *khsae* relationships – requires wealth. Men cannot marry until they can afford to support a wife and family, even where it is expected that women will work before and after marriage. The onus is also upon the groom's family to give gifts to the bride and her family in the meetings leading up to the wedding in order to demonstrate their good faith and their ability to meet the material needs of the prospective couple in their life together.

Compassion and empathy, particularly towards wives and children, were also important characteristics of a 'good' man. Vanna, a 24-year-old housekeeper, reflected several informants' views in her observations on what makes a good man:

> He often helps people who have suffered misfortune. He is happy and likes to speak in a friendly manner. He is handsome, tall and sweetly spoken. He is a man who understands the mind of his wife all the time, he is a counsellor, is a good father, is a good householder, a person many people need.

'Teacher' was the most commonly designated profession in describing a 'good' man. Others mentioned civil servants.[5] This is because government workers are in a position to assist other family members, and clients within the *khsae* system by enabling them to acquire jobs themselves or smoothing the way in the event of bureaucratic hurdles. Education therefore was an important factor for most people. For example Rith, a 26-year-old construction worker, said that a good man 'has a good job because he has a good education' and can help family and neighbours as a result of his own good position. Protection from unscrupulous civil servants and police, as well as from thieves and assailants, has to be purchased in the form of protection money to local gangs or syndicates in urban areas and physical security in the form of fences, gates and secure outbuildings in rural locales. In addition, clients in the *khsae* network must pass on a portion of their produce or business takings to their patrons, who will in turn use their influence in judicial matters or preferment for clients' family members when tenders for construction contracts are being allocated.

As I have discussed elsewhere (Jacobsen 2008), in the Cambodian past it was the norm for men and women to have different yet complementary roles that tended to be valued equally. Since the colonial era this has been replaced with the view that domestic work is women's work and is less important than the work that takes place outside the home (Aing 2004). This has resulted in reluctance on the part of men to perform tasks that are associated more with women than men. On the other hand, globalization has meant that Cambodians are exposed to the feminist discourse on this issue in the West, usually through the medium of television. Many women I spoke to emphasized that good men 'understood' their wives and that as a result would voluntarily assist with household duties 'which are not only women's work but men should do it too'. Teav, a garment factory worker, said that a good man would 'look after his wife during her delivery period by doing housework', whereas others felt that he would 'do things in the house all the time' and 'cook, clean, get children ready for school if she is busy'. Although many male respondents were not as specific as to what good men should be doing in the domestic sphere, the theme of 'understanding' one's wife was again prominent.

This attitude was apparent in research conducted amongst male blue-collar workers for this project. I organized a focus group comprising construction workers and *motodup* (motorcycle taxi drivers) aged between 17 and 32. In response to the question 'How does a good man act at home?', answers indicated that understanding and non-violence were the key attributes required to be described as 'good' in this sphere. Some answers included: he 'understands his wife's heart, knows his wife's difficulties'; 'understands his wife's mind, loves wife and doesn't use violence'; 'understands others, is helpful to others and younger siblings without making difficulties for parents'; 'is a good husband and can find good means to educate children without using violence in the family'; and 'understands his wife's mind and children, and doesn't use violence to solve problem'.

The emphasis upon refraining from violence at home is due in part to the campaigning on the part of non-governmental organizations, which has made domestic violence prevention a priority. Yet it is here that we run into one of the key dichotomies at work in Cambodian society. Although everyone knows that domestic violence is 'wrong', husbands are nevertheless still expected to 'correct' their wives' mistakes or behaviour. Lim, a bank teller, said that a good man should 'not cause quarrels in the family, but advise his wife to give up negative acts and attitude; he should correct the wife's mistakes'. In practice, correction often takes the form of violence in order to punish wives or prevent them from committing acts their husbands perceive as being wrong. In 2006 alone, the Cambodian Women's Crisis Centre received 1,238 female clients seeking assistance for domestic violence, some 74 per cent of their total client base country-wide (Cambodian Women's Crisis Centre 2007: 8).[6]

According to Chantha, a 19-year-old corn vendor, one of the ways that people could distinguish a 'good' man is that he 'doesn't lie or cheat . . . [and] does only good and legal jobs. He is not corrupt.' She added that this was the reason that there were not many 'good' men in Cambodia. Piseth, a civil servant, was even more pessimistic, musing that perhaps 'all good men have died in Khmer society'. As most people cannot eke out a living from their salaries,[7] it is common to supplement one's official income through second jobs or, more often, through practices that many would perceive as corrupt. Drivers' licences, for example, can be purchased from the municipality without a test of any kind. Some universities in Phnom Penh will sell degrees to students who have never entered a classroom. A 'gift' to a teacher at Khmer New Year, when it is common to send baskets of sweets, biscuits and fruit to family and friends, will ensure that a child passes examinations. This integrates yet more people into the complex *khsae* network described above. Men are overwhelmingly perceived to be more likely than women to ask for bribes (Center for Social Development 2005: 39).

One of the questions about a 'good' man that I found most interesting was whether, as in earlier times, an outwardly 'perfect' body reflected moral superiority. Those I spoke to were divided as to whether a good man could be distinguished by outward appearance. Approximately a third of the people I spoke to believed that 'appearance cannot tell you', 'his appearance is just like other people' or 'appearance is not important'. The remaining two-thirds, however, had very definite ideas as to what a good man looked like.[8] The phrase 'proper appearance' (*rup somrum* or *rup dtrou*) came up several times; when questioned, respondents answered that a good man would be tall, neither too fat nor too short, have both his feet, not be disabled and be neither too handsome nor too ugly. As this suggests, extremes and deformities were not something people associated with 'good' men, as accidents or the misfortune of having been born less than perfect would not have befallen them if they really *were* good men.

On the other hand, people were adamant that a 'modern' appearance – *rup samay* – was not something that a 'good' man would seek to acquire. Rather, he would be simple and modest, and dress according to custom. The reasoning behind this belief was that 'good' men were too busy being 'good' – thinking of others, concentrating upon their work and families, and so on – to have time to read fashion magazines, stalk the most fashionable shops for new shipments from Thailand and Malaysia and 'spend all that time to put gel in his hair'. In short, a 'good' man would not be inclined to think too much about his own appearance. Moreover, being *samay* necessarily departs from tried-and-true Cambodian 'tradition' in which 'good' men wear the monks' robes, simple farmers would wear *sampot*, and merchants an approximation of Chinese or Thai peasants' trousers. In this way, everyone would be immediately recognizable and social status easily attributed. Not employing one's sartorial grade – in the case of Cambodian teenagers today, wearing a basic uniform of t-shirts and jeans – confuses the social register.

The 'successful' man

Ultimately, most male informants said that they would rather be 'successful' than 'good', as this was more likely to lead to security for themselves and their families. Cambodian society is divided very clearly into those that have and those that have not, and power relies upon the redistribution of wealth from patrons to clients and the reciprocal acknowledgement of the patron's superior social position. At one end of the spectrum is the mid- to senior-level army or police officer, who can rely upon his salary and the perquisites of being in a position to siphon off 'extras' from state funds to private enterprise; at the other is the *motodup*, a driver-for-hire of a 100-cc motorbike which people in urban Cambodia use in lieu of public transport. *Motodup*s are usually agricultural workers who migrate to the cities following the rice harvest, when their labour is not required in the countryside, and return with extra income. They usually cannot afford to rent accommodation, sleeping in groups on or around their motorcycles at night and eating at street stalls. Yet while separated by economic means, either of these men can be described as a good or bad man. However, only the army officer is considered 'successful', as only he has the power to change people's lives for better or worse.

In contrast with a good man, a 'successful' man (*broh mean joak jey*) is physically distinguishable from other men, being both 'handsome' and 'modern' (*samay*).[9] Samnang, a 21-year-old tailor, thought that a successful man would be dressed 'formally, in a suit or smart trousers and fashionable shirt', while Ly Ly, a seamstress, believed that if she met a successful man, she would know because 'his face is attractive, fresh . . . a handsome appearance that leads him to be successful'. Similarly, Someth, a 43-year-old corn vendor, said that a successful man must have a good physique, while her daughter Chantha described such a man as having 'a pleasing face, attractive, very manly'. When queried further as to what 'very manly' meant, she replied that he would be tall, toned, not overweight, and 'have three mobile phones with different networks'. Anyone who wishes to be thought important carries at least two mobile phones, one for personal use and one solely for business; at very high-level business or political meetings, it is not unusual for a small side table to be placed adjacent to each participant to accommodate the plethora of mobile phones produced from their pockets.

The successful man does not necessarily have to be well educated, although, as a marketing assistant called Lina observed, he would be 'interested in learning new things in society'. In fact, over half of the people I spoke to said that education was not important for success, pointing out, for example, that wealthy merchants do not have a high level of knowledge. In their responses, they emphasized instead the successful man's ability to overcome obstacles. Sopheara, 25, employed in the sales and marketing office of a plastics import company, gave the following example: 'He was born in a poor family, with no money for studying or physical appearance, but he is working at all kinds of jobs, even as a *motodup*, to make enough to finish his BA degree.' Struggling and overcoming adversity are not characteristics of a 'good' man, perhaps because the 'good' man, with his Buddhist morality, would accept his lot in life more readily and fighting against fate contradicts accepting one's *dharma* or duty in life. By contrast, problem-solving and planning were commonly described as traits of the successful man, even by some within the religious community. For example, Sokha, a 26-year-old monk at Wat Lanka, said that he is successful because he is a problem-solver. For him, 'Effort, struggle, patience, and never being sick can identify a successful man.' Other highly educated participants shared the same sentiments. Twenty-year-old Huor and his university friends believe that in order to be successful, 'A man has a specific plan, correct decision-making, and strives.'

Those at the other end of the social spectrum, those working in construction and other low-skilled, low-paid sectors, thought that a successful man had *bunn sak* (high status or social respect), commenting that such a man would have a high-status job and lots of money, or some variation thereof. It is thus success – not virtue or piety – that leads to *omnaich* (power or influence) in Cambodian society. King Sihamoni (r. 2004 to the present), for example, is not ridiculed for being gay; he is seen as 'less manly' because he has not married and produced an heir, thus failing one of the basic requirements of Cambodian manhood.[10] However, because of his *bunn sak*, which contributes to his *omnaich*, he is protected from public ridicule or lack of acceptance as king. Significant too here is the fact that the current Prime Minister of Cambodia, Hun Sen, popularly believed to have hardly any *sel* or morality at all and thus the antithesis of a 'good' man, was universally described as the person with the most *omnaich* in Cambodia (Jacobsen and Stuart-Fox n.d.).[11]

Sex and the successful man

If the 'good' man is family-focused and limits his entertainment to wholesome pursuits, the 'successful' man is bound by no such constraint. In fact, he is expected to assert his masculinity in the time-honoured tradition, described by ex-King-Father Norodom Sihanouk as 'le chaud lapin' (lit. 'the hot rabbit'; a better English approximation might be 'the randy rabbit'). The Cambodian media reaffirms historical and 'traditional' notions of masculinity in that men who are 'successful' are depicted as being surrounded by large numbers of women to whom sexual access is implied. The implication is not only that the 'successful' man can afford to maintain or have access to large numbers of women, but also that his own desire for them is insatiable. This consolidates his identity as a virile man with plentiful economic resources whom women find attractive.

Notions of hospitality and recreation for Cambodian men inevitably include sexual encounters. In the Cambodian past, elite men at leisure – for example, whilst taking a pleasure-cruise along a river in the eighteenth century – would expect to be waited upon by attractive women of their household, or their host's household. Entertainment would consist of performances by women of the household who would play music, sing and/or dance. Only the very elite could expect to maintain households of women; yet even a relatively prosperous rice-farmer could expect to have a few female members of his extended family, or female slaves, whom he could present to male visitors for the duration of their stay in his house. In later eras, as Andaya (1998) has pointed out, this practice evolved into the commodification of such women purely for sexual encounters.

The locations associated with relaxation in Cambodia today are equally sexualized. Brothel-based sex workers and 'taxi girls' (who meet clients in bars and nightclubs) are not the only women assumed to be involved in sex work. Simply by 'choosing' to work in the hospitality sector, 'beer girls' (employed by beverage companies at restaurants to ply their product to customers), waitresses at restaurants and nightclubs, hostesses at karaoke venues and masseuses are also seen to be available (and eager) for paid sex. 'Good' men were most often described as *not* participating in this behaviour, but rather as being faithful and having only one wife. However, most informants considered it to be acceptable for Cambodian men to visit sex workers, arguing that even 'good' men may have sex outside of marriage.[12] As a male law student observed, a 'good' man would 'not have sexual relationships with girls outside marriage except with a taxi girl sometimes'.

Statements such as this reflect a belief that men have inherent biological inclinations that lead them to seek sexual fulfilment with a wide range of women. Thus, by far the most common response to 'what do men to do to relax?' was '*dtou da leng*'. Although this literally means 'go for a walk', *dtou da leng* is a euphemism for going out looking for a 'hook up', be it an innocent flirtation at the riverfront, driving around on motorbikes calling out to girls, singing karaoke, or visiting a brothel. As one man told the researchers from Population Services International:

> We just invited one another by saying, 'Let's go for a walk.' But it was not going for a walk; it was going to find women . . . If I wanted to or my friends wanted to, we just gave the word, 'Let's go for a walk!' . . . We never had clashing ideas in going for walks. If someone wanted to go for a walk somewhere, everyone would go together.
>
> (PSI 2008: 7)[13]

Mid-level police officers, soldiers, civil servants and businessmen patronize 'dancing restaurants', beer gardens, nightclubs and karaoke venues where hostesses will be assigned to dance, order and serve drinks, massage and flirt with customers. High-level politicians usually maintain a *songsar* (sweetheart or girlfriend), or a *prapuon touch* (lesser wife) in a small house or apartment, to which they retire whenever they require 'relaxation'. It is these women who bear the brunt of jealousy from principal wives rather than the 'lower-end' sex-for-cash sex workers who operate out of massage parlours and open-air parks or the brothels catering to blue-collar workers such as Boulding in Phnom Penh.[14] Although many on this spectrum of the clientele ordinarily cannot afford a sex worker visit more than once every few weeks, research has found that it is a normal component of life even for most men employed in low-paid jobs (PSI 2008: 2).

Special occasions were seen as a legitimate reason to visit a sex worker. One *motodup* I spoke to said that Water Festival or the occasion of some windfall were times when 'it is normal to celebrate with friends' by visiting sex workers in a group. His own last trip to Boulding had been when he had won the equivalent of US$12 in a lottery. University students also tend to visit sex workers in a group at the end of the term or school year. Huor and his university friends first visited a sex worker when they found out their secondary school results. He reminisced:

> When we found out we could go to the university, we decided to go and celebrate together. We went to a karaoke place over the river and got a room with a sofa, some Mekong [whiskey], and two girls for the five of us.

In recent years, the association between being a 'successful' man and sex has had serious consequences in Cambodia, as more and more men attempt to assert their own prowess through behaviour that technically makes them 'successful' – without having access to the economic resources required. This has resulted in increasingly high rates of sexual assault against women who are not necessarily involved in the sex sector, although their occupations as waitresses or in other places associated with hospitality and recreation identify them as such. According to 'traditional' models of correct behaviour for Cambodian women, only 'bad' women work in such places; therefore, they are available for 'successful' men, and are fair game (see Jacobsen 2008: 262–9).

Gang rape (involving more than two perpetrators) has been described by Luke Bearup, a gender and development specialist, as 'a fun, bonding experience between males' in Cambodia (*Phnom Penh Post* 2002–3). This most commonly takes the form of *bauk*, a slang term for gang rape of sex workers,[15] but rape of a single victim by large numbers of males occurs outside of the sex sector as well. There has been a worrying increase in the rape of very young children by men known to them. Children, around half of whom were under 12 years of age, comprised the overwhelming majority of victims seen by the human rights organization LICADHO in 2002 and 2003 (LICADHO 2005). The Association pour droits de l'homme du Cambodge reported 375 rapes and sexual assaults against children in 2007 and 280 in 2008 (ADHOC 2009: 24). A possible explanation for the increasing youth of rape victims – and sex workers – is that virginity is believed to have curative and restorative properties, including rejuvenating a flagging libido in older men, a cure for HIV/AIDS, and improving business luck.

'Acting out' what had been viewed in pornographic movies is another rationale often cited for this kind of sexual activity. Lyda, who was raped by her younger brother, causing her to require a blood transfusion and stitches, suggested that he had 'been made crazy by seeing sexy movies online and at friends' houses'. This same explanation was put forward by a program director at the human rights organization ADHOC, who explained that when men who migrate to the cities for seasonal blue-collar jobs get lonely, they:

> Seek companionship with each other in cafés that have strong coffee and films from Thailand and China. Sometimes the movies have sex in them. The combination of the chemical stimulant [coffee] and seeing the sex makes them want to go and try to do the same things.[16]

In this way, successful men validate the manliness of their friends through participation in activities that allow them to feel powerful. At their least harmful, these include *en masse* visits to sex workers. At the other end of the spectrum are the attempts by misguided, oppressed and desperate men to validate themselves through the violation of the most vulnerable. These men are then able to extricate themselves from retribution by paying other men, who are also trying to be 'successful', to intercede on their behalf. Successful men are thus able to bolster their positions through co-opting other men with similar aspirations.

Conflated and conflicting identities

In the analysis that follows, I contrast the tropes of 'good' and 'successful' men with 'real' men in order to present some of the acts and attitudes attributed to men in the media and in the reports of organizations that work in public health, governance and human rights. Cambodian men struggle with what have been described as the 'opposing elements of Khmer masculinity which exist within most men' (PSI 2008: 8). On one hand, men are encouraged (and expected) to act out the 'manhood script' in which they *dtou da leng* with friends, engaging in sexual encounters as part of recreation, abuse their positions by forcing people to pay extra for services to which they are entitled, and 'correct' their erring wives and children through violence if necessary. On the other hand, society lauds the alternative model of a man who is self-controlled and committed to his family and his broader community.

These conflicting scripts reflect the tension between modernity and the perception of tradition at work in Cambodian society. Whereas international development and investment has meant that Cambodia is beginning to catch up with the rest of ASEAN in economic terms, globalization has seen many people – especially those born after the Khmer Rouge regime fell in 1979 – eschew tradition in favour of Westernized models of behaviour that emphasize individual, rather than collective, identity. Yet men are generally unreflective when it comes to these tensions. Of all the male informants interviewed, only Lim commented upon the difficulty in abiding by both sets of expectations, saying 'Sometimes, I listen to what we should do according to our [past] culture; other times, I want to be a man like my friends, and I go out with them to karaoke and other places for sex, because I am a modern man.'

Lim's dilemma is that he cannot move away from the expectations placed upon men, be they 'good' or 'successful'. Cambodian roles, regardless of gender, cannot change drastically from those dictated by social mores of earlier, more truly 'Cambodian' times, as any move away from 'traditional' identities is seen as deeply troubling.[17] There is a sense of urgency that customs, roles and relationships remain unchanged and, should something be found to have altered as a result of civil war or foreign influence, it must be reconfigured to fit into contemporary perceptions of pre-1960s culture. A good example of this is decision-making in the family. There were large numbers of female heads of household in Cambodia during the 1980s (Jacobsen 2008: 239–41) and most respondents claimed that either mothers or both parents had been more responsible for decision-making in the family when they were children. However, by 2006, activists claimed that gender relations within the home had 'reverted' to a more patriarchal model in which men were viewed as the 'final decision makers' and could expect 'deference, respect, and obedience' (Cambodian Women's Crisis Centre 2007: 5).

Attempts to retain (or regain) elements of culture believed to represent a Cambodian 'traditional' identity – such as virginity for women prior to marriage and fidelity after, the onus upon young men to enrol as a novice monk for a period of time, and respecting the *neak ta* and other spirits – are understandable, as Cambodian culture was virtually eradicated by force between 1975 and 1979 and modified to incorporate socialist Vietnamese cultural characteristics between 1979 and 1989. Any further loss of 'traditional' identity, in terms of gender, class or ethnic category, could compromise Cambodian cultural integrity altogether. Although women are more generally perceived to be the 'guardians of culture' in this regard, there are clearly expectations placed upon Cambodian men as well in terms of their behaviour. Cambodia, therefore, is one context in which masculinity does not fit Gilmore's (1990: 230) assertion that 'male ideology (manliness) is a symbolic script, a cultural construct, endlessly variable and not always necessary'. On the contrary, it is seen as culturally essential that the manhood script remain static.

These expectations manifest as good, bad and successful in multiple, overlapping and often conflicting identities that men must struggle to negotiate or fail as men. Before 1975, it was assumed that all young men would spend some months as a novice monk; now, young men will only enter the *sangha* if they can afford to stop working long enough to do so or if their families insist. There is no point, many young men feel, as *sel* – the merit earned through meditation and pious acts such as entering the *sangha* – will not bring wealth or prestige. By extension, few young men want to be 'good' men, as 'good' men are rarely 'successful'. As Keyes (1986: 89–90) found over twenty years ago in Thailand, 'a man who tempers his desires while acting in the world may find himself at a distinct disadvantage to those who accentuate their "natural" maleness'. Indeed, it is difficult to be a 'successful' man without at times being a 'bad' one.

There are no easy answers as to how 'real' Cambodian men will reconcile the multiple and conflicting models of manhood currently bombarding them from all angles through the Internet, television programmes imported from the West and more affluent parts of Asia, and bootlegged copies of Hollywood blockbusters and pornography from all parts of the globe. At the same time, the Cambodian past – including its social norms and gender roles – is persistently asserted as inviolable and bound up with national identity. The Angkorian era continues to represent a distant yet glorious Cambodia that all politicians promise is possible again; the purported chastity and timidity of Cambodian womanhood continues to be a sought-after characteristic in brides for Westernized men; and Cambodian elite men continue to act with impunity, moving forward into a modern world that allows them to satisfy their individual desires, while their less socially elevated counterparts earn reprobation for experimenting with ill-articulated models sourced from elsewhere. As Doyle (2002) has articulated in the Vietnamese context, men will continue to act in ways that enhance their 'maleness' as long as society legitimizes them. Variations on the models of a 'good', a 'successful' and a 'bad' man will undoubtedly emerge as scholars begin a more nuanced analysis of Cambodian men and their issues. However, Cambodian masculinity is unlikely to develop new characteristics that would result in a 'proliferation' of additional models until cultural identity ceases to be as inherently bound up with the survival of a vision of Cambodia that is at odds with the processes of globalization.

Notes

1 Informants were asked to choose their own pseudonyms. Ages and job descriptions have been retained as stated.
2 I have described the women of the palace in great detail elsewhere (Jacobsen 2008).
3 This was true also in the Siamese context (Loos 2005). Ironically, the presence of so many women was perceived as threatening to European notions of masculinity in the colonial period.
4 There are at least three versions of the *Cbpab Srei*, all very similar in content and phrasing. Scholars are unclear as to which was written first. There are also similar codes for other groups; for example, the *Cbpab Koan Chao,* or 'Code of Conduct for High-born Children', spelled out the correct comportment for the children of the palace.
5 One, unexpectedly, said that a good man would work as an artist, as 'he would expect no money, but wants to express his vision'.
6 Rape and sexual assaults are not as likely to be reported.
7 A teacher in an elementary school can expect an official salary of US$45 per month on average.
8 Some were perhaps too specific. Chan, a 22-year-old student at the Build Bright University in Phnom Penh, said that his father 'does only good things, is fat and 1.65 metres tall. My uncle who is a farmer also does good deeds and is a bit thin.'
9 Interestingly, there was not a high correlation between those who believed that 'good' men could be differentiated by appearance and those who identified physical characteristics for a 'successful' man.
10 It is common in Cambodia for a gay man to marry a woman and have at least one child in order to fulfil his obligations to his family.
11 Indeed the only safety for Cambodian men is to have sufficient *omnaich* that nobody will dare cast aspersions on their ability to act as 'real men'.
12 Of the fifty-two male informants, only fifteen said that it was not acceptable for *any* man to visit sex workers. Conversely, only five of the thirty-four women said that it was acceptable for any man, whether good or not, to visit sex workers.
13 The expectation that men will *dtou da leng* with friends means that gay men have as many opportunities (if not as many venues) to engage in M2M sexual encounters as their straight counterparts do to engage in heterosexual ones. However, gay men are becoming more confident about being public about their sexual orientation and Cambodia celebrated its first Gay Pride Week in May 2009.
14 One of the reasons that many Cambodians find it acceptable for men to visit sex workers is that, if they did not 'release their feelings' with them, 'respectable' women would be at risk of violence as (unmarried) male passions would inevitably find an outlet somehow. At the same time, sex workers are frowned upon for 'tempting' married men who are trying to concentrate on their families. A 1998 ban on prostitution within Khan Daun Penh, in the centre of Phnom Penh, was viewed as a positive move for strengthening family relationships as 'prostitution distracts husbands from their wives' and relocating sex workers to the periphery of the city, necessitating a long journey, would deter husbands from visiting them (Khmer Women's Voice Centre 1998: 9).
15 *Bauk* can mean 'to open', 'to switch on' or 'to drive'; another very similar word, spelled with a different vowel, means 'to cheat'.
16 ADHOC reiterated this assertion in their most recent annual report, stating that 'We observe that a dramatic increase in rape-related offences . . . [is caused by] rampant influx and display of pornographic films as local authorities are ineffective in their crackdown on obscene materials and law enforcement. Perpetrators often used drugs and alcohol, the use of which has become increased in society in general' (ADHOC 2009: 25).
17 I am referring here to Mead's (1934) classic definition of role-taking as implementing the generalized other's expectations and values in determining self-behaviour.

References

ADHOC (2009) 'Eighth annual human rights situation report', Phnom Penh: Association pour droits de l'homme du Cambodge (ADHOC-Cambodian Human Rights Association).

Aing Sokroeun (2004) 'A comparative analysis of traditional and contemporary roles of Khmer women in the household: a case study in Leap Tong village', unpublished MA thesis, Royal University of Phnom Penh.

Andaya, B. W. (1998) 'From temporary wife to prostitute: sexuality and economic change in early modern Southeast Asia', *Journal of Women's History* 9(4): 11–35.

Cambodian Women's Crisis Centre (2007) 'Global report 2006', Phnom Penh: CWCC.

Center for Social Development (2005) 'Corruption and Cambodian households: household survey on perceptions, attitudes and impact of everyday forms of corrupt practices in Cambodia', Phnom Penh: Center for Social Development.

Cœdès, G. (1937–66), *Inscriptions du Cambodge*, 8 vols., Paris and Hanoi: Imprimerie de l'Ecole Française d'Extrême-Orient and Imprimerie Nationale.

Connell, R. W. (2005) *Masculinities*, 2nd edn, Crows Nest, New South Wales: Allen & Unwin.

Doyle, N. (2002) 'Why do dogs lick their balls? Gender, desire and change – a case study from Vietnam', in F. Cleaver (ed.), *Masculinities Matter! Men, Gender and Development*, London and New York: Zed Books, pp. 186–208.

Ebihara, M. (1984) 'Societal organization in 16th and 17th century Cambodia', *Journal of Asian Studies* 15(2): 280–95.

Fenstermaker, S. and West, C. (eds) (2002) *Doing Gender, Doing Difference: Social Inequality, Power, and Resistance*, New York: Routledge.

Gilmore, D. D. (1990) *Manhood in the Making: Cultural Concepts of Masculinity*, New Haven and London: Yale University Press.

Jacobsen, T. (2008) *Lost Goddesses: The Denial of Female Power in Cambodian History*, Copenhagen: NIAS Press.

Jacobsen, T. and Stuart-Fox, M. (n.d.) 'Power and political culture in Cambodia', unpublished paper.

Jennar, P. N. and Pou, S. (1976) 'Les *cpap* our < codes de conduite > khmers II: *cpap prus*', *Bulletin de l'Ecole Française d'Extrême-Orient* 63: 313–50.

Keyes, C. F. (1986) 'Ambiguous gender: male initiation in a northern Thai Buddhist society', in C. W. Bynum, S. Harrell and P. Richman (eds), *Gender and Religion: On the Complexity of Symbols*, Boston: Beacon Press, pp. 66–96.

Khmer Women's Voice Centre (1998) *8 March*, Phnom Penh: Khmer Women's Voice Centre.

Ledgerwood, J. L. (1990) 'Changing Khmer conceptions of gender: women, stories, and the social order', unpublished PhD thesis, Cornell University.

—— (1996) 'Politics and gender: negotiating changing Cambodian ideas of the proper woman', *Asia Pacific Viewpoint* 37(2): 139–52.

LICADHO (2005) 'Rape and indecent assault 2004', Phnom Penh: Cambodian League for the Promotion and Defense of Human Rights (LICADHO).

Loos, T. (2005) 'Sex in the inner city: the fidelity between sex and politics in Siam', *Journal of Asian Studies* 64(4): 881–909.

Mead, G. H. (1934) *Mind, Self and Society*, Chicago: University of Chicago Press.

Minh Mai (2001) *Cbpab Srei-broh* [c.19th century], Phnom Penh: Phsep pseay juon koan khmei.

Phnom Penh Post (2002–3) 'You can say that again! – 2002's quotable quotes', 20 December 2002 – 2 January 2003.

Pou, S. (2005) 'The concept of *avatāra* in the *Rāmāyaṇa* tradition of Cambodia', *Orientalia Loveniensia Periodica* 31: 123–35.

PSI (2008) *Informed Decisions: Recent Evidence Provides Programmatic Guidance for HIV Prevention Intervention in Cambodia*, Phnom Penh: PSI.

Zhou Daguan (1992) *The Customs of Cambodia* [13th century], trans. J. Gilman d'Arcy Paul, 2nd edn, Bangkok: Siam Society.

6 Violence, masculinities and patriarchy in post-conflict Timor-Leste

Henri Myrttinen

I ran into Alberto (not his real name) in one of the beachside restaurants which have sprung up along the beach east of Dili, the capital city of Timor-Leste. Settling down with a few beers, we inevitably started talking shop and got onto the topic of my research – masculinity and gender-based violence. It turned out to be a sore spot for my informant, a university-educated, well-travelled, middle-class East Timorese who mostly worked as a consultant for international development agencies and NGOs:

> BULLSHIT! I'm fucking tired of this fucking bullshit! All these *malae* [internationals] coming here and labelling us East Timorese men as violent! I'm sick of it! Timorese culture has always been a peaceful one, we never had violent conflict in the past! And this western gender-stuff . . . Man, back in the old days there was a system that worked, where everyone knew their place and their roles![1]

Back-pedalling to defuse the situation, I ventured that perhaps it had been the long-term impacts of the experience of the invasion of Timor-Leste by Indonesia in 1975 and the subsequent twenty-four years of military occupation and resistance, and being part of the militarized New Order society that had made violence such a visible part of East Timorese society. Lighting an (imported Indonesian) cigarette, my informant burst into laughter:

> Dude, no way! No way! Those Indonesians were pussies! They couldn't teach us that shit! Man, we used to beat up the Indonesians every day in school, man! Every day! They're just too soft!

In retrospect, this scene at the little beachside restaurant crystallized many of the contradictions which I encountered over the years while working on issues of male identity and violence in Timor-Leste. Alberto's comments highlight the paradoxes and complexities surrounding gender-based violence and the interplay of male identities with militia and gang violence.[2] The simultaneous legitimization and de-legitimization of the use of violence intersects with narratives of agency and lack of agency as well as the amalgamation of the traditional with the modern, of the local with the global.

In this chapter, I examine a number of these apparent paradoxes involving masculinities and violence, particularly gender-based violence, in Timor-Leste. Gender-based violence has formed the bulk of reported crime and of cases brought into the judicial system in Timor-Leste since crime statistics began to be compiled under the United Nations administration from 2000 onwards and after Independence was achieved in 2002 (Cristalis and Scott 2005; TLAVA 2009; UNTAET 2002). During the period of the United Nations Transitional Administration in East Timor (UNTAET),[3] 40 per cent of reported crimes were categorized as gender-based violence, while a study on court cases in Dili District Court over a two-month period in 2004 by the Timorese NGO Judicial System Monitoring Programme (JSMP) found that 55 per cent of cases involved violence against women, of which 78 per cent involved serious sexual assault (TLAVA 2009).[4] These figures represent only a fraction of the actual cases, as most gender-based violence cases are handled through the informal justice system and thus are never reported to law enforcement agencies. If they are reported, they may be registered under other categories such as assault, manslaughter or murder. Law No. 7/2010 on Domestic Violence uses a broad definition of the term, including psychological violence, neglect and abuse of economic dependence, and considers domestic violence a public crime and makes it mandatory to report it to the police. But until it was passed, cases involving gender-based violence were dealt with according to pre-existing Indonesian legislation, which, in practice, has meant using a threshold of 'whether blood flows' from a beating to determine whether it is a case for police action. Of the reported cases, the overwhelming majority of the perpetrators have been men (Abdullah and Myrttinen 2009; TLAVA 2009).

In spite of the lack of reliable numerical data, local and international actors, including the government, UN agencies, NGOs and urban and rural communities, consider gender-based violence to be a major problem (Myrttinen *et al.* 2010a; TLAVA 2009). Two key explanations for male violence dominate accounts of gender-based violence in Timor-Leste. The first, a cultural/historical argument, suggests that male violence, particularly gender-based violence, is the product of a deeply patriarchal society in which violence has become an accepted 'way of life'. The second, the socio-economic argument, suggests that young, socio-economically marginalized men are prone to violence because they have few other avenues to express their anger and frustration. I argue, however, that the picture is more complex and messy than is suggested by either of these accounts. Problematizing these two narratives in the light of changing masculinities and patriarchal structures in Timor-Leste, I argue that the intersections between masculinities and violence cannot be blamed merely on culture, on history or on socio-economic conditions alone, though all of these do play a role. Violence has become a normalized tool, especially for men, for seeking redress to real and perceived grievances in both the private and the public sphere but also for challenging or confirming social power structures. As such, it was viewed by my interviewees with ambivalence – on the one hand accepted as a part of life but on the other condemned as unacceptable. A common strategy for bridging this gap was to downplay or deny one's own participation in acts of violence.

Because violence against women has been at the centre of much of the gender debate in Timor-Leste and the relationship between masculinity and violence is still inadequately understood, in this chapter I focus on the ways in which East Timorese men understand and explain violence, particularly that which is directed at women. I begin by examining the levels of public and private violence in Timor-Leste and attitudes towards it. Next, I discuss the gendered social order, the role of violence in it, and how this has been affected by the nation's history of colonization, occupation and resistance. Turning then to the present day, I examine how the political crisis and socio-economic transformations have challenged traditional notions of masculinity and patriarchy and the role played by violence in these processes.

The ubiquity and ambiguity of violence

The assertion that a direct link exists between violence and male role expectations and behaviours has achieved a level of conventional acceptance both at a global level and in Timor-Leste in particular. Acts of gender-based violence are mostly committed by men – and the public violence of the gangs, martial arts groups (MAGs) and ritual arts groups (RAGs) which defined public life in Dili between May 2006 and February 2008 was mostly a male phenomenon.[5] Explaining this apparent link, is however, not straightforward. The concept of violence is seen differently across cultures and historical periods. The question of whether a particular act constitutes violence is frequently disputed, not least between perpetrators and victims. As Hearn (1998: 15) puts it:

> The definition of violence is contested. This contestation is itself part of the process of the reproduction of and indeed opposition to violence . . . [V]iolence is not *one thing*; it is not a thing at all. Violence is simply a word, a short-hand that refers to a mass of different experiences in people's lives [Emphasis in original].

For the purposes of this chapter, I concentrate on direct violence, defined as the deliberate use of coercive physical, psychological or verbal force to cause injury or abuse, a definition that coincides with the local East Timorese perceptions of violence I encountered during my research. Violence is about reasserting and/or renegotiating power relationships. It is an extreme form of communication (Cramer 2006: 284). While violence is often seen as a tool of the more powerful, paradoxically violence can also be used to overcome feelings of powerlessness, frustration or vulnerability (Isdal and Råkil 2002: 104). Those who feel personally, politically and socio-economically marginalized may vent their frustrations by resorting to physical violence in both the public and the private sphere. In Timor-Leste violence is commonly regarded by local and outside observers as a part of public and private life.

Since gaining their independence, the people of Timor-Leste have dealt with politically, economically and socially motivated public violence by gangs and martial arts and ritual arts groups. In the aftermath of the 2006 political crisis in Timor-Leste, a UN Commission of Inquiry concluded that the Portuguese and Indonesian eras both 'created and subsumed internal divisions within Timor-Leste. Political competition within Timor-Leste has been historically settled through violence' (United Nations 2006: 16). Although this assessment does not take into account many of the non-violent means by which political differences are settled in Timor-Leste, including traditional conflict resolution and reconciliation methods (cf. Babo-Soares 2004), the statement resonates with many local assessments of violence.

It was not uncommon for the respondents in my research to see violence perpetrated by males as an integral part of life. As one gang leader noted:

> You know, that's the way we Timorese are, whenever there's a problem we resort to violence. We lash out. It's our culture. Hot-blooded, hard-headed. We Timorese never confess, never repent anything. And that's a problem. We always find someone else to blame for our faults.
>
> (Interview, 2007)

Much of the attention on public violence has been on Dili, but male violence is also considered to be a normal part of life in more rural settings. As a martial arts group member in Zumalai village stated:

> Yeah, on market days there's always violence, always . . . There's drinking, there's gambling, and the guys from the other martial arts groups show up, someone says something, one thing leads to another and yeah, then there's a fight.
>
> (Interview, 2007)

These observations were confirmed by a former gang member from Los Palos, who framed his participation in gang violence in terms of normality, of gaining status, of dealing with frustration – but also as a kind of necessity:

> I set up a gang with my friends because everyone was in a gang. It was cool, you know, sexy. Everyone did it. We got drunk, we took out our frustrations. We also had to do it to protect our neighbourhood.
>
> (Interview, 2007)

Although violence is regarded as a part of everyday life, attitudes towards it are ambivalent. On one hand, the use of violence is generally condemned and individuals tend to deny or downplay their personal participation in violent acts. However, at the same time, its use is seen as an acceptable, or at the very least understandable, disciplining measure or as a legitimate means to address existing political, economic or social grievances (Grove *et al.* 2007; Myrttinen 2010; UNFPA 2005).

An incident that occurred during my field research underlines this contradiction. A young gang member in Dili who had been dumped by his girlfriend went downtown and decapitated a member of a rival gang with a samurai sword as a means of venting his frustration. While many of my respondents viewed his reaction as being excessive, they also saw it as being understandable on the other hand because the young man in question was after all *sakit hati* (upset or offended, lit. to have a sore liver). Similarly, in interviews with both former militia members and former resistance fighters, the militia violence of 1999 was partially 'explained' as resulting from the militia members feeling *sakit hati* after losing the referendum. Again, excessive violence was seen as being regrettable, but also an understandable reaction to extreme frustration (Myrttinen 2010).

These tensions between condemning violence (or denying one's part in it) and considering it to be acceptable are also expressed in the following comments by a local martial arts group leader in Baucau. He first described at length his group's non-violent nature, describing it as a 'peaceful group' that 'didn't resort to violence'. Echoing the international discourse on such things, he went on to note that the group was 'open to all religions and races, [and has] no political agenda. We are an international brotherhood, we are for peace; we are for respect. We are a spiritual group.' Minutes later, however, he contradicted himself when discussion turned to the current conflict in which his group was involved against a rival group:

> Well, when they started to move into our territory in 2000, that's when it all started. We just had to retaliate. We always get a bad reputation and the police discriminate against us, but they are biased. We need to defend ourselves, defend our territory.
>
> (Interview, 2007)[6]

These paradoxical accounts of violence, of denouncing yet approving it, recurred in numerous accounts of violence in the private sphere as well.[7] Research that I conducted in 2010 in Dili and Liquiçá districts confirms that domestic violence is at times socially accepted within the family (see Myrttinen *et al.* 2010b: 29–30). Acknowledging that male violence was part of the natural order, one young woman interviewed in the context of that study said:

> it is right for a husband to beat his wife, for if she does something wrong, she will need to be taught to do the right thing . . . I would never strike back at my husband, for that would be like striking God on the face.
>
> (Interview, 2010)

However, this perception is not representative of all community attitudes and it is an over-simplification to see gender-based violence in Timor-Leste as merely the product of violent men and subservient women. Although high levels of gender-based violence are a serious concern, this does not imply that all men in all relationships are violent. Such a view also overlooks the extent to which community attitudes change over time. Following a crackdown on the various groups after the February 2008 shootings of renegade Major Alfredo Reinado and President José Ramos-Horta, public violence by gangs and martial arts and ritual arts groups has decreased, as has public acceptance of the violence (Myrttinen *et al.* 2010b). In terms of public attitudes, this has also been true of gender-based violence. In the words of a village administrator from Liquiça district:

> In the past, we did not consider domestic violence a problem; it was considered a normal part of life. Now however, after the awareness-raising campaigns [by the government and NGOs] we understand that it is a crime, and that we need to take steps to end it.
>
> (cited in Myrttinen *et al.* 2010a: 25)

These comments suggest that the interplay between masculinities and public and private violence in Timor-Leste must be problematized rather than taken for granted. It also emphasizes that – in a society where the average citizen is too young to vote and where a young woman working for a foreign aid organization wields more power than traditional village elders or elected government officials – simply invoking a traditional 'way of life' glosses over the particular historical factors that shape patterns of gender-based violence.

Patriarchal gender order

The high levels of gender-based violence in Timor-Leste society are attributed to a range of social, cultural and historical factors (Dewhurst 2008; Hovde Bye 2005; Streicher 2008; TLAVA 2009; UNFPA 2005). But one of the key contributing factors for the high levels of gender-based violence identified in reports is Timor-Leste's hierarchical gender order, exemplified by a study by the United Nations Population Fund (UNFPA), entitled *Gender-based Violence in Timor-Leste: A Case Study*, which emphasizes the 'patriarchal organization of society and strongly held beliefs that men are the heads of the families' as causes of gender-based violence (UNFPA 2005: 7). Patriarchy – a hierarchical gendered social order which systematically places the interests of men over women – is seen as playing a key role in facilitating high levels of male violence, especially in the private but to a lesser extent also in the public domain. The essence of this argument is that, in patriarchal systems, male domination over women is seen as the norm, and the use of violence to maintain this order as acceptable. The UNFPA concludes that 'there are traditional beliefs that violence is a normal, almost inevitable, part of domestic relationships – a traditional saying is *"bikan ho kanuru baku malu"* / "a dish and a spoon will hit each other"' (UNFPA 2005: 7–8).

Although culture and tradition are often invoked in both defending and critiquing the extant gender order, there is little reliable information available on pre-1974 Timor-Leste society, in part owing to the lack of local written histories. Timorese warrior culture is a recurring (but mostly poorly researched) topic in colonial-era sources, but other forms of violence, including gender-based violence, were not a topic of interest.[8] Hicks' (2004) work, which is based on field studies in pre-1974 Timor, is an exception in as much as he mentions sanctions for the rape of women in which the male family members of a rape victim receive compensation payments (ibid.: 102). The fact that other forms of gender-based violence are not mentioned in colonial-era sources may well reflect past tendencies to overlook domestic violence as a problem. Timorese victims of gender-based violence were also unlikely to take their cases to the colonial Portuguese police or subsequently to the occupying Indonesian security forces.

Available sources such as Hicks (2004) and Traube (1986), which draw on fieldwork in pre-Independence and pre-invasion Portuguese Timor, stress the binary nature of gender relations, in which men and women have strictly ascribed complementary roles – but, at least in the patrilineal societies studied by Hicks and Traube, within a context of male political and social dominance. Writing about the post-Independence period, Hovde Bye (2005: 50) has argued that women are also complicit in maintaining a potentially violent gender order:

> In a culture such as the East Timorese, there exists a hierarchical division between women within families according to generations and in-laws. Newly-wed women are on the bottom of the hierarchical ladder, and are thus subjected to subordination not only by men, but also by older women. Traditionally, increased status and rewards accrue to women later in life when their sons get married and their new daughters-in-law move into the family. Then they come to dominate the young women, and finally can exercise power over someone. This tradition can result in compliance from the older women to the patriarchal system, since they finally are in a position of power of privilege, while the younger women comply because they know that one day it will be their turn.

In contemporary Timor-Leste, the subordinate position of young women continues to be reinforced by cultural beliefs and practices, such as bride price (*barlaki*). As a young woman I interviewed in Becora reflected:

> I guess a lot of men do feel frustrated and trapped by their obligations. They are expected to pay a *barlaki* they can't afford, to get a proper job which they can't find, to fulfil their obligations to their elders, their uncles and so on . . . then they take out their frustrations on those who are in a weaker position. But on the other hand, they are also given more space to act out that way. It's sort of socially accepted.
>
> (Interview, 2007)

Referred to in Tetum as *barlaki, barlake* or *burlaque*, the 'bride price' or dowry system varies from region to region. It has generally had a far more complex meaning than a mere dowry, as it has traditionally been a key element of defining relations not only between husband and wife but between their two respective families for the future. Through the marriage process and attendant payment of *barlaki*, the relationships between the two families involved are redefined as those of the 'wife-givers' and the 'wife-takers' (*umane* and *fetosa'an*) in a complex system of mutual and recurring obligations going far beyond merely the initial dowry payment (Loch 2007: 172–6).

While there has been a move away from the *barlaki* system especially amongst the urban middle classes, the tradition is still seen by many as being binding. Increasingly, however, young men are unable to pay the traditional dowries, adding to their general sense of frustration. East Timorese women's rights activists tend to see *barlaki* 'as one of the underlying reasons for the problems many married women are facing' (Cristalis and Scott 2005: 20). A survey by the International Rescue Committee (IRC 2003: 19), on the other hand, found that only 9 per cent of the women polled saw the *barlaki* payment as having a negative impact on the way the husband treats his wife. One way of interpreting this discrepancy is to view it as evidence of a gap in perceptions and interpretations between the women's rights movement and the majority of the population with respect to the tradition. While women's organizations stressed how *barlaki* underlined a sense of men's ownership of women and therefore opened the door to abuse, the women polled by the IRC either had not experienced this link or, more worryingly, might have come to expect violence as part of marriage (Cristalis and Scott 2005: 92, 103).[9]

Studies of gender-based violence also cite debts incurred by *barlaki* payments, along with poverty, unemployment and shared housing, as contributing to high gender-based violence levels (e.g. Dewhurst 2008; Hovde Bye 2005; TLAVA 2009; UNFPA 2005).[10] However, as the extent of male dominance and male violence in 'traditional' East Timorese society cannot be reliably gauged, the apparent link between traditional masculinities and the prevalence of gender-based violence is by necessity *ex post facto* speculation which draws on a limited amount of research on 'traditional' gender relations.

Colonization, occupation and violence

The traditional gender order, whatever its precise form, did not exist separately from the Portuguese colonial power, the Catholic Church or, after the 1975 invasion, the Indonesian state and its military forces. Any understanding of gender-based violence must therefore also explore the intersection between patriarchy, the role of the Catholic Church (which emphasizes the need to keep families together often in spite of violence), and the history and culture of violence associated with occupation and colonialism. Traditional society was not left untouched by the colonial experience, especially after the intensification of Portuguese colonial rule in the first decades of the twentieth century. An even more cataclysmic experience was that of the Indonesian invasion and occupation from 1975 to 1999, which affected society and individuals to a far greater degree than colonial rule had.

The acceptability of the use of violence as a tool to address grievances was subject to changes brought in by both the Portuguese and the Indonesian regimes. Olivio Da Costa, secretary general of the East Timorese men's organization Asosiasaun Mane Kontra Violensia (Association of Men against Violence), describes a historical legacy of male dominance from the traditional power of men over Portuguese and Catholic influences to the militarizing experience of the Indonesian occupation:

East Timorese society has traditionally been patriarchal with male political power, polygamy and men in control over women, sometimes with force. This patriarchy was strengthened by the Portuguese colonial power and by the Catholic Church. During the Soeharto years, violence was everywhere and the educational system was highly militarized, teaching violence as a method to solve your problems.

(Interview, 2010)

Similarly, but placing even more of a stress on external rather than internal factors, the East Timorese researcher José Trindade argues:

It was the Portuguese colonizers who really brought violence to Timor-Leste. They used the local *liurai* (local rulers) as tax collectors and these beat up those who couldn't pay taxes under pressure from the Portuguese. The colonizers also introduced beatings in schools as disciplinary measures – and this was passed on to the families. The Indonesian occupiers continued to use the same system, only then the violence was everywhere, all the time.

(Interview, 2010)

Unfortunately there are no baseline studies available of gender-based violence in pre-colonial or colonial Timor-Leste to prove or disprove quantitatively the impact of the colonial regime on its prevalence. As mentioned above, when violence was mentioned in colonial-era sources, it tended to be focused on traditional Timorese warrior culture and/or uprisings, not on gender-based violence.

The experience of the years of occupation and resistance have shaped the lives of East Timorese men and women as well as the social sense of the acceptability of the use of violence for political and social means. As underlined by both Da Costa and Trindade in their observations of colonial and occupied Timor, the Portuguese and Indonesian rulers (and, during their brief sojourn, the Imperial Japanese Army) normalized the link between the upholding of authority and the use of violence, sometimes directly and sometimes by investing the power to use violence to local proxies (see CAVR 2005; Cribb 2002; Fox 2006; Hill 2002). During the Indonesian occupation, awareness of sexualized violence tended to be focused on the systematic gender-based and sexual violence perpetrated against the East Timorese civilian population by the Indonesian occupation forces and, in 1998–9, local proxy militia forces.[11] It was only in the wake of the 1995 Beijing UN Women's Conference that domestic violence began to be first publicly discussed by nascent Timorese women's organizations such as Fokupers (Communication Forum of East Timorese Women – Forum Komunikasi Perempuan Timor Loro Sa'e, Fokupers). This was not met with unanimous support amongst East Timorese activists, many of whom felt that the focus should be kept solely on the acts of gender-based violence committed by the Indonesian occupation forces (Cristalis and Scott 2005: 91–2).

As in other societies in this kind of situation, for many men in Timor-Leste the years of conflict and occupation made living up to traditional expectations of masculinities extremely challenging. Dolan (2002: 64) points out in his study of masculinities in northern Uganda how in the 'context of on-going war, heavy militarisation and internal displacement it is very difficult, if not impossible, for the vast majority of men to fulfil the expectations contained in the model of masculinity' prevalent as the idealized form in society. However, as Dolan also argues:

> the normative model of masculinity . . . exercises considerable power over men, precisely because they are unable to behave according to it, but cannot afford not to try to live up to it. The relationship between the social and political acceptance which comes from being seen to conform to the norm, and access to a variety of resources, is a critical one in a conflict situation.
>
> (Dolan 2001: 11)

While the life of the young men in the outskirts of Dili is not as dire as the life of young men in northern Uganda, there are definite similarities. Throughout the occupation and the resistance, both the imposition of authority and the challenging of it were most visible in acts of violence, a pattern which has continued in many ways in the post-Independence years.[12] Violence has also become normalized as a response to personal, social, political and economic frustrations, in both the public and the private sphere (Cristalis and Scott 2005: 103; Myrttinen 2010: 49; Streicher 2008: 45).

Taking it out on women

Following the end of the transitional UNTAET administration on 20 May 2002, newly independent Timor-Leste struggled socio-economically and politically to establish itself. Though it was largely regarded as a success story by the international community, tensions between various factions in the security forces, within the political elite and between communities from different parts of the country, simmered beneath the surface. Triggered by the sacking of almost 600 soldiers from the army, a violent crisis unfolded in April and May 2006, which led initially to the deaths of thirty-seven people and prompted 150,000 people to flee into Internally Displaced Persons camps (Lothe and Peake 2010: 431–4).

The street violence of 2006–8 in Dili has often been cast as young, male and socio-economically marginalized (Kostner and Clark, 2007: 4; Niner, 2008). In addition to cultural and historical explanations for male violence, frustration born of socio-economic marginalization, lack of education, unemployment and poverty are often cited as factors in the violence. A World Bank report on the violence ascribed it to 'uneducated, unoccupied, unemployed and excluded' youth (Kostner and Clark 2007: 4). In a study of East Timorese youth attitudes to the street violence, Grove *et al.* gave similar reasons for violent male behaviour. According to this report, violent young men were motivated by:

> social jealousy; no jobs or prospects; don't go to school; offered food, *tuak* [palm wine], jobs [in return for committing acts of violence]; bored, unoccupied

[*sic*]; sitting on street and 'looking for action'; no moral education from family; don't have 'strong minds' . . . stupid and don't think clearly.

(Grove *et al.* 2007: 7)

The sense of one's own socio-economic disempowerment compared to the new wealth of the political elites is seen as a reason for past, current and potential future violence. As East Timorese researcher Nelson Belo put it:

There is a great deal of frustration, especially amongst the young men who were in the resistance. They feel that they sacrificed their education, their career chances, their lives in the past and now have nothing to show for it. They see the new wealth of their former leaders but also of those who fought against independence. There's a lot of anger there, and that leads to violence. It's a time-bomb.

(Interview, 2010)

This is complicated by the fact that, even in post-Independence, urban, 'modern' Dili, East Timorese men's position in society continues to be largely defined through membership in networks of male patronage, the ties and obligations of which form the basis of society.[13] As Dinnen (2000: 8) has argued for a number of Melanesian societies, there are 'many competing sources of authority and allegiance at local levels, with the claims of the state being merely one among many'. In a sense, male identity (and the range of responses available to an individual in any given situation) in particular becomes 'over-determined' by obligations to clientist networks of patronage controlled by 'the big people' (*ema bo'ot* in Tetum), which include political elites and traditional leaders.

Most of the young men I researched were born and raised in an urban environment. These young men who were involved in the gangs, martial arts groups and ritual arts groups are unable to – and not necessarily willing to – live up to the real or imagined traditional forms of rural East Timorese masculinity, which are based heavily on ritual, adherence to tradition and a lifestyle of subsistence farming. Nor could the young men fulfil fantasies of male warrior glory through participating in a resistance struggle as their fathers, older brothers and uncles may have done, for that struggle was over. In line with the findings of other studies on East Timorese youth (cf. Grove *et al.* 2007; Streicher 2008; Wigglesworth 2007), many of my respondents were seeking to attain the ideal of the male urban professional, working in a white-collar job in an air-conditioned office, with a house and a car and a family. But given the dire economic situation of the mid-2000s and the lack of skills and education amongst the young men, these forms of modern urban masculinity were by and large closed to them.

Amongst many of the interviewees, there was a strong sense of entitlement to better socio-economic conditions and subsequent frustration at not achieving it, frustration which found public and private violence as one of its outlets. Gang members and informants associated with MAGs and RAGs also regularly identified their frustration with their socio-economic situation as a driving factor for violence in the public, but especially the private, sphere. As the leader of one of the bigger gangs concluded:

> The main reason for domestic violence is economic. There are no jobs for the youth, they see others getting rich, they feel like side-lined spectators in their own country. And some of us fought for this country! But yeah, there's a lot of frustration and then something happens, the wife says something or does something, and they take it out on her.
>
> (Interview, 2008)

Yet though socio-economic realities need to be taken into account as contributing factors to male violence in both the public and the private sphere, it would be mistaken to cast violence simply as a problem of the lower classes. Many of the groups behind the street violence of 2006–8 had the backing of economic and political elites and a number of the leaders of the groups held steady jobs and had university degrees (Myrttinen 2010; Scambary *et al.* 2006). So, too, do the perpetrators of domestic violence.

Patriarchy in flux

In the decade since the 1999 referendum on independence, life in Dili has been in many ways visually dominated by the massive international presence, which has also had an ambiguous impact on gender relations (Koyama and Myrttinen 2007). The international peacekeeping force has been seen as a reassuring presence; as unwanted occupiers; as examples to be emulated (for instance, by the local police force) or fought against (Myrttinen 2010: 265). It is as part of this context that campaigns by the Timor-Leste government and the UN administration, as well as by local and international NGOs, have publicly raised gender issues, especially gender-based violence.

   The opening up of Timor-Leste to global influences has also led to an increased visibility of imported global media images, icons and fashions. These new influences have especially had an impact in urban areas, where masculinities are arguably more in flux than in rural areas, given the continuing existence of more traditional possibilities of fulfilling gender role expectations in the latter. Imported masculine role models and icons include the real and the fictional; the violent and the non-violent. They may be pop stars such as Bob Marley or the Indonesian band Slank or more violent symbols and role models such as Ernesto 'Che' Guevara, Jean-Claude van Damme, Vin Diesel, Rambo and a host of East and Southeast Asian martial arts movie stars and characters, such as Bruce Lee (Myrttinen 2010: 265). These icons – and others, such as Nazi symbols – are often associated with very different values in Timor-Leste compared to Western contexts and are often used as symbols shorn of their historical legacy, a legacy which is often unknown to their users. Wearing a Che t-shirt in Timor-Leste does not necessarily imply a left-wing political outlook; in fact it can be worn by people who consider themselves militant anti-communists. Equally, no inherent contradiction is seen in wearing the Nazi flag on one's jacket together with the peace sign. During the resistance years, the icon of Bob Marley was often associated with the armed resistance of the Falintil guerrilla more than with peace and love. These imported masculine icons and ideals often become mixed with more traditional visions of East Timorese masculinity.

A common link between these icons is what perhaps could be termed the 'coolness of agency'. They have all come to symbolize, in one way or another, masculine resistance, protest and agency (see also Myrttinen 2008). This agency can be seen as being in direct contrast to the perceived powerlessness and lack of agency of many of the gang, martial arts and ritual arts group members I interviewed and more broadly of East Timorese youth. However, the two essentially Western concepts of hegemonic and protest masculinity cannot be directly transferred from the Western, post-industrial societies in which they were developed into the non-Western context of post-conflict Timor-Leste.

The two main types of masculine role models brought in by the foreign presence have been that of the militarized peacekeeper and that of the white-collar UN or INGO official, both of which have been emulated by their East Timorese counterparts – and been possibilities closed to the young men I researched. If one takes the upper-middle-class white-collar urban office worker as the current form of hegemonic masculinity in East Timorese society, then in some ways the masculinities enacted in the various gangs, MAGs and RAGs can be seen as a form of protest against this. These new structures, which young East Timorese men have joined by the thousands (Scambary *et al.* 2006), can also be seen as a reinvention of old models of male patronage networks, albeit with a more modern look. The dress and style of the young men which underline rebelliousness, their choice of language (rejecting the official Portuguese) and their stated resentment against the elite *ema bo'ot* could seem to support this reading. They can also be seen as a way of renegotiating gender hierarchies. In their protest against the *ema bo'ot*, the young men in the gangs, MAGs and RAGs can be seen as questioning these obligations. On the other hand, however, their ties to the political elite reaffirm the traditional networks externally while the neo-traditional structures of the groups constitute internal reaffirmation (Myrttinen 2010).

As this suggests, the two categories of hegemony and protest are thus not as easily separable or antagonistic as, for example, in Connell's (1995) accounts of hegemonic businessmen and protest masculinity bikers. Rather, there is much more a symbiosis, even a degree of overlap, between the new political and economic elite and the gangs, MAGs and RAGs of Timor-Leste. Furthermore, the amalgamated enactments of masculinities in these groups which mix the traditional with the global are not challenging what could be seen as the hegemonic model but rather existing in parallel to it. Given the massive societal changes brought about by three and a half decades of decolonization, military occupation, resistance, modernization, globalization and a massive international presence, the questions of what constitutes hegemonic masculinity and how power dynamics within the patriarchal social structure are defined are being renegotiated to a far greater degree and at a far faster pace than in the more settled context of Western societies.

Awareness-raising campaigns and legal measures, such as the passing of a Law on Domestic Violence in 2010, have started a process of seeing gender-based violence as a serious social problem rather than as a 'natural' part of life. But, as discussed above, gender-based violence in the domestic sphere is not regarded as incompatible with either hegemonic or protest masculinity. It tends to be seen by both hegemonic and protest groups as an undesirable phenomenon on the rhetorical level but as a normalized part of life on the practical level, especially where it stops 'before blood flows'. The difference is more in the attitudes to public violence which, using the terms of hegemonic and protest masculinities with the above-mentioned caveats in mind, can be seen as a further dividing line between the two. The protest masculinities of members of gangs, martial arts groups and ritual arts groups are closely linked, at least in the public mind. Such open, out-of-control public violence does however not fit the East Timorese conceptualizations of hegemonic masculinity. As de Silva (2005: 27) observes for Sinhala culture in Sri Lanka, hegemonic masculinity is linked to a 'sedateness of bearing which does not easily lend itself to violence . . . risking the body is often the idiom of minions and underlings who bloody their hands carrying out the project of hegemonic masculinity'. Similarly in Timor-Leste, gang, MAG and RAG members saw themselves as the manipulated tools of the *ema bo'ot*, and their public and private violence as a product of it. The issue of one's own agency, of consciously choosing whether to act violently or not, be it in relation to public or private violence, was almost always denied or glossed over (Myrttinen 2010: 161–2).

Conclusion

Timor-Leste society has suffered, and continues to suffer, from high levels of violence committed mostly by men, in both the public arena and the private sphere. This violence is often explained by referring to the country's violent past, socio-economic grievances and a patriarchal culture in which the hegemonic forms of masculinity condone the use of violence. While these can be seen as partial explanations, they often do not take into account that even men who have experienced the violence of conflict and occupation are socio-economically marginalized and uphold patriarchal values are not automatically violent in the public or private sphere.

What is seen as simply being an unchanging culture which is 'traditionally patriarchal' is actually the product of various historical and social processes and as such is in constant flux – as are the gender role identities of those partaking in the construction of the gendered social orders. The gendered structure of East Timorese society and the gender roles and expectations are amalgamations of the perceived traditional, the imported 'modernity' of the Indonesian occupation, media influences and the current international presence as well as the long-term societal impacts of colonization, occupation and resistance.

The enactments of masculinities, the gendered social order and the attitudes towards public and private violence are the products of immense societal changes which continue to redefine Timor-Leste. As the gender roles, expectations and hierarchies change, so do perceptions of the acceptability of the use of violence, especially by men, in the public and private spheres. As yet, however, violence continues to be seen ambiguously as both acceptable/understandable and deplorable, and as such as part of the repertoire of both hegemonic and protest masculinities, in as far as the terms are transferrable to Timor-Leste.

Notes

1 Most of the narrative in this chapter is based on fieldwork conducted between 2006 and 2010. The main focus of the research was with young urban men who were involved with gangs, martial arts groups (MAGs) and ritual arts groups (RAGs). I have used pseudonyms for all respondents associated with gangs, martial arts groups and ritual arts groups. With the exception of the opening section, which was a conversation held in English and given verbatim, all interviews were carried out in Indonesian and translated by the author. Stylistically and grammatically I tried to stay as true to the original as possible. All of the interviews quoted here were individual interviews.

2 For gender-based violence, I rely on the following definition by Ward (2002: 8–9): 'Gender-based violence is an umbrella term for any harm that is perpetrated against a person's will; that has a negative impact on the physical or psychological health, development, and identity of the person; and that is the result of gendered power inequities that exploit distinctions between males and females, among males, and among females.'

3 Following the 30 August 1999 referendum on East Timorese independence and the violent wave of destruction perpetrated by the Indonesian military and their proxy militias, the territory was placed under the interim administration of UNTAET until gaining full independence on 20 May 2002.

4 Reliable figures on the incidence of gender-based violence are, however, notoriously difficult to come by for a number of reasons. Official data are missing altogether for the years 2005 and 2006 due to the breakdown of a large part of the police services during the ensuing political crisis (on the crisis and collapse of the police force, see for example Lothe and Peake 2010; Scambary 2009; United Nations 2006). Where official figures do exist they are in part dependent on NGO reporting. For example, in a 2003 study of gender-based violence, a quarter of female respondents reported having been physically assaulted over the past twelve months (International Rescue Committee 2003).

5 Exact figures of casualties are not available, but for the approximately two years between April 2006 and February 2008 the public acts of violence led to the displacement of around 100,000 people and to the deaths of approximately 100 people (Scambary 2009).

6 A few days earlier a young man from the respondent's group had almost had his leg chopped off with a machete – in retaliation for a previous attack.

7 Similar contradictory attitudes are also evident in other reports on violence in Timor-Leste (cf. Grove *et al.* 2007; Hovde Bye 2005; Myrttinen 2010; Myrttinen *et al.* 2010b; Streicher 2008; UNFPA 2005).

8 One of the more comprehensive studies of traditional East Timorese warrior culture is de Castro (1864). Later colonial observers reproduced sections of this study in their own descriptions of colonial Timor.

9 A further factor may have been a reluctance to criticize a custom which is seen as being a central part of local culture.

10 It is important to note that cases of gender-based violence are not only to be found in poorer households. A prominent example of a member of the political elite is former

Minister of Health Sergio Lobo, who was indicted for repeated cases of domestic violence against his wife, only to be acquitted by the Dili District Court for 'cultural reasons' (Cristalis and Scott 2005: 98–9). Rumours also abound in Dili of senior members of the political elite committing acts of domestic violence and sexual harassment, though these cannot be fully substantiated.

11 The most comprehensive documentation of sexual violence during this period is found in the final report of the Commission for Reception, Truth and Reconciliation (CAVR 2005).

12 It should, however, be remembered that the East Timorese resistance also used non-violent means and, at the risk of stating the obvious, that not all East Timorese primarily resort to violence to address grievances.

13 For the gangs, martial arts groups and ritual arts groups, this involved re-enacting reinvented traditional roles of leaders (*liurai*), practitioners of traditional magic (*matan do'ok*) and warriors (*asuwain*) within the group structures. Traditions of ritual and black magic were invoked and mixed with influences from East Asian martial arts movies (Myrttinen 2010: 223–6 and 261–3).

References

Abdullah, S. and Myrttinen, H. (2009) '"Now they have guns, now they feel powerful": gender, small arms and violence in Timor-Leste', in V. Farr, H. Myrttinen and A. Schnabel (eds), *Sexed Pistols: Gender Perspectives on Small Arms and Light Weapons*, Tokyo: United Nations University Press, pp. 177–208.

Babo-Soares, D. (2004) '*Nahe biti*: the philosophy and process of grassroots reconciliation (and justice) in East Timor', *Asia Pacific Journal of Anthropology* 5(1): 15–33.

CAVR (2005) 'Chega! Relatório da Comissão de Acolhimento, Verdade e Reconcilição de Timor-Leste: Executive Summary', Dili: Comissão de Acolhimento, Verdade e Reconcilição de Timor-Leste.

Connell, R. W. (1995) *Masculinities*, Cambridge: Polity Press.

Cramer, C. (2006) *Civil War Is Not a Stupid Thing: Accounting for Violence in Developing Countries*, London: Hurst.

Cribb, R. (2002) 'From total people's defence to massacre: explaining Indonesian military violence in East Timor', in F. Colombijn and T. Lindblad (eds), *Roots of Violence in Indonesia*, Singapore: Institute of Southeast Asian Studies, pp. 227–42.

Cristalis, I. and Scott, C. (2005) *Independent Women: The Story of Women's Activism in East Timor*, London: Catholic Institute for International Relations.

De Castro, A. (1864) 'Une Rébellion à Timor en 1861', *Tijdschrift voor Indische Taal-, Land-en Volkenkunde* 13(4): 398–411.

De Silva, J. (2005) *Globalization, Terror & the Shaming of the Nation: Constructing Local Masculinities in a Sri Lankan Village*, Crewe: Trafford Publishers.

Dewhurst, S. (2008) '"Violence is just a part of our culture": explaining enduring violence in post-Independence Timor-Leste', unpublished MA thesis, University of York.

Dinnen, S. (2000) 'Violence and governance in Melanesia: an introduction', in S. Dinnen and A. Ley (eds), *Reflections on Violence in Melanesia*, Canberra: Hawkins Press, pp. 1–16.

Dolan, C. (2001) 'Collapsing masculinities and weak states: a case study of northern Uganda', unpublished draft on ACORD website, www.acord.org.uk/r-pubs-CollapsingMasculinities. doc (accessed 15 July 2010).

—— (2002) 'Collapsing masculinities and weak states: a case study of northern Uganda', in F. Cleaver (ed.), *Masculinities Matter! Men, Gender and Development*, London: Zed Books, pp. 57–83.

Fox, J. (2006) 'Ceremonies of reconciliation as prelude to violence in Suai', in C. Coppel (ed.), *Violent Conflicts in Indonesia: Analysis, Representation, Resolution*, London: Routledge, pp. 174–9.

Grove, N., Zen, K., Bucar, E., Moniz Cardoso Pereira, L., Fernandes, G. and Amaral, N. (2007) *Like Stepping Stones in the River: Youth Perspectives on the Crisis in Timor-Leste*, Dili: Plan Timor-Leste.

Hearn, J. (1998) *The Violences of Men*, London: Sage.

Hicks, D. (2004) *Tetum Ghosts and Kin: Fertility and Gender in East Timor*, Long Grove: Waveland Press.

Hill, H. (2002) *Stirrings of Nationalism, Fretilin 1974–1978: The Origins, Ideologies and Strategies of a Nationalist Movement*, Sydney: Otford Press.

Hovde Bye, H. (2005) 'The fight against domestic violence in East Timor: forgetting the perpetrators', unpublished MA thesis, University of Tromsø.

International Rescue Committee (2003) 'Prevalence of gender-based violence in Timor Leste', Research Report, Dili: IRC.

Isdal, P. and Råkil, M. (2002) 'Volden er mannens ansvar: behandling av mannlige voldsutøvere som tiltak mot konemishandling', in M. Råkil (ed.), *Menns vold mot kvinner-behandlingserfaringer og kunnskapsstatus*, Oslo: Universitetsforlaget, pp. 100–28.

Kostner, M. and Clark, S. (2007) 'Timor-Leste's youth in crisis: situational analysis and policy options', Dili: The World Bank.

Koyama, S. and Myrttinen, H. (2007) 'Unintended effects of peace operations on Timor-Leste from a gender perspective', in C. Aoi, C. de Coning and R. Thakur (eds), *Unintended Consequences of Peacekeeping Operations*, Tokyo: United Nations University Press, pp. 23–43.

Loch, A. (2007) *Haus, Handy & Halleluja: Psychosoziale Rekonstruktion in Osttimor; eine ethnopsychologische Studie zur postkonfliktuösen Dynamik im Spannungsfeld von Identität, Trauma, Kultur und Entwicklung*, Frankfurt am Main: IKO Verlag.

Lothe, E. and Peake, G. (2010) 'Addressing symptoms but not causes: stabilisation and humanitarian action in Timor-Leste', *Disasters* 34(3): 427–43.

Myrttinen, H. (2008) 'Sketching the militias: constructions of violent masculinity in the East Timorese conflict', in D. Zarkov (ed.), *Gender, Violent Conflict and Development*, New Delhi: Zubaan Publishers, pp. 180–204.

—— (2010) 'Histories of violence, states of denial: militias, martial arts and masculinity in Timor-Leste', unpublished PhD thesis, University of Kwazulu-Natal.

Myrttinen, H., Guterres, D. A. and Exposto, P. (2010a) 'Gender baseline study for Liquica District – RDPL II', Dili: Agencia Española de Cooperación Internacional para el Desarrollo.

Myrttinen, H., Schlicher, M. and Tschanz, M. (2010b) 'Häusliche Gewalt ist nicht Teil unserer Tradition!', *Suara*, 2/2010, Berlin: Watch Indonesia.

Niner, S. (2008) 'Major Alfredo Alves Reinado: cycles of torture, pain, violence', *Austral Policy Forum*, 08–02B, Melbourne: Nautilus Institute.

Scambary, J. (2009) 'Anatomy of a conflict: the 2006–7 violence in East Timor', *Conflict, Security & Development* 9(2): 265–88.

Scambary, J., da Gama, H. and Barreto, J. (2006) 'A survey of gangs and youth groups in Dili, Timor-Leste', Report commissioned by AusAid Timor-Leste, Dili.

Streicher, R. (2008) 'The construction of masculinities and violence: "youth gangs" in Dili, East Timor', unpublished MA thesis, Freie Universität Berlin.

TLAVA (2009) 'After the guns fall silent: sexual and gender-based violence in Timor Leste', Timor-Leste Armed Violence Assessment, Issue Brief Number 5/09, Dili: TLAVA.

Traube, E. (1986) *Cosmology and Social Life: Ritual Exchange among the Mambai of East Timor*, Chicago: University of Chicago Press.

UNFPA (2005) *Gender-based Violence in Timor-Leste: a Case Study*, New York: UNFPA.

United Nations (2006) 'Report of the United Nations Independent Special Commission of Inquiry for Timor-Leste', Geneva: United Nations.

UNTAET (2002) 'Gender equality programme: UNTAET Fact Sheet 11', Dili: United Nations Transitional Administration in East Timor.

Ward, J. (2002) 'If not now, when? Addressing gender-based violence in refugee, internally displaced, and post-conflict settings: a global overview', *The Reproductive Health Response in Conflict Consortium*, online document. Available at www.rhrc.org/resources/gbv/ifnotnow.html (accessed on 10 July 2010).

Wigglesworth, A. (2007) 'Young people in rural development', in D. Kingsbury and M. Leach (eds), *East Timor: Beyond Independence*, Victoria: Monash University.

7 The biggest cock

Territoriality, invulnerability and honour amongst Jakarta's gangsters

Ian Wilson

I followed Bang Cep on his nightly rounds of the food stalls surrounding the bus terminal. This was Bang Cep's territory and he walked with an exaggerated swaggering confidence. Vendors he approached for their daily 'protection' fee greeted him politely, but with their eyes betraying an apprehension bordering on fear. At Pak Dede's fried tofu stall Bang Cep loudly berated him for his lateness in paying his dues, slamming his ring-encrusted hand on the flimsy wooden stall to emphasize the point. Eyes downcast, Pak Dede muttered an apology, promising to pay in full, with interest, the next day. Perhaps owing to my presence, Bang Cep didn't follow up with the beatings and 'bitch slaps' he was infamous for. I returned to Pak Dede's *warung* later that evening for dinner. Asking him about the encounter with Bang Cep, he let out a pained sigh, 'Yeah, as you saw that's what we have to deal with. We don't like it, but what can we do? People say he is *kebal* (invulnerable), plus he is close to the police. Either way, if it weren't him it would be someone else. For now at least he is the biggest cock (*yang paling jago*) around here, and unless we want to get bashed we do what he says.'[1]

Extortion, intimidation and beatings at the hands of *jago*, literally a 'cock' or 'rooster', but colloquially a descriptor for a type of local strongman, constitute an unsavoury aspect of everyday life in urban and rural centres throughout Indonesia. As a social personage, the *jago* has been a recurring social and political actor in both recent and more distant history. Despite associations with criminality, in Indonesian popular culture the *jago* is also often romanticized as a champion of the people and an embodiment of the virile and virtuous man, a Hobsbawmian 'social bandit', whose acts of violence are motivated by a deep sense of justice, honour and order, one that transcends that of the law and the state. At the same time the *jago*, and his modern equivalent the *preman*, is frequently the object of public fear due to his brutality and to his role as sub-contracted instrument of state control during the New Order regime, and more recently as freelance entre-preneur in violence for political parties, religious groups and business interests. This points to the contradictory nature of *jago* masculinity, which is a sub-cultural identity encapsulating specific notions of honour, territoriality and violence, but also a reproduction and extension of the hegemonic institutionalized masculinity of state power, the embodiment of a reactionary and oppressive social and political order.

There is now a growing body of academic work examining the construction of masculine identity within various gangs and criminal sub-cultures (Bourgois 1995; Hagedorn 1998; Messerschmidt 1993). In his groundbreaking work on the relationship between masculinities and crime, Messerschmidt (1993: 85) contends that 'crime' by men is a form of social practice, a resource for 'doing' masculinity when other resources are unavailable. Acts of crime and violence, such as street gangs protecting their turf, are grounded in idealized notions of 'hegemonic masculinity', what Connell (2002) has defined as a normative type of masculinity occurring in specific times and places which demands conformity to certain characteristics. In the context of male gang culture these characteristics commonly include, amongst other things, frequent use of violence, volatile notions of honour, group solidarity and 'toughness'. With other hegemonic masculinities (such as those associated with formal employment or university education) inaccessible to them, socially marginal communities are, according to Schwendinger and Schwendinger, more likely to 'subscribe to violent macho ideals' (cited in Messerschmidt 1993: 110). Bourgois (1995), for example, has argued that the misogynist and violent sub-culture of El Barrio gangs in East Harlem emerged as a response to the de-industrialization of the urban economy and subsequent inability to reproduce rural based notions of masculinity, an outcome of structural conditions producing social and economic marginalization resulting in a life 'in search of respect'. However, unlike the marginal criminal crack-dealer gangs examined by Bourgois, *jago* have occupied a far more central position in national discourses regarding masculinity and power.

Based upon fieldwork in Jakarta, this chapter seeks to make a modest contribution to this body of work through an examination of *jago* masculinity. After examining some of the characteristics and elements constituting *jago* masculinity, the chapter looks at the historical background of the *jago* and their changing relationship with the colonial and post-colonial state. A central contention will be that *jago* masculinity, or *kejagoan*, is acted out through the securing, control and defence of territory (*lahan*), calculated acts of symbolic violence, and the 'fortifying' of the body through the acquisition of supernatural power.

As Blok (2001) has argued, concepts of male honour are closely related to processes of state formation. With the strengthening of the New Order state the *jago*'s volatile notion of masculine honour, expressed through control over resources and territory through the use of force, became a threat to the state's monopolization over violence, resulting in it being emasculated via violent purges before being reconstituted as an obedient auxiliary of state power (Blok 2001: 21). In so far as the ideas and practices of masculinity, violence and territorially bound notions of honour found within the world of *jago* have informed hegemonic notions of masculinity embodied and enforced by the state, in particular the authoritarian New Order regime, *jago* as social and political actors have been subject to both political incorporation as agents of state authority and social marginalization via stigmatization as a manifestation of deviant criminality. As this chapter suggests, the ability of the *jago* in particular periods and spaces to render the state at least temporarily redundant as a source of dispute settlement and the maintenance of social order has made them an embodiment of an ideal-type masculinity.

In contemporary Indonesia, the relaxing of state control combined with the politicization of localized ethnic and religious identities has seen a resurgence of *jago* identity as a form of 'protest masculinity' by those on the economic and social margins, defined by Poynting (2007: 511) as 'compensatory claims to imagined powerfulness on the part of marginalized young men experiencing social injury at their lack of real power, expressed through a hypermasculine style'. With the post-1998 collapse of centralized state power, assertions of place-based distinctiveness became the new grounds for 'securing rights to territories and resources' (Elmhirst 2001). Wee and Jayasuriya (2002: 3) have argued that in Southeast Asia shifts in centre–periphery relations and the 'rescaling' of the state, often brought about by policies of decentralization, have seen a trend towards localism and the ideology of 'indigenism', which they define as the 'articulation of rights that come from belonging to a place', in contestations over resources. Drawing from latent class and ethnic resentments over the perceived institutionalized inequalities of the New Order and the failure of the post-New Order state adequately to redress them, local cultural idioms of masculinity and power such as the *jago* have been revived and gained increasing currency amongst disenfranchised young men in Jakarta's slums and poor neighbourhoods. In the context of decentralized and democratized Jakarta, post-New Order *jago* identity has become an assertion of exclusivist rights over resources in a given place.

Turf, honour, potency and the economic use of violence

In the world of *jago* notions of masculinity, honour and virility are inextricably bound with those of territoriality and the body. A *jago*'s power, like that of the state, is in large part judged by the extent of his monopolization over *lahan* or turf. This *lahan* is defined in spatial terms: a street, neighbourhood, market or bus terminal, within which the *jago* gang controls the extraction of *pungli* or *jatah preman*, illegal fees imposed usually on the pretext of offering protection from 'criminals' and/or other *jago*. Often *jago* also profit from a range of other illicit activities such as prostitution, gambling and *miras* (illegally produced or distributed alcohol). The territorial power of *jago* and *preman* is established via a combination of symbolic displays of violence and machismo, the cultivation of belief in their magical power and physical skill in fighting, and, within the context of a strong state, their relationships and networks of patronage with those holding formal authority such as the police, the military and government officials. With these attributes, a *jago* will begin to accumulate followers and expand his territorial power.

Developing a 'name' (*punya nama*) is perhaps the single most valuable asset of a *jago*. The defence of one's honour (*harga diri*) and face (*muka*) from perceived insult is inextricably linked to this name and the ability to exert power over turf. This territorial power is exercised by extracting dues from residents and the imposition of a protection regime in which the *jago* takes on a role as self-appointed enforcer of social order. The importance of *punya nama* has especially become the case in the context of the increasingly competitive private security industry in Jakarta, where a reputation for getting things done and an ability to maintain 'order' is crucial to securing contracts in an increasingly competitive market. It is equally crucial, however, in other locations such as markets and bus terminals.[2] Without such a reputation a *jago* is no longer a *jago*, simply a wannabe or *sok jago*.

There are a number of volatile and violent traditions linked to the preservation of masculine face in Indonesia. On the island of Madura, for example, honour killing is institutionalized in the violent tradition of *carok*, a culturally sanctioned death duel or murder in retaliation to a loss of social face or slight upon a man's reputation.[3] *Jago* and *preman* are commonly defined by the alleged tendency to use violence as both a first and last resort. However, for those seeking to make a living as a *jago* the use of actual physical violence is highly calculated and measured, even in instances when 'face' is at stake. Violence is a tool of communication, useful in so far as it helps in the establishment and maintenance of a name and territory. Once this name is consolidated, the necessity to rely upon violence as the central means of maintaining territorial dominance diminishes significantly. As one gang leader in South Jakarta explained:

> Of course you need to kick arse sometimes, otherwise people might start to think you are too soft. If someone insults you in front of others you need to whack them then-and-there. If someone has an attitude they have to be made an example of. But the difference between a real *jago* like me and some snotty nosed thug (*preman ingusan*) is that I know exactly who, when and how to kick arse. There is an art to it. Petty thugs are too excessive and indiscriminate in their use of violence. People may fear them but they don't respect them. In the end this always results in their undoing.
>
> (Interview, Jakarta, 2005)

The 'art', then, of the *jago*'s violence is to find a balance between 'fear and respect', to balance the necessity of ruthlessly suppressing challenges to his territorial domain and upholding honour, while not going so far as to alienate himself from the immediate community, unnecessarily antagonize rivals or the police. The potential for violence is greater than the actual use of it. The established *jago* no longer has to rely upon constant displays of violence which, especially in the later stages of his career, bring with them increasing risks of physical defeat at the hands of younger stronger opponents. Some informants suggested that in certain circumstances inaction or inscrutableness is deliberately employed as a sign of power, drawing on the martial arts derived maxim that the more one 'knows' the more humble one becomes (*makin berisi makin berunduk*).

Successful *jago* are commonly surrounded by a cultivated mythos, usually revolving around embellished accounts of battles with rivals or daring escapades, similar to what the oral historian Rusyana (1996) has referred to as 'fight events' (*peristiwa pertarungan*), oral accounts of physical violence that over time and the oral process of dissemination undergo transformation and frequent elaboration, elevating the protagonist to the status of a culture hero. Circulation of these accounts of fighting prowess acts both to attract followers and to deter competitors, as in the following account from a Bandung *jago*:

> At the time the gang from Cimahi attacked our neighbourhood. They were trying to make a name for themselves and take control of our turf. When the trouble started Kang Aang came out into the streets, not to attack but to try and stop things getting worse by preventing the Cimahi crew from coming into our street. From Cimahi there were – I couldn't count how many as they mixed in with those shopping at the market. Fights started to break out between the Cimahi *crossboy* and locals.[4] Kang Aang was set upon by a group of the Cimahi gang. At that time I wasn't involved, though I had several machetes with me. I passed them to Kang Aang who proceeded to use them on his attackers. He did it with such ease and beauty . . . dak dak dak!! Within moments all of them were taken care of. How did he do it? I don't really know. It must have been because he had already been on a journey to seek knowledge (*merantau cari ilmu*) and had become a true master. I was deeply moved. At that moment I knew that I wanted to become his disciple.
>
> (Interview, Bandung, 1999)[5]

An interrelated element in the establishment of the *jago*'s name is fostering the belief that he possesses an array of magical and supernatural abilities. These can include a number of fantastic skills such as invisibility, the ability to be in two places at once, mind-reading and hypnotism. The most important of these however is *ilmu kebal*, physical invulnerability from weapons such as knives and firearms. The skin of the *jago* is believed to be literally impenetrable, closing and sealing the boundaries between self and others. With *kebal* the body of the *jago* is transformed into an immutable site of power. The accumulations and transmission of *ilmu kebal* are a distinct political currency linked to the political authority derived from the perceived ability to control threats and disruptions to the social order, and to resist corrupting hegemonic forces.

Traditionally the pursuit of *kebal* was achieved after a long period of tutelage and ascetic trials under the direction of a recognized master or *guru*. In Banten, for example, a region with a long history of *jago*, known locally as *jawara*, *kebal* aspirants are required to undergo a variety of ascetic exercises such as extended periods of fasting, meditation and retreats to places believed to be infused with supernatural power such as caves or forests. They are also expected to maintain a state of ritual purity, abstaining from activities and relationships believed to sap spiritual and supernatural power such as the consumption of alcohol, gambling and excessive fraternization with women, including sexual intercourse.[6] Social interaction with women outside of one's immediate family is in this context considered a temptation, a distraction from the task of accumulating power and a potential drain on reservoirs of supernatural strength. In some *jago* traditions, such as the *warok* strongmen of Ponorogo in East Java, prohibitions on association with women has developed into something resembling a misogynist cult, with *warok* taking on a young male assistant in lieu of a wife (known as a *gemblak*) who is chosen because of his effeminate appearance and in some instances identifies as transgendered (Wilson 1999).

The close proximity to rival *jago*, the constant tensions over turf boundaries and the general volatility that ensues in crowded urban centres such as Jakarta have resulted in the emergence of 'fast-track' methods for achieving *kebal* such as is described in the following field notes extract:

> I asked Pak Edi, a gang leader in South Jakarta, about his reputation for being *kebal*. He recounted that as a young man he sought tutelage under a number of guru. After extensive periods of fasting, sensory deprivation and prayer he achieved physical invulnerability to sharp weapons and bullets. The downside of this, he explained, was the requirement for a continued state of 'purity' that demanded abstinence from alcohol and womanizing. Due to his own fondness for both, he set about developing a more 'scientific' method which by-passed the need for moral piety. 'The benefit of this method', he stated, 'is that you don't have to be 100% "clean". Even if you have been drinking, gambling or playing with women it still works!' After asking him to explain further, he suggested that I undergo the 'procedure': 'Who knows what might happen in the streets, especially as a foreigner, you need to be protected. Anyway, all real men (*laki sejati*) must possess *ilmu*.' I agreed, and was immediately alarmed as his assistant produced a strange tangle of electric cords and metal plates. Plugging the cord into an electric socket, I was instructed to place my foot on top of one of the plates. Pak Edi held the other plate under his own foot, and immediately his leg began to quiver from the electric current. Tentatively I placed my other foot down on the tile floor earthing the current, sending my limbs into mild spasms as electricity pulsed through my body. While trying to resist the natural urge to let go, Pak Edi firmly grasped my forearms, closed his eyes and muttered a jumbled mantra, a mixture of Arabic, Indonesian and Javanese. With the soles of my foot feeling as if they were about to combust, Pak Edi finally let go and I jerked back into my chair, my arms quivering uncontrollably for several minutes. 'That's it!' he said with a smile. 'Now you don't have to worry about being stabbed!'
>
> (Field notes, Jakarta, August 2007)

Such devices bypass the need for lengthy apprenticeship or ritual asceticism, providing a method that sits easily with the conditions of the urban *jago*, as well as severing the link between the maintenance of supernatural power and forms of religious piety and moral prohibitions at odds with the more hedonistic lifestyles. In his early 50s, with a portly frame and a persistent smoker's cough, Pak Edi was respected and feared by younger and more physically fit local men, who commonly referred to him as *sakti* (possessing supernatural power) and *berwibawa* (charismatic/authoritative). With this unique 'modern' method for achieving *ilmu* he began drawing followers from outside of his neighbourhood in Kebayoran Lama, some from as far away as Surabaya. His reputation for *ilmu* helped him to expand his gang's network with a minimum of conflict, to include branches in other parts of the city. Like most *jago* leaders, Pak Edi rejects any suggestion that his group is criminal, insisting that the security and protection they provide to the community from thieves, pickpockets and drug dealers is a valuable service for which they receive modest 'voluntary contributions' from local businesses and vendors. Further consolidating his reputation as *kebal* was his close relationship to the local military commander, who has allowed his group to set up a command post in the grounds of his office. Closeness to the authorities in a sense makes one invulnerable from the law and official sanction, and also makes one a mediator between them and the local community.

Armed with *kebal*, the body of the *jago* is fortified against the dangers of external attack, transforming the physical body into a virtual fortress. As one mantra for obtaining invulnerability from Banten intones, 'my head is black rock, my forehead is coral' (*hulu aing batu wulung, tarang aing batu karang*) (Interview, Serang, 1999).[7] According to Onghokham (2003: 115), invulnerability constituted a notion of power in Java counter to those of political elites that was in theory accessible to any prepared to undergo the rigours and trials involved in obtaining it. Hence invulnerability cults were treated with suspicion by both the colonial and the post-colonial state, in particular the New Order, which saw them as potential sites of informal power challenging that of the state.

In times of social and political upheaval where fears emerge regarding the maintaining of personal and social boundaries, belief in invulnerability practices continues to resurface as a last line of bodily defence against social breakdown. For example during the tumultuous period of social and political upheaval surrounding the resignation of Suharto in 1998, popular tabloids were full of advertisements for 'instant *kebal*' through mantras sent via SMS, as well as short-course 'executive packages' run by *jago* seeking to profit from uncertainty. That *kebal* has frequently proved to be a completely ineffective form of physical protection has not diminished faith in its efficiency.[8] Perhaps the enduring power of belief in invulnerability is related less to its practical uses than it is to its centrality to notions of the empowered, potent and masculine body embodied in the figure of the *jago*.

The *jago* in Indonesian history

The *jago* of pre-colonial times was said to possess physical prowess in the form of skills in martial arts (usually the indigenous martial art of *pencak silat*), and was believed to have access to a swag of magical and supernatural abilities, such as invulnerability and invisibility, which he achieved through tutelage under a *guru* or extended periods of ascetic retreat and deprivations. A mix of personality cult and criminal gang, groups of *jago* came and went in accord with the fortunes of their leader. Their social capital came in their embodiment of cultural ideals regarding physical and spiritual potency and intimate knowledge of local conditions, whilst their political capital was found in their proficiency in the use of violent force and ability to mediate between peasant society and higher authorities. While it was common practice for *jago* to raid and plunder neighbouring villages, they were often fiercely protective of their own community and for this reason commanded loyalty and respect, albeit underpinned by fear of the consequences if this loyalty was betrayed. *Jago* were both protector and exploiter of the local community. According to Schulte Nordholt (2002: 40), this resulted in the general population reaching the pessimistic conclusion that 'power and crime were synonymous'.

The initial arrival and gradual expansion of Dutch colonial rule did little to disturb the *jago*. It was only in the nineteenth century with the advent of a bureaucratically organized government that their role shifted (Schulte Nordholt 1991: 77). Rather than being the object of repression, *jago* became, according to Schulte Nordholt and van Till (1999: 68), 'an integral part of the colonial power structure', resulting from a 'stagnating process of state-formation'. The colonial administration was based in Batavia, but had little effective reach into the rural heartland of Java. In order to consolidate their rule the Dutch established a parallel indirect government headed by indigenous officials to govern Java (Sutherland 1979). At the village level, monopoly over force was the preserve of the *jago*, hence any effort to establish 'order' by necessity had to involve their incorporation. Without an adequate police force to support them and with shallow roots in the area in which they were assigned, indigenous officials effectively became clients of the *jago* to gain some degree of control over the countryside. As long as the appearance of 'order' was maintained, *jago* could continue with their banditry, theft and extortion unhindered. This incorporation, however, was not without disruptions. The volatile nature of *jago* bands saw them frequently emerge as sites of rebellion, such as in the Banten peasant uprising in 1888 (Kartodirdjo 1966).

In colonial Batavia *jago* also emerged as powerful figures constituting what Cribb (1991: 15) has described as 'a network standing outside of the hierarchy of government authority, antagonistic to it yet not overtly hostile'. In a society based almost entirely upon trade where most of the indigenous population worked as labourers, bosses and their entourage of overseers and *jago* enforcers were central to the economic life of the city. As Cribb (1991) has stated, the world of labour control blended with the criminal underworld but was also a necessary component of social control. It was in this context that the Dutch-derived term *vrijman* (free man), later to become *preman*, entered common parlance to describe a new breed of urban *jago*, a freelance entrepreneur in force who 'is not in the service of the Dutch East India Company, but has permission to be in the Indies, and carries out trade for the sake of the VOC' (Ryter 1998: 50–1).[9] In a society bound by law, the *vrijman* existed in a legal and conceptual grey zone, operating both inside and outside of the law. For this reason they were admired as one of few groups with autonomy from colonial power, but also feared owing to their intimate connections with it. Despite, or perhaps because of, their central role in the colonial power structure, the banditry of *jago* figures such as Si Pitung, Sakam and Si Gantang saw them exalted as heroes of the people (Schulte Nordholt and van Till 1999). With little organized opposition to colonial rule, even the self-serving criminal predation of *jago* was quickly mythologized as Robin Hood-like social banditry, conducted by 'men of honour' on behalf of the poor.[10] As Blok (2001:21–2) has argued, the social bandit myth is an expression of a dormant protest element; 'the myth of the bandit represents a craving for a different society, a more human world in which people are justly dealt with and in which there is no suffering'.

Owing to their skill in coercion and localized territorial power, violent entrepreneurs such as the *jago* have been essential allies for the consolidation of political power, while embodying the contradictions that come with their informal status. In times of crisis of hegemony where political and social institutions are in flux such as during the revolution for Indonesian independence, *jago* sought to benefit from breakdowns in social order, and aligned themselves ideologically with dominant or emergent social and political forces in order to facilitate integration within them and to consolidate and legitimate rackets. Conversely, colonial and post-colonial elites and aspirants for power have sought to harness the localized territorial power of *jago* in the establishment and maintenance of particular configurations of social order and the suppression of forces that threaten to disrupt them. *Jago* bands and militias were at the forefront of resistance to Dutch attempts to reinstate colonial rule after World War II and many later formed parts of the embryonic Indonesian armed forces.

In post-Independence Jakarta, in lieu of a functioning police force, *jago* operated as an informal source of authority and enforcers of a particular kind of personalized social order that revolved around the maintenance of a local territorial protection regime. This order was inextricably bound to notions of 'honour' and face rather than any normative notion of the rule of law. If a 'crime' was committed in the territory of a *jago* gang without their consent, or someone else began demanding protection dues (*jatah*), it was considered an insult to their territorially defined sense of honour, a challenge to their authority. In such instances the *jago* would seek out the perpetrator and regain face by fighting or publicly humiliating them. According to one former Jakarta *jago* from the 1950s, they were *palang dede*, or 'pillars of the community' (Interview with Irawan, Jakarta, 2005). So long as one *jago* gang remained dominant and the presence of the state remained minimal, this 'order' was maintained. In instances where there was a contestation between *jago* over territory, this was often resolved via rule-bound 'duels', as described in the following account from a Bandung *jago* of the 1960s:

> There was no ganging up or hitting from behind (*main keroyok*) like nowadays but it was a duel till the matter was resolved. The duellists would take an oath, sealed with blood that whatever the outcome there would be no revenge on the part of their family or followers. The fights were one-on-one until one party either conceded defeat or didn't get up. *Ilmu* played a big part, and we all carried *jimat* (talismans) that had been 'filled' with magical power. If the police showed up we would say that we were just doing *silat* training, and usually that's all they wanted to know. If they asked more questions we answered them with packets of cigarettes and some cash. We may have been rough around the edges, but we had a strict code of ethics, and that's why we got respect.
>
> (Interview, Bandung, 1999)

From *kriminal* to regime assistant

During the late 1960s and early 1970s many of the gangs and youth organizations that had been mobilized by the military as part of the bloody anti-communist purges which led to General Suharto's appointment as President in 1967 had now returned to their neighbourhoods, and a combination of a lack of work, absence of opportunities and boredom meant that many continued with the criminal activities which had sustained them. Like the militias in the revolution, they had profited handsomely from the disorder by extracting, stealing and appropriating property from putative communists. In times of upheaval the law of the *jago* prevailed. However, a new 'order' had now come into effect and different laws applied.

In response to a perceived increase in gang-related violence, in 1972 General Soemitro, the Commander of the Command for the Restoration of Security and Public Order (Kopkamtib), ordered that 'groups and gangs of teenagers' be disbanded.[11] As Ryter (1998) has argued, the disbandment of gangs was intended not to eliminate crime per se, but to lay the way for reconstituting and regularizing the gangs in a manner that was conducive to strengthening state power. During the 1970s, a host of youth organizations and state-sanctioned martial arts groups emerged throughout the country that provided a new institutionalized framework for *jago* and gangs. Many, however, continued to operate outside of these institutionalized spaces.

The increasing territorial power of *jago* and gangster networks that emerged in the late 1970s, mainly in the context of their role as private security providers, created anxiety within the regime, who feared they could evolve into a structural threat, such as the Yakuza in Japan or the Sicilian Mafia. The response from the New Order state was unequivocal. Starting in 1982, a wave of terror swept the *jago* world with the appearance of thousands of mutilated bodies in streets throughout the country. Known as the 'Mysterious Shootings' (*Penembakan Misterius*, or Petrus), according to the media the victims were *gali*, an acronym of 'gangs of wild kids', many of whom were identified and targeted because of their tattoos, a sign that the state argued was an indelible mark of abject criminality. A new term entered state rhetoric and the popular media replacing that of *jago*, namely *kriminal* (Bertrand 2004). In contrast to the troublesome but honour-bound identity of the *jago*, the *kriminal* was defined as amoral, brutal and beyond redemption or use. *Jago* masculinity, in so far as it involved the assertion of territorial power outside of state control, was recast as 'evil' even though it was the state itself, in the arbitrary brutality of Petrus, that went beyond the bounds of conventional morality. Barker (1998) argues that a central purpose of the Petrus killings and *kriminal* discourse was the deterritorialization of the power of the *jago* and its reterritorialization within the organs of the state. The New Order sought to recuperate the local authority of the *jago*, Suharto reasserting his authority as the 'king of the *jago*', literally Indonesia's biggest cock.

In the wake of Petrus, *jago* were increasingly institutionalized within state-created bodies such as the youth organization Pemuda Pancasila or as uniform-wearing *Satpam* security guards. In this way the territorially based masculinity of the *jago* was first criminalized via its recasting as *kriminalitas* and then reintegrated in the hegemonic masculinity of the state, reframed as obedient and loyal youth (*pemuda*) within a nationalistic and militaristic patriarchy. The rationale of groups such as Pemuda Pancasila was almost uniformly the same, to provide 'guidance' (*pembinaan*) and help direct the 'aspirations' of members towards the twin state goals of 'unity' (read 'security') and development. This fundamentally affected the performance of *jago* masculinity. The *jago* was one who was in part defined by his freedom from social obligation, including that of adhering to the law. However, *jago* were now bound by the necessity to make themselves useful to those in formal power and appear publicly obedient to state ideology. This undermined their own autonomy as well as changing their relationship to the local community, the territory over which they ruled. The new relationship has been characterized as one of *bekking* (backing), whereby *jago* could operate their localized protection regimes so long as the spoils were divided with state officials and they agreed to act as state agents, conducting surveillance and intimidation on the state's behalf. Without state backing a *jago* could not expect to last long. Duels over turf and honour were a threat to 'stability', with territorial divisions determined by patronage from bureaucrats and the military. A reputation for *kebal* also ran the risk of claims of subversion. Invulnerability for the *jago* now meant obedience to the state.

The increasing confluence post-Petrus between state power and that of the *jago* was reflected in the shift in the popular meaning of the word *preman*. Up until the mid-1980s '*berpakaian preman*' referred to a policeman or soldier out of uniform, an officer wearing his civvies. Gradually, reflecting the corrupt and repressive nature of the regime, it took on connotations of criminality and violence. By the 1990s *preman* was synonymous with street thugs, gangsters and an extensive network of rackets run by criminals but coordinated by the state. Unlike the *jago*, the *preman* was a figure who was publicly reviled, embodying the intersection between criminal violence and state power that increasingly came to characterize public perceptions of the New Order. As Ryter (2005: 1) has said, 'If politicians and soldiers were revealed as essentially *preman*, so *preman* were revealed as politicians and soldiers.' Towards the end of the New Order this situation reached the extent that 'the thin line between criminals and soldiers (and politicians) seemed to vanish' (ibid.).

Democratization, *jago* identity and 'protest masculinity'

During the New Order the power of the *jago*, while in part determined by the cultivation of a local reputation, was ultimately dependent upon favourable relationships with the official embodiments of masculine power: police, military and political elites. In the post-New Order environment, however, the fragmentation of previous patronage networks and the unravelling of the New Order criminal state, together with the new dynamics of decentralized, democratized Indonesia, have created numerous spaces in which *jago* and *preman* masculinities can thrive. Freed from dependence upon backing or sanction by state elites, many groups have grown substantially, with branches, franchises and networks of supporters spread throughout the city. The model of the territorial *jago* gang, which protects its constituents while preying upon its neighbours or those labelled 'outsiders', has translated well in the context of intensified local political struggles for control over turf and resources that have characterized post-1998 Jakarta. As Kusno (2004: 2384) has argued, the 'loosening' of political power at the centre has resulted in a proliferation of non-state groups in Jakarta formed around identities that 'are all linked by a sense that the nation-state no longer commands any power to protect and rule, or, at best, the political elites only safeguard their own interests'. The state is in this sense perceived as weak and emasculated, no longer able to perform its protective function, provide for the welfare of its citizens or suppress challenges to its authority. In this context, the localized territorial monopoly over violence of the *jago* gang, freed from the constraints of acquiescence to state authorities imposed during the New Order, can and has evolved into more pervasive and alternate forms of social organization and identity.

Neighbourhoods and streets throughout Jakarta are peppered with an array of flags and banners from these various groups that are used colourfully to demarcate the complex divisions of territory, mini *jago* regimes in the midst of urban sprawl. This informal bureaucratization of territorial control, which in part reproduces elements of the territorial command system employed by the military during the New Order, has had the effect of diminishing the importance placed upon rites of initiation, individual displays of potency and personal mythologies of prowess. In what amounts to a kind of *jago* franchise system, local gangs or groups of individual youths affiliate with a larger group that already has an established name, allowing them as it were to ride on the tails of others' success. As one member of the Jakarta ethnic gang the Betawi Brotherhood Forum (Forum Betawi Rempug, FBR) explained, 'That's life in Jakarta, if you don't step on someone you will get stepped on. On my own I'll just end up a victim, but together we are a force to be reckoned with' (Interview with FBR member, Jakarta, 2008). Group identity and violent solidarity are believed to compensate for perceived powerlessness in a city where social standing is determined by wealth and connections to political and social elites. After making an oath of loyalty to the group and its leaders the member has access to a network of solidarity and back-up when faced with rivals, competitors or resistance from locals to the imposition of protection.[12] Like the methods for instant *kebal*, this has become a relatively easy way of establishing and monopolizing a local territorial domain, a space in which *jago* 'honour' and masculinity can be performed. The group name also acts as a deterrent to sanction from local police, who are generally reluctant to confront those groups with a large membership (Interview with police officer, Jakarta, 2007).

In the interests of protecting the name and honour of the group and expanding its territory, members will deploy to fight, and many will die, alongside fellow members whom they have never met.[13] One senior member described the importance of preparedness to 'sacrifice at all costs' in the interests of upholding the group name:

> If someone tries to take over an area under our control, insults us, or harasses our members then we have to retaliate with full force. If we lose a few in the

process, well that's the price you pay in war. If we don't we lose face by looking weak, especially if the group is smaller than us or doesn't have much of a name.
(Interview with senior FBR member, Jakarta, 2008)

Refusal or reluctance to participate in honour-related violence results in immediate expulsion from the group. One member who declined to take part in a reprisal on a smaller rival, after they had killed two FBR members who were part of a failed turf takeover bid, not only was expelled as a 'traitor' but also was subject to constant verbal and physical harassment in his neighbourhood from other FBR members, ultimately forcing him to move.[14] Despite his reputation as a seasoned fighter, according to those meting out the abuse his decision revealed him as 'a coward', 'weak' and 'not one of us'. His argument, that the FBR had unnecessarily provoked the incident and that it was best to avoid further unnecessary loss of life, was considered irrelevant. Adherence to group solidarity overrides rational considerations.

These groups also provide a ready-made *jago* identity that has a strong appeal to the thousands of socially and economically marginal young males occupying Jakarta slums and poor neighbourhoods. This identity has emerged as a protest at the weakness of the post-New Order state and its failure to improve social conditions, but has also intersected with broader discourses regarding decentralization and demands for greater autonomy at the local level. Some such as the FBR invoke the imagery of the legendary Si Pitung, the 'Robin Hood' bandit of colonial Batavia popularized in a series of movie adaptations screened in the 1970s. Drawing also upon belief in *ilmu kebal*, FBR's former leader Fadloli el Muhir fostered an image of himself as a modern-day Si Pitung who had come to restore the dignity of the Betawi, Jakarta's socially and economically marginal indigenous population and, in the words of one senior member, 'take back the land, rights and dignity that had been stolen by the New Order' (Interviews with FBR member, Jakarta, 2005).[15] As if to confirm the New Order state's suspicions towards *kebal* as a potential site of informal power challenging its own, after reports circulated in East Jakarta in 2002 that Fadloli had remained unscathed after being attacked by a machete-wielding mob of Madurese gangsters, arch rivals of the FBR, hundreds of men flocked from surrounding *kampung* to join the group.

No longer petty crooks, the urban poor, delinquents or what popular media often describes as 'society's trash', FBR members are now, according to the group's leadership, part of a lineage of 'noble bandits' and 'warriors' fighting injustice, providing disempowered men, in the words of Standing, with 'a sense of extreme masculinity, importance and even order' (Standing 2006: 122). The carrying of machetes in public by FBR members, a criminal offence in Jakarta, is perceived by members not as a deliberate provocation or threat but as the fulfilment of ideal-type Betawi masculinity, an attempt to re-establish an imagined order in which the *kampung* is protected and ruled by an honourable *jago*. This is embodied in the group's slogan of 'let's become *jawara* in our own neighbourhood'.[16] The group's stronghold areas are in some of the poorest parts of Jakarta, where police presence and government services are minimal, and membership is made up overwhelmingly from the unemployed or informal-sector workers, lacking social status or regular income. *Jago* masculinity is not only a means by which to command respect and fear and to make a living, but an assertion of autonomy and sovereignty from the state.

Similar constructions of idealized hypermasculinity as a response to social and economic marginalization can be seen in Islamist vigilante groups such as the Defenders of Islam Front (Front Pembela Islam, FPI), whose uniform of white robes and turbans is adapted from popular representations of Javanese Islamic warrior saints such as Sunan Kalijaga as well as informed by globalized images of the jihadist. The FPI's frequent violent attacks on bars, clubs and other places of 'sin' are fuelled by this desire for 'respect', an aggressive reassertion of an idealized gendered identity by men and youths occupying Jakarta's social and economic margins.[17] Vigilantism, which as Abrahams (1998) has argued flourishes on the frontiers of the state, is an alternate form of social ordering whose existence is driven not just by a functional or regulatory vacuum of state power, but also by anomie and negative attitudes towards the state. When gaps emerge between institutional and moral orders, as is common in times of rapid social and political change, violent vigilantism often emerges. In Jakarta vigilantism has emerged as a reaction to the perceived failure of the post-New Order state to provide physical safety and economic security, hence the need for citizens to fight crime and establish 'order' themselves. The result has been what Barker (2007: 93) describes as 'a patchwork of jurisdictions, each with its own "morality"'. Rejecting the state's label of their own violence as criminal, the FPI vigilantes represent themselves as a virtuous vanguard protecting society from moral and social decay. As one FPI member explained, 'If they [the state] won't uphold decency and order then we will' (Interview with FPI member, Jakarta, 2007). On a more fundamental level, however, the attraction of vigilante groups such as the FPI for many young men is their focus upon 'action'. Through acts of violence orchestrated for maximum media exposure, what Al-Zastrouw (2006: 81) has described as 'symbolic radicalism', FPI members very publicly perform their idealized notion of a violent masculine order. Through these invented traditions of urban social order, which are largely authoritarian and anti-democratic in character, *jago* have reified themselves as a pillar of a territorially defined community, an honourable and masculine protector rather than a predator. As one gang member explained:

> We are from the street, so we know who the trouble-makers are. Most of them we know personally. We say to them, ok if you want to make trouble here you will have to deal with us. Respect us or else! Usually that's enough as they are scared of us. But if they still go and make trouble we wipe them out. Like this one pickpocket, we went round to his house and bashed him good!
> (Interview, Jakarta, 2007)

Conclusion

Jago masculinity as a product of structural conditions, most significantly degrees of state formation and penetration, and cultural ideals regarding masculine power has persisted throughout Indonesian colonial and post-colonial history. The authoritarian New Order regime sought to appropriate the local territorial power and potency of the *jago*, institutionalizing them as loyal and obedient youth within the hegemonic patriarchal masculinity of the state. At the local level, however, notions of spiritual power, face and violence integral to *jago* identity continued to inform men regarding the construction of honour and face. While the state could not completely co-opt *jago* it did create the conditions whereby a *jago*'s strength was ultimately dependent upon their networks of political patronage; a metaphorical 'leash' that could be pulled when necessary. With the breaking of this leash post-1998, *jago* masculinity has aggressively reasserted itself in forms moulded by the dynamics of a decentralized social and political environment: a contradictory identity that is at once reactionary and hegemonic, reproducing a kind of local-level authoritarianism not dissimilar to that of the New Order state.

In their reformulation of the concept of hegemonic masculinity, Connell and Messerschmidt (2005: 849–51) recognize the importance of geographic location in constructions of hegemonic masculinity that are embedded in specific social environments. In the local face-to-face arenas of the urban *kampung* and streets of Jakarta *jago* masculinity frequently remains hegemonic. The *jago* is king of his domain, even if that domain is limited to a neighbourhood, bus terminal or street corner. Outside of this domain, however, the position of *jago* can quickly shift from hegemonic to socially marginal. In middle-class neighbourhoods, housing estates or up-market malls, for example, *jago* are considered a criminal menace, 'trash' to be removed and excluded via police raids and private security patrols. With economic disparity making the hegemonic masculinities of these spaces of affluence, consumerism and global mobility more inaccessible than ever to working-class men (a reality constantly emphasized via billboard advertising, under the literal shadow of which *kampung* dwellers live), *jago* masculinity is a means for demanding respect and achieving social status with a minimum of resources. It is in this respect also protest masculinity, an assertion of autonomy and a claim to power for those marginalized and disenfranchised by Indonesia's democratic transition and the opening up of markets.

Notes

1 Pseudonyms are used throughout this chapter.
2 Since 1998 there have been an increasing number of instances of street vendors attacking and even killing *preman* considered to be excessive in their use of violence or extraction of protection dues.
3 For a detailed study of the *carok* traditions in Madura see Wiyata (2002).
4 The term *crossboy* originated in the 1950s, referring to fans of James Dean and Elvis Presley. During the 1960s and 1970s it became synonymous with troublesome youths and petty criminals (Ryter 1998: 59).
5 The informant became the first *anak buah* of Kang Aang. Known in the neighbourhood as the 'human experiment', he bares with pride numerous scars and twitches caused by damaged nerves resulting from his apprenticeship. Another witness to the attack said that the Cimahi gang were the children of military and that was why they had the nerve to attack an area well known for its tough *jago*.

6 Amongst practitioners of *kebal* it is almost universally asserted that women are not able to achieve invulnerability. Many notions of *kebal* trace origins back to yogic ideas of *sakti* that were believed to be achieved by the accumulation and storing of semen (see Wilson 1999).

7 Other mantras are drawn from the Quran, such as *Sura al-Besi* which is believed to make the aspirant's body as hard and impenetrable as iron. The possession of a mantra is often a closely guarded secret, a kind of 'secret weapon'. Like Achilles' heel, the revealing of the source of a *jago*'s supernatural power opens the possibility that a rival may find the key for neutralizing it.

8 At several displays of *ilmu kebal* which I attended, practitioners sustained serious injuries after being hit over the head with bottles or cut with machetes. Quickly whisked out of view of those in attendance, the explanation given for the failure of *ilmu* to protect them was that they had 'not been concentrating' or that there had been a 'spiritual disturbance' caused by a rival group.

9 A similar meaning is attached to *warok*, the strongmen from Ponorogo, East Java, a term which is said to originate from the Javanese words *uwal* and *rokan* meaning to be free from forced labour (Wilson 1999).

10 In her study of Si Pitung, van Till (1995) discovered that there was little evidence to suggest that Pitung was 'pro-peasant' and in fact his gang often targeted the weakest and poorest.

11 Established by Suharto in 1965, Kopkamtib was granted almost limitless extra-judicial powers to maintain 'security', unburdened by the constraints of law or accountability.

12 Groups such as the FBR conduct fortnightly mass *bai'at* oath-taking ceremonies, where as many as two or three hundred are inducted as new members at the same time.

13 The FBR has 'hotline' numbers for a fast-response team made up of seasoned fighters who will deploy when called. For example, after a FBR banner was torn down by locals in a neighbourhood in Cilandak, several hundred FBR members from throughout Jakarta descended on the area to restore this apparent slight on the honour of the group, beating up those involved. In another instance, when a member had his car repossessed due to late loan repayments, the manager of the credit company administering the loan was forcibly abducted and only released after agreeing to give a repayment extension.

14 Those dishing out the abuse believed that the recipient's humiliation was further compounded by the fact that he was forced to move to the home of his wife's parents, something they claimed a real *jago* 'would never do' (Interviews with FBR members, Jakarta, 2008).

15 Within the space of six months after the incident, the membership of the FBR increased from several hundred to over 15,000. The FBR currently has around 300,000 members spread throughout the greater Jakarta region.

16 The slogan plays upon the dual meaning of *jawara* (*juara*) as 'champion' and also as a common name in Jakarta and West Java for a *jago* strongman. These imaginings recall Lombard's description of the narrative of *cerita silat*, a popular form of martial arts literature dating back to the 1920s: 'In silat stories there is no center of power, no state, no police, and no uniform justice. People busy with everyday activities in their village or neighborhood are constantly made fools of by bandits from surrounding areas that control the mountains and forest, and who also, from time to time, loot and extort. In this pessimistic world fortunately there appear a number of chosen people – the *pendekar* – who live a nomadic and solitary lifestyle, are blessed by the ascetic practices they perform, and possess supernatural powers. Endowed with silat techniques, they are able to temporarily break the grip of evil power and provide security to the oppressed' (Lombard 1996: 332–3).

17 In interviews with FPI members, a constant reason cited for involvement in the group was a desire to be respected within their community as 'holy warriors'. Many came from backgrounds as petty criminals or the long-term unemployed and joined the group as a form of redemption for past 'sins'.

References

Abrahams, R. (1998) *Vigilant Citizens: Vigilantism and the State*, Cambridge: Polity Press.

Al-Zastrouw, N. (2006) *Gerakan Islam Simbolik: Politik Kepentingan FPI*, Yogyakarta: LKiS.

Barker, J. (1998) '"State of fear": controlling the criminal contagion in Suharto's New Order', *Indonesia* 66 (October) 7–42.

—— (2007) 'Vigilante and the state', in T. Day (ed.), *Identifying with Freedom: Indonesia after Suharto*, New York: Berghahn Books, pp. 87–93.

Bertrand, R. (2004) 'Behave like enraged lions: civil militias, the army and the criminalization of politics in Indonesia', *Global Crime* 6(3–4): 325–44.

Blok, A. (2000) 'The enigma of senseless violence', in J. Abbink, and G. Aijmer (eds), *Meanings of Violence: A Cross Cultural Perspective*, Oxford: Berg, pp. 23–38.

—— (2001) *Honour and Violence*, Cambridge: Polity Press.

Bourgois, P. (1995) *In Search of Respect: Selling Crack in El Barrio*, Cambridge: Cambridge University Press.

Connell, R. W. (2002) *Gender*, Cambridge: Polity Press.

Connell, R. W. and Messerschmidt, J. W. (2005) 'Hegemonic masculinity: rethinking the concept', *Gender and Society* 19(6): 829–59.

Cribb, R. (1991) *Gangsters and Revolutionaries: The Jakarta People's Militia and the Indonesian Revolution,* Sydney: Allen and Unwin.

Elmhirst, R. (2001) 'Resource struggles and the politics of place in North Lampung, Indonesia', *Singapore Journal of Tropical Geography* 21(3): 284–306.

Hagedorn, J. M. (1998) 'Frat boys, bossmen, studs, and gentlemen: a typology of gang masculinities', in L. Bower (ed.), *Masculinities and Violence*, Thousand Oaks, CA: Sage, pp. 152–67.

Kartodirdjo, S. (1966) *The Peasants' Revolt of Banten in 1888: Its Conditions, Course and Sequel*, The Hague: Martinus Nijhoff.

Kusno, A. (2004) 'Whither nationalist urbanism? Public life in Governor Sutiyoso's Jakarta', *Urban Studies* 41(12): 2377–94.

Lombard, D. (1996) *Nusa Jawa: Silang Budaya, Kajian Sejarah Budaya, Bagian II: Jaringan Asia*, Jakarta: Gramedia Pustaka Utama.

Messerschmidt, J. W. (1993) *Masculinities and Crime: Critique and Reconceptualization of Theory*, Lanham, MD: Rowman & Littlefield.

Onghokham (2003) *The Thugs, the Curtain Thief, and the Sugar Lord: Power, Politics, and Culture in Colonial Java*, Jakarta: Metafor.

Poynting, S. (2007) 'Protest masculinities', in M. Flood, J. Kegan, J. Gardiner, B. Pease and K. Pringle (eds), *Encyclopedia on Men and Masculinities*, London: Routledge, pp. 511–12.

Rusyana, Y. (1996) *Tuturan tentang Pencak Silat dalam Tradisi Lisan Sunda*, Jakarta: Yayasan Obor Indonesia.

Ryter, L. (1998) 'Pemuda Pancasila: the last loyalist free men of Suharto's order?', *Indonesia* 66: 45–73.

—— (2005) 'Reformasi gangsters', *Inside Indonesia* 82 (April–June), available at: http://insideindonesia.org/content/view/177/29/ (accessed 14 November 2010).

Schulte Nordholt, H. (1991) 'The *jago* in the shadow: crime and "order" in the colonial state in Java', *RIMA* 25(1): 74–91.

—— (2002) 'A genealogy of violence', in F. Colombijn and J. T. Lindblad (eds), *Roots of Violence in Indonesia: Contemporary Violence in Historical Perspective*, Leiden: KITLV Press, pp. 33–60.

Schulte Nordholt, H. and van Till, M. (1999) 'Colonial criminals in Java, 1870–1910', in V. Rafael, *Figures of Criminality in Indonesia, the Philippines and Colonial Vietnam*, Ithaca, NY: Southeast Asia Program, Cornell University, pp. 47–69.

Standing, Andre (2006) *Organised Crime: A Study from the Cape Flats*, Pretoria: Institute of Security Studies.

Sutherland, H. (1979) *The Making of a Bureaucratic Elite: The Colonial Transformation of the Javanese Piyayi*, Kuala Lumpur: Heinemann Educational Books.

Van Till, M. (1995) 'In search of Si Pitung: the history of an Indonesian legend', *Bijdragen KITLV* 152(3): 462–81.

Wee, V. and Jayasuriya, K. (2002) 'New geographies and temporalities of power: exploring the new fault lines of Southeast Asia', City University of Hong Kong Working Paper Series No. 30.

Wilson, I. (1999) 'Reog Ponorogo: spirituality, sexuality and power in a Javanese performance tradition', *Intersections: Gender and Sexuality in Asia and the Pacific* 2 (May), available at: http://intersections.anu.edu.au/issue2/Warok.html (accessed 14 November 2010).

Wiyata, L. (2002) *Carok: Konflik, Kekerasan dan Harga Diri orang Madura*, Yogyakarta: LKIS.

8   Defending the nation

Malay men's experience of National Service in Singapore

Lenore Lyons and Michele Ford

The military is both a site for the reproduction of hegemonic masculinity and a space within which dominant forms of masculinity are institutionalized. Often described as 'the last bastion of masculinity' (Sasson-Levy 2008: 297), the military is also one of the main institutions involved in the construction and expression of citizenship. Military service has the potential to link masculinity with the political concerns of the state because the ultimate test of 'manliness' is the willingness to die defending one's country (Higate and Hopton 2005: 436). The figure of the warrior is thus a key symbol of both masculinity and nationalism: embodying the characteristics of physical strength, endurance and aggression, the soldier is the epitome of the patriotic citizen. At the same time, however – as in civilian life – the military is characterized by a hierarchical order based on occupation, gender, sexuality, class and ethnicity that reflects and reproduces social stratification. This hierarchy of belonging and loyalty produces multiple, dynamic and contradictory military masculinities that defy a straightforward correlation between hegemonic masculinity and nationalism.

Sasson-Levy (2003: 320) argues that 'studying the military from the standpoint of its marginalized groups reveals not only counter hegemonic conceptions of masculinity and state, but also exposes tense, often contradictory and clashing relationships among the military, the state and masculinity'. In the post-9/11 world, the figure of the Muslim man has been positioned very publicly in many countries as a subversive masculine form with the potential to threaten global and national security. Singapore is no exception. Negative representations of Muslim men and boys are muted by a state-sponsored programme of multiracialism that admonishes Singaporeans to avoid statements which may lead to racial or religious tension. However, these claims for multicultural harmony stand in stark contrast to the state's own public statements about the status of Muslim men. Since Independence in 1965, the ruling People's Action Party (PAP) has continually expressed its concern that religion and ethnicity, as primordial markers of identity, could act as powerful sites of fissure within the body politic if conflict were to erupt between Chinese-dominated Singapore and its Muslim neighbours. These anxieties about Muslim men's loyalty in a situation of regional conflict have shaped Singapore's national security model, which is built on a system of compulsory national service for all Singaporean male citizens and permanent residents but which actively discriminates against Malay Muslims by limiting their access to leadership and combat roles (Bedlington 1981; Peled 1998; Huxley 2001). Yet while this systemic discrimination against Singaporean Muslim national servicemen (NSmen) is an 'open secret' (Huxley 2001), little attention has been paid to the ways in which Malay Muslim soldiers understand and perform their masculinity in a context where their loyalty to the nation-state is constantly questioned.

This chapter explores the relationship between military service, masculinity and citizenship as experienced by Malay men in Singapore, drawing on data collected in interviews with men from middle- and lower-income backgrounds over a four-year period to 2008.[1] For the purposes of this discussion, we concentrate primarily on our encounters with professionals aged between 25 and 34 who completed National Service in the 1990s and early 2000s. Although these men represent less than 8 per cent of the Malay population of Singapore (Leow 2001), their status as potential community leaders makes them a significant group in the eyes of the state. They have experienced rapid social mobility and the majority espouse a distinctly middle-class outlook in terms of their aspirations and perceptions of their social and economic opportunities. At the same time, it is not possible to describe their class position solely in these terms since this label obscures the complex nature of inter-generational differences in education and income levels within Singaporean house-holds. The parents of these men generally work in the service and manufacturing sectors – and while they have benefited from higher levels of education (including access to university), and subsequently higher wages, like most Singaporeans they continue to live in the family home until they are married.

Focusing on these ethnically marginal middle-income professional men, we explore the nexus between class and ethnicity in the construction of Malay mas-culinities and in the juxtaposition of those masculinities against hegemonic middle-class Chinese norms. Our interest is in the ways in which these masculinities are linked, contested and mutually constructed through the ambiguities and contra-dictions that surround Malay men's simultaneous inclusion and marginalization within the military. Following Hirose and Pih (2010: 192), who argue that 'the boundaries between hegemonic and marginalized forms of masculinity are much more interactive than oppositional', we examine the ways in which subaltern Malay masculinity supports and contests hegemonic Chinese masculinity. Our analysis demonstrates that while National Service is a site for the construction of a subaltern masculinity built on physical strength and on personal and national loyalty under-pinned by religious faith, it is also a space in which hegemonic Chinese masculinity is reinforced and institutionalized.

Hegemonic and subaltern masculinities

The PAP's management of ethnicity and potential ethnic conflict in Singapore has been dependent upon a strategy which privileges selected 'race' identities and not others.[2] Diversity within racial categories is downplayed, and shared cultural and linguistic heritages within racial groups are emphasized.[3] Singapore's economic success since Independence is routinely attributed to aspects of Chinese culture –

often presented under the rubric of 'Asian values' – such as thrift, hard work, desire for education and filial piety. Minority races are expected to maintain a sense of racial/cultural separateness, as expressed through markers such as diet, dress, religion and language, while jettisoning those aspects of culture that do not meet the desired attributes of the national identity (Barr and Low 2005). This cultural deficit is used to explain the Malay community's continuing economic and social disadvantage when compared to other racial groups (Rahim 1998; Kamaludeen Bin Mohamed Nasir 2007).

Amongst the Malay men with whom we spoke, race and religion are constant markers of identity. Malayness and Malay masculinity are invoked against a hegemonic model of Chinese masculinity, in which Malay men frequently compare and contrast themselves with the politically, culturally and numerically dominant Chinese. The men were keenly aware of the stereotypes that circulate about them – they are said to lack intellectual capacity and motivation; to be better with their hands (a reference to physical and technical skills) and less capable in academic areas; and to be 'laid back' and not interested in hard work.[4] These stereotypes reflect a widely held view in the non-Malay community that Malay men lack the key cultural and biological attributes that would enable them to succeed in the modern Singaporean economy (Li 1998).[5] The men in our study saw laziness as a defining stereotype of Malayness while simultaneously painting a picture of all Chinese as hardworking, high achievers. The men felt that, despite their academic and professional success, they did not measure up to the idealized vision of Chinese masculinity. As Zulfikar commented when asked to talk about Chinese masculinity, 'I guess Chinese guys are like normal. Stereotypical. What we expect of normal society.' Zulfikar and others we spoke to nonetheless strove to achieve what they described as a 'normal' way of 'being a man'.

Studies of Chinese masculinity in other cultural contexts emphasize patriarchal paternalism and the hierarchal relationships implicit in Confucianism as central defining features of Chinese men's gendered identities (cf. Louie and Edwards 1994; Louie 2002; Hibbins 2005). Louie (2002) argues that traditional discourses of Chinese masculinity are premised on the concept of *wen-wu*, literally translated as 'cultural attainment – martial valour'. As a basic organizing principle of Chinese masculinity, *wen-wu* favours a balance between intellectual and cultural achievements, and physical and martial strength.[6] Although it is important to recognize that Chineseness varies in different historical, geographical, political and cultural contexts, the *wen-wu* framework is useful in articulating traditional and historical elements of Chinese heterosexual masculinity. In Singapore, as elsewhere, it is the object of intense political and cultural contestation (Ang and Stratton 1995; Ang 2001). At the same time, idealized (Chinese) Singaporean masculinity is actively promoted via a state-driven model of paternalism built on traditional Chinese patriarchy (Heng and Devan 1995) and *wen-wu* has been reinterpreted through iterations of PAP-led educational policy which at various times has sought to promote Confucianism within schools (Chong 2002).

As Barrett's study of the US Navy has shown, constructions of masculinity do not only vary across job specialties, but these 'versions of masculinity are relationally constructed through associations of difference' (Barrett 1996: 129). Until recently, military service in Singapore was deemed incompatible with the dominant model of Chinese masculinity with its emphasis on entrepreneurship and academic achievement. Malay men see their long history of involvement in the Singapore Armed Forces (SAF) as a sign of superior masculinity, arguing that, in comparison to the Chinese, Malay men are physically capable, technically minded, and loyal to the nation, but this view is not shared by the dominant Chinese community or those within the senior echelons of the military and government. Outside their own community, Malay men's masculinity is the subject of denigration and their religion is a source of state concern about possible internal security threats to the nation – concerns which constantly mediate Malay men's experiences of National Service.

Between nation and Islam

Enloe (1980) has noted that, in ethnically divided societies, the elite shapes its armed forces according to an 'ethnic state security map' which distinguishes between loyal ethnic groups, which occupy combat roles, and a range of others who either are placed at the margins of the military or are excluded from service. While the armed forces promote images of universalism and egalitarianism, this ethnic state security map works to 'reproduce ethnic stratification, not to break it down' (Smooha cited in Sasson-Levy 2003: 324). States may use and manipulate ethnicity to maintain authority and preserve the existing political order, with the result that ethnic identities are enhanced rather than diminished. For example, in Israel, Ashkenazi men are placed at the centre of the army and the Mizrachim at the periphery; Druze and Bedouin soldiers are located at the margins of the military while Palestinian citizens of Israel (both Muslim and Christian) are not enlisted (Sasson-Levy 2003: 324). In this way, differential recruitment policies help to define hegemonic and subordinate masculinities.

Similar 'race'-based policies have applied in independent Singapore. During the colonial period, Malays were actively recruited into the military and police and these professions provided an important means of upward mobility for the Malay community (Bedlington 1981: 261). As a result, Malays constituted the backbone of the armed forces in the 1960s. But by 1970 – with well-publicized exceptions – the recruitment of Malays into the SAF had ceased as a result of concerns about the dangers associated with Malay 'over-representation'. Tense relations with Malaysia, race riots in both Singapore and Malaysia in the 1960s, and Confrontation with Indonesia contributed to the PAP's fear that a Malay-dominated military would be unwilling to defend Singapore in the event of conflict in the region (Bedlington 1981; Peled 1998). Although the policy was not made public, Malays in the armed forces and police were only too aware of it, as they found their career prospects cut short by removal from combat positions to logistic and ceremonial roles, offers of early retirement and reduced promotional prospects, especially after 1975 when Mandarin replaced English as the language of senior commanders, and promotion to rank of captain and above required a pass in a Mandarin exam (Peled 1998: 113).

A phased reintegration of Malays began as the threat from Malaysia diminished and the numbers of Chinese soldiers increased, and between 1977 and 1985 the proportion of Malays in the SAF doubled. However, restrictions remained in place on Malay recruitment into critical areas such as the Air Force and the Commando Unit until the 1990s (Peled 1998; Huxley 2001). Today, Malays are under-represented – and Chinese over-represented – among higher-ranking officers of the SAF (Huxley 2001). As Ali observed, 'If you go to the more "secret" units such as armour, all are Chinese. If you compare the Guards and the Commandos, or the STAR unit [an elite crack unit] in Police, there are no Malays.' Similarly Farid, who served in the medical corps, commented:

> With respect to social strata, there is a problem, because in the navy, in the 1970s, it is full of Malays. There is more Malays and Indians than *manjens* [Tamil, lit. yellow, i.e. Chinese]. But now there are so many Chinese in navy. You don't even see one Malay. Even Air Force.

According to Walsh (2007: 273), SAF intelligence even uses Malay-speaking Chinese as analysts to read Malay newspapers rather than take advantage of the language skills of ethnic Malay soldiers.

Representatives of the state openly attribute this marginalization of Malay men in the SAF to outstanding questions about their loyalty to the Singapore nation. As then Minister for Trade and Industry, and later Prime Minister, Lee Hsien Loong asserted in a public debate over the issue of Malay recruitment in February 1987, 'greater participation in the SAF will follow greater integration, not the other way round' (Lee cited in Siddique 1989: 570). This is so, Lee stated, because:

> If there is a conflict, if the SAF is called upon to defend the homeland, we don't want to put any of our soldiers in a difficult position where his emotions for the nation may come in conflict with his emotions for his religion because these are two very strong fundamentals, and if they were not compatible, then they will be two very strong destructive forces in opposite directions . . . We don't want to put anybody in that position where he feels he is not fighting a just cause, and perhaps worse, maybe his side is not the right side.
> (*Straits Times*, 23 February 1987, cited in Peled 1998: 123)

Discrimination against Malay men serving in the armed forces is also evident during National Service, which is compulsory for all male citizens and permanent residents of Singapore upon reaching the age of 16½ years.[7] Elite (Chinese) men are deliberately streamed into the more prestigious and more operationally important sectors of the armed forces. According to Walsh (2007: 276), scholarship winners (who are almost entirely Chinese) are quarantined into special scholar platoons, and thus have very little to do with Malay soldiers even during basic training.[8] In short, in what Peled (1998: 106) describes as the 'Trojan horse' dilemma, the state demands military service of its male citizens yet harbours security concerns and mistrust of the loyalty of Malay Muslims bearing arms.

Traditionally cloaked in questions of defending sovereign boundaries against regional aggressors, the motivations for structural discrimination against Malays have more recently become complicated by concerns about terrorism. These concerns, while not documented in the scholarly literature on the SAF, were apparent in our interviews. Iqbal, who was completing his National Service at the time of the 9/11 attacks in the US, recounted an event in his camp when an email was circulated stipulating that Malays were not to be part of a bioterrorism exercise. As a result, no Malays were allowed to do guard duty. When the NSmen concerned questioned their superiors as to why they were excluded from these kinds of activities, they were asked whether Islam came first in their lives, implicitly justifying the directive in terms of their potential complicity in threats posed by terrorists. Fadi reported a similar story from his time in the medical corps, when the first Malay doctor to receive a SAF scholarship to study at the National University of Singapore was reportedly asked to leave a strategic meeting during exercises on bioterrorism on account of his religion.

Our informants' responses suggest that anti-Malay policies in the defence sector are not always legible to perpetrators, or even sometimes to targets. Mustafa, who served in logistics, explained that things had changed from the time of his uncle, whom he argued *had* faced ethnically based discrimination. As evidence, he pointed to Malay and Indian officers in his own unit. Others justified the predominance of Chinese in senior positions and in strategic divisions in terms of their numerical strength and personal superiority. When asked whether Malays could serve as fighter pilots, Hakim, who served in a support unit, observed:

> There's no fighter pilots because . . . uh . . . I don't know . . . I guess maybe there's no one who is eligible, who can really go in, because you got to fight for one Malay, and you got to fight against three or four Chinese, if you follow the ratio, so you got to be the best of the best.

Hafiz, who served in a logistics unit, also invoked the language of meritocracy:

> The Chinese are able to produce more talent. I feel that they are more studious. In terms of getting a degree, it's a necessity for them but it's not a priority for us now. Not at the same level as the Chinese. In terms of fishing out talent, Chinese families have more.

Echoing these sentiments, Mustafa explained away the disproportionate number of Malays in his logistics unit as being simply a matter of preference, saying that 'A lot of Malays want to go there. It's an easier life than in commando or combat.'

However, many others we spoke to were highly aware of the structural origins of these patterns, and what they said about them as Muslim men.[9] Jamal told the story of a friend who wanted to serve in an A-class vehicle unit that dealt with tanks and other combat vehicles. When he approached his superior, Jamal's friend was told in no uncertain terms that he could not be posted there because he was Malay.[10] In another example, Khairul, who served in the police force, described the experiences of a relative who had been placed in officer cadet school during the first nine months of his National Service, only later to be posted to 'some logistics place' as a storeman. Khairul believed that the redeployment was directly related to his relative's religion.

In some cases, streaming presents itself in terms of the inability of the SAF to meet Malay and other Muslims' religious requirements. Malik, who served in the medical corps, asserted:

> There [are] definite indicators of discrimination in terms of where they can go. That is quite clear. I was wrongly sent to some unit to conduct training but I was not supposed to be there. They said it was a mistake by my officer. And I realized that they did not have a Muslim cookhouse. So that in itself is a clear indication in terms of the structure – Muslims are not allowed to be in certain areas in the army.

In a similar story, Zainul described the experiences of a friend who was told that he could not sign up for the navy because pork was served.

Within mixed units, differential positioning of Malay NSmen on religious grounds is generally made material through personalized and apparently incidental restrictions on religious practice. However, restrictions on religious practice are also justified by official documents and handbooks. For example, the *BMT: NS Guidebook for Muslims* (Ariff *et al.* 2000) promises that Muslim NSmen will be able to practise their religion during all stages of National Service, including Basic Military Training. However, it also warns that it is important that they not be overly rigid in their practice, so as not to interfere with the operational requirements of their unit (Ariff *et al.* 2000: 13). As one informant commented, the opportunity to observe the rituals of Islam were 'not seen as constant', but rather as something to be squeezed in if there is time during National Service. It is not surprising, then, that most informants agreed that time for prayers or the demands of fasting were not taken seriously. As Malik remarked, citing the tendency to schedule outdoor training on Fridays, which made it impossible to attend Friday prayers, 'It's not something they consider when they plan the training programme.'

Some informants felt that there was some room for discretion with regard to accommodation of their religious practices, particularly where their superiors were also Muslim. Fadi, for instance, told a rare tale of an entire unit that was required to begin their day earlier to accommodate fasting soldiers – a concession he attributed to the fact the higher ranks of the unit were dominated by Malay Muslims. However, others were adamant that it made little or no difference whether or not a unit commander was Muslim. For example, Hafiz commented that:

> CO [commanding officer] for my Company is a Malay Muslim . . . My mum did ask him about how they are all going to treat the Muslims in the fasting month. He said, 'Don't worry. We will take care of them.' This was his actual words. And then, this is the actual life experience. And then on the next day, they had this thing where they assess our fitness lah – the IPPT [Individual

Physical Proficiency Test]. During the running, I asked one of the staff sergeants whether those who are fasting can be excused and he said, 'That's your own problem.' In the end we still have to run. Because of that, all of us went to the same hard training, [and] some of us had to break the fast.

There was also a perception that Muslim servicemen who had made it into senior positions in the regular army were least likely to identify with other Muslims. Farid stated:

I divide the senior officers and the mid-level ones. The senior officers are more with the non-Muslims. They try not to be aware, that kind of thing. They try to pretend that issues with the Muslims are not really outstanding. They let the junior officers take charge. In BMTC [Basic Military Training Centre], in my experience, usually, because I was there in Tekong [an offshore island where the BMTC is located] for two and a half years, the junior officers like the warrant are always being the *imam* [leader for congregation prayers] and all that, but the senior officers they never go, or don't join us or they take a secret launch to the mainland to the mosque. They never call us. They do their own things. It's because they don't want to be seen as pro-Muslim senior officers. That's what I feel lah. They try to distance themselves from the others for religion. It's always the junior officers who take charge, during fasting month and all that. The major and colonel happily break fast at home.

In this example, Farid points to the ways in which senior Malay officers deliberately choose to downplay or hide their religiosity in order to avoid the perception that they are 'too Muslim' and thus a potential threat. Through their actions, officers encourage other Muslim soldieries to put the SAF, and the nation, above Islam. The message to Malay NSmen is clear: it is effectively impossible to be a 'good citizen soldier' and a 'good Muslim' at the same time. In this way, the expression and practice of religious faith becomes an option that, if exercised by an NSman, demonstrates his lack of commitment to protecting the nation. As Malik told us:

I would say because people do not understand the importance of it. They think it's an option while NS is a duty to the nation which you have to fulfil so you have to forgo your duties as a Muslim. It's not the right perception.

Such experiences stand in direct contrast to government rhetoric which claims that National Service is a means to break down the barriers between Singapore's different 'races'. Indeed, the state explicitly positions compulsory military service as a builder both of nationalist sentiment and of community solidarity. As Singapore's first Minister of Defence Goh Keng Swee said in 1967, 'Nothing creates loyalty and national consciousness more speedily and thoroughly than participation in defense and membership of the armed forces' (cited in Peled 1998: 97–8). A closely related objective of National Service is the building of a strong multiracial society through shared experience:

Apart from fulfilling military requirements, National Service has the wider object of integrating a multiracial, multilingual and multireligious community committed to Singapore and to the well-being of its citizens. It follows the direction begun in schools, where an integrated community is educated together, where young people of all races study together, to forge a national identity.

(*Singapore Year Book 1971*: 104)

Da Cunha (1999: 461) argues that for this reason universal conscription is a 'leveller' of social class in Singapore. This claim is also made in other contexts. For example, in her study of young men who performed compulsory military service in Finland, Lahelma (2005) asserts that conscripts saw the military as a positive force in breaking down class barriers because it brought men of all backgrounds and education levels together in one place and dressed them in uniforms that eliminated the clear markers of class difference. Similarly, a number of our informants felt that the chance to live and work at such close quarters with fellow Singaporeans of different ethnic backgrounds was a positive levelling experience. As Jamal commented:

I was brought up by father that the Chinese will always say, 'Oh the Malays, they are no good.' So I went into BMT [Basic Military Training] with that sort of mentality . . . [I thought that] if I were to cock up something, they [would] react to me in that way because I am Malay. It's an unhealthy way of thinking lah. Whenever I feel that things are being unfairly towards me, I thought it's because of skin colour and stuff like that but then I realize at the end that [they] treated me the same as the others. They are actually helping me. There is no difference.[11]

However, while close contact may break down prejudice for some NSmen, for others it simply reinforces it. Farid remarked:

I don't like the marginalization in the army. I am the only guy who spoke Malay in the whole platoon. There was once an M16 course. The *manjen* sergeant when he is talking, he talked Chinese all the way. So I don't understand a shit thing lah. So I told him, 'Sergeant, can you repeat in English so that I don't have to shoot your head?' I told him that if I don't know how to handle the weapon and I shoot your head, you cannot blame me what – how the hell am I supposed to know [how to use it safely] if you speak Chinese. And at that time was fasting month, so I was pissed off lah. You know my fuse was also very short at the time. What the hell is happening? This is not a China army or the PLA [Chinese People's Liberation Army].

While not discounting the value of positive experiences, it is clear, then, that an overly strong emphasis on the levelling effects of compulsory military service ignores the ways in which class, ethnicity and religion converge to reinforce normative constructions of difference. As Musa told us, while National Service 'does bring races together' in a unit where they are 'all brothers', it also 'makes Malays more aware of what oppression is'.

Marginality is a constant trope in the narratives that the men in this study construct about what it means to 'be a Malay' in contemporary Singapore. Discrimination against Malay NSmen further serves to highlight the men's marginal position within the SAF and wider Singaporean society. And yet, while the men we spoke to were able to provide detailed descriptions of discrimination, they were uncomfortable describing these as instances of racism or prejudice. They are caught in a double bind – they want to challenge the veracity of the many negative stereotypes used to label the Malay community, and particularly Malay men, but they also rely on those same stereotypes to secure their own 'exceptional' status in relation to education and employment opportunities, as well as achievements, within the Malay community. National Service allows them to fulfil the dominant ideals of masculinity in political and cultural terms by performing the role of model citizens and 'manly' men. However, their access to dominant models of masculinity is always fragile and premised on their ability to internalize and demonstrate the 'superior' values of hard work and leadership. Streaming of Malay men into less demanding, less sensitive or less prestigious areas of the military hinders their ability to achieve and perform these traits. When they fail to measure up to their own – and Singaporean society's – definition of a 'normal man', they attribute their personal failings to an inherited cultural inferiority. In this way, military service both undercuts and supports Malay men's marginality.

A subaltern masculinity based on strength and loyalty

Thus far, we have focused on the interplay between marginal Malay and hegemonic Chinese masculinities and demonstrated the ways in which hegemonic power relations are structured within the SAF. We have observed how in the context of the SAF, and of National Service in particular, hegemony is achieved through domination and coercion, as well as through Malay men's inscription of inferiority. This discussion, however, only reveals one aspect of the ways in which hegemony is achieved. Our research reveals that National Service is also a site for the construction of a positive model of Malay manliness which seeks to challenge the dominance of hegemonic Chinese masculinity. This subaltern masculinity, while relying on Chinese masculinity as its counterpoint, inverts the negative marker of religion to assert Malay men's superior morality and loyalty.

In her study of Bolivia, Gill (1997: 527–8) claims that military service is 'the most important prerequisite' for the development of a successful subaltern manhood among indigenous men because it serves as a 'counterpoint to the degradation experienced from more dominant males and an economic system that assigns them to the least desirable occupations'. In the process, she argues, it provides a channel through which they can 'contest more genteel notions of masculinity associated with upper-class males who avoid military service altogether'. In Singapore, compulsory military service has provided both Chinese and Malay men with an avenue for the expression of a dominant and socially valued form of manhood. But, significantly, it is also a site for the construction of a subaltern Malay masculinity linked to the positively ascribed values of respect, responsibility and loyalty, as well as to dominant ideas of manliness based on masculine strength, leadership and survival.

Many of the men we spoke to described the process of actively constructing a subaltern model of military masculinity based on racially based notions of technical ability, physical attributes and morality which stood in opposition to dominant representations of Chinese hegemonic masculinity. The foundation of this subaltern masculinity is the expression of pride in having served in the SAF.[12] Hakim observed:

> It has been instilled that when you serve NS you are doing something for the country. So you have to do it for two years, don't know how many hours, of blood and sweat, and tears you see. Something to be respected about – it brings respect.

For those who have it, this feeling may be reinforced by a sense of achievement during the period of service itself. Samad, who served in a support unit, felt that he had grown up: 'I got mature. How to be independent. To respect people. To respect whatever. Moral values. You experience a lot of things you can't do out of army.' For him and many others, National Service was integrally tied to the achievement of manhood, which in this context means 'growing up' (learning to respect others) and 'being respected' (demonstrating one's commitment to the nation). This sense of pride and achievement was contrasted to the supposed widespread attitude amongst Chinese NSmen that military service was a waste of time, an attitude that many Malay NSmen read as an indicator of moral lack and a failure to achieve manhood on the part of Chinese men.

For many of our informants, the physical changes that accompanied their period of National Service were a visible marker of their achievement of manhood. They described their pride and enjoyment in the physical dimensions of life in the military, nominating Basic Military Training (BMT) as the best part of National Service. While physically gruelling, it was a time when, as Ramli, who served in logistics, commented, 'They try to bring the best in you lah. In terms of physical and mental lah.' For some, BMT offered an opportunity to shine. Reflecting on his first day in the BMTC on Tekong Island, Hafiz recalled:

> I feel so pumped up. I am learning combat. Training to be a soldier. On the first day, I seem to have a head start. When I was in secondary school, I was in NPCC [National Police Cadet Corps]. So all the basic drills I know. In terms of the weapons, some of my friends were in NCC [National Cadet Corps], so they know the M16. I learn from them. On the first day, I was pumped up. So ready to go and try my best. It's like I feel I was on top of my game. I could easily see that some of my sergeants were trying to steer me to take some form of leadership.

For others, exposure to potential physical danger was a highlight. Farid valued the skills of survival and tough decision-making, while for Talib, it was taking responsibility and having the sense of a job well done, especially during guard duty when he was trusted to handle live bullets. Reflecting on his experience of basic training, Hakim also recalled his feelings of manliness and personal worth when he realized the seriousness of his mission:

> The first time I hold the rifle, you know the M16. Wow this thing can kill, you know, it's not play thing. Yeah . . . it's . . . even there's one part, we actually go to a guard night. I realize that guard is a real, serious type you see. Anything can happen. That kind of feeling is like, wow, so it's a term that you need to be better for your country . . . I mean it's for your life, for your country, for your people . . . so that's the macho part. With all this team of people, like-minded people together, coming to do something together, to achieve something together. For me that's the goodness part, the macho part you see.[13]

Macho-ness was also expressed in the men's physicality, and they described their feelings of pride in their physical appearance during the BMT phase. They felt that their bodies were stronger and fitter, and that, in particular, they looked good in uniform. For example, Ghani, who was completing National Service in the police force at the time he was interviewed, said:

> For police it's a white shirt, the belt, black pants, shoes. It's cool. Really cool! And the belt is quite cool lah. I quite like it. Can you imagine if you come out and wear the uniform, it's quite cool lah. It's not green or brown. People's perception of police officer walking around – they say 'ah, police officer'. You have a gun and everything, so it's really cool lah.

During National Service, physical strength and aptitude are a strong source of pride for Malays, who contrast their own innate abilities with those of weaker, more scholarly Chinese.[14] When asked if the reason there was only one Malay pilot in the SAF was because there were no suitable candidates, Samad responded, 'I don't think that is the reason lah. I mean you need sharp minds. Sharp eyes. If the air force is technical, then I bet the Malays will be in the technician side [laughs].' In his comment, Samad suggests not only that active discrimination against Malays is the reason for the lack of fighter pilots, but that Malays would make better pilots because of their technical superiority to the Chinese. Hafiz also took up this theme:

> I don't mean to be ah, like a racist lah, but Malay man is much more macho than those geeky Chinese people. [laughs] I think in terms of flying and operating vehicles, it's clear that Malays are much more better. In terms of driving, we are better. We are more technically sound. If we are given a chance to fly a jet, we would do a hell of a job.

Our informants not only describe Chinese men as physically weak but – in a direct counter to the government's reading of Islam as a threat to national identity – question Chinese Singaporeans' ultimate loyalty to the nation. For Farid and Hakim, job mobility is a sign of disloyalty to an employer and 'materialism', by which they mean a focus on amassing wealth, is a character trait that demonstrates the Chinese community's lack of allegiance to the nation. As Hakim commented:

> The Malays are the most loyal men. Yeah! Generally speaking lah. The Chinese they are not loyal you see . . . they have good bargain elsewhere, they go somewhere else! For Malays you work from age 20 to 60, you would still work as a postman. Not the Chinese! So you see who are [more] loyal.

Farid echoed this point, claiming that the minorities are more loyal because 'Generally, the Chinese is a materialistic culture . . . [In times of war] they run away lah. The minorities stay. Chinese will run. Simple as that.'

An important part of this project is the men's efforts to read their religious affiliation against the grain. As Fadi commented:

> Popular media portray Islam as a negative vehicle driving people to do bad things. They are afraid that these Muslims will turn radical and learn about sensitive secrets. But if they really study the religion, they should know that Islam teaches you to be loyal to your country. So if people who are actually religious, they will be loyal to your country cos the religion teaches you to be loyal to your country, defend your country. If he follows the religion properly, he will be loyal. It's just the mindset.

Malay men's superior loyalty was also said to be expressed in their attitudes towards sex and in their relationships with their wives and girlfriends, which they felt meant that they were more morally upright than their Chinese counterparts. Our informants claimed that sexual promiscuity was openly accepted, and in some cases encouraged by their Chinese and Indian officers, who would use sexually explicit language and show the men sexual photographs on their mobile phones. In some cases, officers would even taunt the men with descriptions of their planned sex acts with the NSmen's girlfriends. It was also commonly expected that NSmen would use the services of sex workers when deployed overseas. Farid explained, for example, that it is Standard Operating Procedure for condoms to be handed out to troops going overseas for training or service. One of his jobs as a medic in the Tekong Medical Centre was to pack 20–30 kilograms of condoms whenever a group headed to Thailand or Taiwan for training. He claimed that it was a fact of life in the camps that was never discussed despite the fact that the boxes always returned empty.

Some of our informants connected Chinese soldiers' sexual practices directly with the question of loyalty. Picking up on the theme of overseas service, Fadi commented:

> They actually give out three packets to those going overseas. I am thinking, if you promote these kinds of things, what about those who are married? Some of them are married. You give them these, you are encouraging disloyalty. It's the wrong mindset.

For Fadi and others, monogamy and sexual abstinence were indicators of Malay men's superior loyalty to their partners, their families, and ultimately the nation. While they acknowledged that some Malays engaged sex workers, they claimed that it was overwhelmingly Chinese men who engaged in this form of behaviour. Malay men's actions, they argued, were circumscribed by Islam, which provided clear guidelines on appropriate behaviour:

> Malays, because they are brought up as Muslims. They say *haram* [prohibited], *dosa* [sin], cannot. But a number of Chinese like one-night stand, have sex with multiple partners. Same like Malay guys. But it's safe to say that there are more Chinese doing this than Malays.

For Malay men the reassertion of a positive subaltern masculinity in contrast to hegemonic Chinese masculinity is reliant on a questioning of Chinese men's sexuality. Not only were the Chinese considered to be 'less loyal' because they engaged in extra-marital sex, but they were also considered more likely to be homosexual.[15] Fadi, who worked in a unit that dealt with male rape cases, reported that most soldiers who came before his unit were Chinese, commenting that he was 'not sure if this is a race thing or what'. As in other contexts, the tension between a desire for homosociality and a fear of being associated with homosexuality is a key site for producing straight masculine identities in Singapore.[16] Awareness that, despite their marginalized positions within the military, straight Malay men nevertheless occupied a position above gay men in the 'pecking order', contributed to a sense of hierarchy that constituted a significant part of their subaltern discourse of masculinity.

For our Malay Muslim informants, questioning hegemonic Chinese masculinity via the suggestion of homosexuality feeds on three quite discrete discourses. First, Islam takes a strong normative position on the question of same-sex relationships between men, which our informants espoused to a greater or lesser extent. Second, homosexuality presents a significant challenge to the way that straight Malay men, some of whom are seen as 'soft' (*lembut*), perform their masculinity. When asked to describe what is meant by *lembut*, Fadi replied that 'Maybe it's nature. Yeah it's their nature of being soft . . . soft spoken, soft in attitude, in everything', going on to contrast both being soft and being gay with soldiers who were *lembek*, or soft in the sense of being unfit (but obviously mentally tough because basic training was so much harder for them).[17] Softness among men is socially accepted in the Malay community, and – in contrast to Western stereotypes – rarely associated with homosexuality. As Hakim emphasized, while some soft men are gay, not all gay men are soft:

> Some men are not men you see [laughs] Yeah! They can be tough, but some men are really not men [laughs]! That's the scary part! After weeks of being there doing the trainings, things . . . happen.

However, in the military context, Malay softness nevertheless creates ambivalence. As Fadi commented:

My friend, he is an officer. Not my friend, sorry. I know him . . . He is very *lembut*. I find out later on that he is one. He is both feminine and gay. I thought at first he is feminine only. If he had declared, he would not go for officer course.

Despite their reportedly 'relatively rare' encounters, Malay men actively participated in the everyday banter that contributes to the denigration of homosexuals. They were conscious, however, that their comments should exclude 'softer' Malay men.

Third, and most pertinent to the question of hierarchies of loyalty, is the fact that homosexuals are treated with great suspicion by the state. If homosexuals declare themselves to be sexually active, they are treated as medical invalids (PES C) and put on 'less strenuous activity' in non-combatant positions. Some of our informants traded tales (perhaps urban myths) of straight men who declared that they were homosexual in order to avoid National Service. But, as Talib observed, this was a dangerous strategy as chances were that those attempting to use it would get caught: 'They trace you. Wherever you go. They trace you all the way. There is a unit in charge of that. They trace you. If they say you are 302, you better be 302 till you die.' As Fadi noted, highly educated gay men – who are more likely to be chosen as officers – are reluctant to declare their sexual orientation for fear of later discrimination in the workplace. Our informants advised that for Malay men, whose loyalty to the nation-state is already questioned, coming out to the military authorities is even more problematic, perhaps in part also explaining their eagerness to assert their heterosexuality.

For our informants, asserting a subaltern Malay masculinity is a work in progress that relies on continual comparison against a dominant Chinese masculine ideal. Acutely aware of the common stereotypes that are used to explain Malay men's economic and political marginalization, the men depict an image of Malay soldiers as physically and morally superior to their Chinese counterparts. In defiance of dominant discourses of the threat posed by Islam, Malay men use their religion as a positive marker of difference from Chinese men. Religious faith is thus not a source of treachery but rather a means to demonstrate a Malay man's superior loyalty to the nation, standing as it does in stark contrast with the materialism and promiscuity they associate with the Chinese.[18] In a context in which Muslim men's loyalty is already questioned by the state and where militaristic Islam is associated globally with terrorism, drawing on religious faith – but particularly on Islam – in this way is potentially dangerous. The men are keenly aware of this risk, and respond by framing Islam as a source of personal and private strength rather than an overt vehicle for the expression of subaltern masculinity. As a result, although Muslim NSmen are forced to choose daily between their religion and their country, open defiance of officers within the military is rare.

In the face of their marginalization, then, the men draw on their religious faith as a way of recouping a sense of masculine power. By asserting positive models of subaltern masculinity built on Islam, however, they also contribute to the ongoing vilification of gay men within the military, and thus the reassertion of normative heterosexuality.

Conclusion

As a warrior, the Malay NSman is fundamentally flawed – try as he may, he fails to live up to the hegemonic ideal embodied by dominant Chinese masculinity. Instead, Malay men's subaltern masculinity reveals their ambivalent position in Singaporean society. National Service provides them with an opportunity to embody the hegemonic masculine ideal by handling weapons, developing physical strength, wearing a uniform and demonstrating loyalty to fellow soldiers and the nation. At the same time, however, their marginalization is expressed in their positioning in lower-status, less combat-sensitive areas of the military. After their Basic Military Training, the majority of Malay men are deployed into logistics and civil defence services. The men understand their location in these units to be a product of two inter-related factors – first, as members of a (Muslim) minority group they are a potential threat to a Chinese-dominated state; and second, their marginal status as a minority group means that they have less access to the social capital required to succeed in more prestigious, combat roles.

Malay subaltern masculinity, as it is described here, does not subvert the existing hegemony because the men also gain from National Service. They see it as a positive experience where boys grow up, learn respect and gain knowledge of the world, and thus as a means to achieve the status of normative Singaporean manhood. At the same time, however, their achievements are always partial because of their marginal location in class and ethnic hierarchies. The state ensures the loyalty of non-hegemonic men, while at the same time maintaining their marginalization within the army and the state. National Service provides an opportunity for Malay men to construct a positive model of Malay masculinity. But it also contributes to the process of reinscribing patterns of Malay disadvantage.

In his study of Chinese American masculinities, Chen (1999: 586) argues 'hegemony is anything but generic, referring as it does to a distinctive kind of domination'. Our study of Singaporean Malay Muslim masculinities exposes the daily practices through which the hegemony of Chinese masculinity is achieved and subverted. National Service is a key site not only for the production of loyal male citizens, but also for the institutionalization of Malay marginality and Chinese superiority. This process, however, is never complete. For some men, the expression and performance of marginal masculinity is also a site for the construction of an alternative subaltern masculinity that challenges the taken-for-granted assertion that Chinese men's superiority is also a sign of their greater loyalty to the nation. Relying on the idea that Malay men make 'more loyal citizens', subaltern Malay masculinity challenges the link between hegemonic masculinity, citizenship and nationalism. However, it also contributes to the valorization of National Service and thus to the ongoing maintenance of a Chinese-dominated military and state.

Notes

1 The research on which this chapter is based was funded by Australian Research Council Discovery Project grant, In the Shadow of Singapore: The Limits of Transnationalism in Insular Riau (DP0557368). We thank Mike Donaldson and Keith Foulcher for their

comments on an earlier draft, and Mohamed Fairoz bin Ahmad for his assistance in conducting a number of the interviews referred to in this chapter. Some interviews were conducted in English and some in Malay, some in focus groups and some individually. English conversations are reported verbatim with no editing for grammar except where the original form would interfere with understanding. Pseudonyms have been used throughout.

2 'Race' is used in Singapore to refer to official state ethnic categories. Its usage implies that ethnic groups are marked not only by cultural and linguistic differences, but also by biological differences. For a discussion of the ways in which the term is used in popular and state discourses in Singapore see Lai (1995). Our use of 'race' in this chapter reflects its common usage in Singapore.

3 Under a policy of multiracialism all Singaporeans must identify with one of four official race categories – Chinese, Malay, Indian and Other – or CMIO multiracialism (Lai 1995). The Chinese are the dominant ethnic group (75 per cent), with a large minority of Malays (14 per cent), and a smaller minority of Indians (9 per cent). 'Others' include Eurasians and Europeans (Singapore Department of Statistics 2007). The vast majority of Muslims are Malay (Singapore Department of Statistics 2000).

4 In his study of youth in the army, Leong Choon Cheong notes that Chinese national servicemen describe Malay men as 'lazy, unintelligent, unhygienic, and aggressive' (cited in Rahim 1998: 57–8).

5 The men recognized these as distinctly gendered stereotypes that describe Malay men but not Malay women.

6 Another equally important aspect of *wen-wu* is the privileging of a bounded desire, a restricted sexuality, one that stands in marked contrast to the ideals of Western heterosexual masculinity, namely that of an active excess.

7 Men must serve two years of National Service and continue to be called up for active reservist training until the age of 40 or 50, depending on rank.

8 Walsh argues that the fact that these groups are not exposed to the benefits of cross-cultural learning associated with a fully integrated military service is 'especially significant' because many high-ranking officers are very influential in Singaporean society after their military career is over (Walsh 2007: 276).

9 Note, however, a distinct tendency among informants to claim that 'friends' had been discriminated against while they had not. Similar tendencies have been reported in other situations where sensitive topics are discussed.

10 It is widely known that Malays are only permitted to repair B-class vehicles, which have no weapons installed (Interview with Abdullah).

11 Similarly, Samad reported that there were no Malay or Chinese cliques during his time in BMT. Instead, divisions were greatest between the 'cool ones' and 'those who give trouble'. He did note, however, that Chinese NSmen with experience mixing with Malays and Indians outside NS tend to be more open to inter-ethnic friendships while in the BMTC.

12 While some of our informants held critical views about how NS operated, the majority expressed strong positive sentiments about the importance and value of conscription.

13 For many, the glamour of training quickly wears off. In Hafiz's case, it did not last beyond his basic training. His subsequent placement after basic training gave him 'no sense of fulfilment', since all he did all day was 'read papers, eat, sleep, read papers'.

14 Positive accounts of Malay men's 'innate' physical attributes and sporting prowess act as a source of community pride, and also serve to channel boys and young men into naturalized roles in commodified sports cultures (particularly soccer) that in turn reinforce 'positive' racism. The dominance of Malay players in the national soccer league, for example, is both a reminder of ethnic stereotyping and a source of ethnic pride (see Lyons and Ford 2009).

15 According to Hafiz, homosexual acts were relatively rare during National Service because 'this type of men is given certain positions or units to go to'. He went on to say

that gay men generally did not serve in combat or infantry units because 'in such situations where they are trained to be tough, there are a lot of rubbing going on [men in close contact with one another], where morale plays a large part in this type of vocation. Having people like this is not good cos you might not know what will happen. It's just the army or governments way of protecting [us].'

16 See Chapter 4 for an account of this dynamic among Chinese Singaporean sex tourists and for a more detailed overview of the literature.

17 The characterization of Malay men as 'soft' has a long tradition. Colonial authorities described Malay men as effeminate and unsuited to waged labour (Crinis 2004). This view continued to be deployed by the new ruling elite in the early years of Independence. For example, Holden (2001: 420) claims that in former Prime Minister Lee Kuan Yew's memoir, *The Singapore Story* (1999), Indian and Malay men are portrayed as 'effete, governed by emotion and appetite, and unable to apply the disciplinary practices necessary for the founding of a new nation'.

18 In her study of the Israeli context, Sasson-Levy (2002: 366) observed a similar phenomenon. Mizrachim working class constructed a positive form of subordinate, anti-militaristic, 'home-based' masculinity by rejecting the ethos of Zionist sacrifice and constructing a masculinity that runs against the Israeli discourse of citizenship.

References

Ang, I. (2001) *On Not Speaking Chinese: Living between Asia and the West*, London: Routledge.

Ang, I. and Stratton, J. (1995) 'Straddling east and west: Singapore's paradoxical search for a national identity', in S. Perera (ed.), *Asian and Pacific Inscriptions: Identities, Ethnicities, Nationalities*, Melbourne: Meridian, pp. 179–92.

Ariff, Mohd Ikram Mohd, Mohd Iqbal Abdullah, Azhar Erimo and Zaiman Putra Ahmad Ali (2000) *BMT: NS Guidebook for Muslims*, Singapore: Majilis Ugama Islam Singapura (MUIS) and PERDAUS.

Barr, M. D. and Low, J. (2005) 'Assimilationism as multiracialism: the case of Singapore's Malays', *Asian Ethnicity* 6(3): 161–82.

Barrett, F. J. (1996) 'The organizational construction of hegemonic masculinity: the case of the US Navy', *Gender, Work and Organization* 3(3): 129–42.

Bedlington, S. S. (1981) 'Ethnicity and the armed forces in Singapore', in D. C. Ellinwood and C. H. Enloe (eds), *Ethnicity and the Military in Asia*, New Brunswick, NJ: Transaction Books, pp. 242–66.

Chen, A. S. (1999) 'Lives at the center of the periphery, lives at the periphery of the center: Chinese American masculinities and bargaining with hegemony', *Gender & Society* 13(5): 584–607.

Chong, T. (2002) 'Asian values and Confucian ethics: Malay Singaporeans' dilemma', *Journal of Contemporary Asia* 32(3): 394–406.

Crinis, V. (2004) 'The silence and fantasy of women and work', unpublished PhD thesis, University of Wollongong.

da Cunha, D. (1999) 'Sociological aspects of the Singapore Armed Forces', *Armed Forces and Society* 25(3): 459–75.

Enloe, C. (1980) *Ethnic Soldiers: State Security in Divided Societies*, Harmondsworth: Penguin.

Gill, L. (1997) 'Creating citizens, making men: the military and masculinity in Bolivia', *Cultural Anthropology* 12(4): 527–50.

Heng, G. and Devan, J. (1995) 'State fatherhood: the politics of nationalism, sexuality, and race in Singapore', in A. Ong and M. G. Peletz (eds), *Bewitching Women, Pious Men:*

Gender and Body Politics in Southeast Asia, Berkeley: University of California Press, pp. 195–215.

Hibbins, R. (2005) 'Migration and gender identity among Chinese skilled male migrants to Australia', *Geoforum* 36(2): 167–80.

Higate, P. and Hopton, J. (2005) 'War, militarism, and masculinities', in M. S. Kimmel, J. Hearn and R. W. Connell (eds), *Handbook of Studies on Men and Masculinities*, Thousand Oaks, CA: Sage, pp. 432–47.

Hirose, A. and Pih, K. (2010) 'Men who strike and men who submit: hegemonic and marginalized masculinities in mixed martial arts', *Men and Masculinities* 3(2): 190–209.

Holden, P. (2001) 'A man and an island: gender and nation in Lee Kuan Yew's *The Singapore Story*', *Biography* 24(2): 401–24.

Huxley, T. (2001) *Defending the Lion City: The Armed Forces of Singapore,* St Leonards: Allen and Unwin.

Kamaludeen Bin Mohamed Nasir (2007) 'Rethinking the "Malay problem" in Singapore: image, rhetoric and social realities', *Journal of Muslim Minority Affairs* 27(2): 309–18.

Lahelma, E. (2005) 'Finding communalities, making differences, performing masculinities: reflections of young men on military service', *Gender and Education* 17(3): 305–17.

Lai Ah Eng (1995) *Meanings of Multiethnicity: A Case-Study of Ethnicity and Ethnic Relations in Singapore*, Kuala Lumpur: Oxford University Press.

Lee Kuan Yew (1999) *The Singapore Story: Memoirs of Lee Kuan Yew*, New York: Prentice Hall.

Leow Bee Geok (2001) *Census of Population 2000: Education, Language and Religion (Statistical Release 2),* Singapore: Singapore Department of Statistics.

Li, T. M. (1998) 'Constituting capitalist culture: the Singapore Malay problem and entrepreneurship reconsidered', in R. W. Hefner (ed.), *Market Cultures: Society and Morality in the New Asian Capitalisms*, Boulder, CO: Westview Press, pp. 147–72.

Louie, K. (2002) *Theorising Chinese Masculinity: Society and Gender in China*, Cambridge: Cambridge University Press.

Louie, K. and Edwards, L. (1994) 'Chinese masculinity: theorizing Wen and Wu', *East Asian History* 8: 135–47.

Lyons, L. and Ford, M. (2009) 'Singaporean first: challenging the concept of transnational Malay masculinity', in D. Heng and S. M. K. Aljunied (eds), *Reframing Singapore: Memory, Identity and Trans-Regionalism*, Amsterdam: Amsterdam University Press, pp. 175–94.

Peled, A. (1998) *A Question of Loyalty: Military Manpower Policy in Multiethnic States*, Ithaca, NY: Cornell University Press.

Rahim, Lily Zubaidah (1998) *The Singapore Dilemma: The Political and Educational Marginality of the Malay Community*, New York: Oxford University Press.

Sasson-Levy, O. (2002) 'Constructing identities at the margins: masculinities and citizenship in the Israeli army', *Sociological Quarterly* 43(3): 357–83.

—— (2003) 'Military, masculinity, and citizenship: tensions and contradictions in the experience of blue-collar soldiers', *Identities: Global Studies in Culture and Power* 10(3): 319–45.

—— (2008) 'Individual bodies, collective state interests: the case of Israeli combat soldiers', *Men and Masculinities* 10(3): 296–321.

Siddique, S. (1989) 'Singaporean identity', in K. S. Sandhu and P. Wheatley (eds), *Management of Success: The Moulding of Modern Singapore*, Singapore: ISEAS, pp. 563–77.

Singapore Department of Statistics (2000) *Singapore Census of Population 2000, Advance Data Release No. 2, Religion,* Singapore: Singapore Department of Statistics.
—— (2007) *Singapore in Figures 2007,* Singapore: Singapore Department of Statistics.
Singapore Year Book (1971), Singapore: Government Printing Office.
Walsh, S. P. (2007) 'The roar of the Lion City: ethnicity, gender, and culture in the Singapore Armed Forces', *Armed Forces and Society* 33(2): 265–85.

Index

An environmentally friendly book printed and bound in England by www.printondemand-worldwide.com

PEFC Certified

This product is
from sustainably
managed forests
and controlled
sources

www.pefc.org

This book is made entirely of sustainable materials; FSC paper for the cover and PEFC paper for the text pages.

#0399 - 091214 - C0 - 234/156/12 - PB